Mythology and Ideology of the Basque Language by Antonio Tovar

Series Editor
Pello Salaburu

Mythology and Ideology of the Basque Language

Antonio Tovar

Translated by Jennifer R. Ottman

With an introduction by Joaquín Gorrochategui

Basque Classics Series, no. 9

Center for Basque Studies
University of Nevada, Reno

This book was published with generous financial support obtained by the Association of Friends of the Center for Basque Studies from the Provincial Government of Bizkaia.

Basque Classics Series, No. 9
Series Editors: William A. Douglass, Gregorio Monreal, and Pello Salaburu

Center for Basque Studies
University of Nevada, Reno
Reno, Nevada 89557
http://basque.unr.edu

Cover and series design © 2015 by Jose Luis Agote
Cover painting: Jose Luis Zumeta

Library of Congress Cataloging-in-Publication Data

Names: Tovar, Antonio, author. | Ottman, Jennifer (Jennifer Rebecca) translator.
Title: Mythology and ideology of the Basque language / Antonio Tovar ;
Translated by Jennifer Ottman ; With an introduction by Joaquin Gorrochategui.
Other titles: Mitología e ideologíia sobre la lengua vasca. English
Description: Reno : Center for Basque Studies, University of Nevada, [2016] |
Series: Basque Classics series ; no. 9 | Original publication in Spanish: "Mitología e ideología sobre la lengua vasca." | Includes bibliographical references and index.
Identifiers: LCCN 2015038636| ISBN 9781877802348 (hardcover : alk. paper) |
ISBN 9781877802355 (pbk. : alk. paper)
Classification: LCC PH5023 .T63513 2016 | DDC 499/.92--dc23 LC record available at http://lccn.loc.gov/2015038636

Contents

Note on Basque Orthography

The standard form to refer to the Basque language today is Euskara. Most English-language texts on the Basque Country have traditionally employed only the French and Spanish orthographic renderings of Basque place names. Here, in light of the standard Basque orthographic renderings of these same place names by the Basque Language Academy (Euskaltzaindia), we will endeavor to use these Basque versions, with an addition in parentheses of the French or Spanish equivalents on first mention in each chapter.

Some exceptions to this rule include the use of Navarre (Nafarroa in Basque, Navarra in Spanish) and Lower Navarre (Nafarroa Beherea in Basque, Basse Navarre in French); the hyphenated bilingual cases of Donostia-San Sebastián, Vitoria-Gasteiz, and Iruñea-Pamplona; and occasions where French or Spanish place name variants are used to make a linguistic point. In the latter case, the Basque equivalents appear in parentheses after the French or Spanish place name.

Introduction

JOAQUÍN GORROCHATEGUI

This small book on ideas about the nature and origin of the Basque language up to the early twentieth century is a highly erudite essay,[1] even if the motivation for its composition was ultimately political. Its erudition is guaranteed by the professional credentials of its author, Antonio Tovar, one of twentieth-century Spain's most polymathic intellectuals and men of letters, at the same time that its reason for being was the fruit of his passionate political commitment, which originated in his early years and, modulated over the course of his life by criticism and experience, led him to take an interest in all aspects of public life, especially those related to culture.

The work of a seasoned scholar, based on vast reading over many years, this slim volume was the product of a single burst of composition—like almost all Tovar's works—at a particularly critical moment in Spain's recent history, when, following the dictator Franco's death in 1975, the country was eagerly seeking a democratic political system that could overcome the consequences of the Spanish Civil War and guarantee the peaceful coexistence of the full spectrum of political views. At that time, the so-called Basque problem, manifested in its rawest form by the terrorism of the separatist organization ETA (Euskadi Ta Askatasuna, "Basque Country and Freedom"), was an unavoidable factor in Spanish politics. It can be said that the Basque Country had been in open rebellion against Franco's regime since the late 1960s: countless strikes in all economic sectors, constant sabotage,

---

1. A number of the topics that appear in this book are also discussed in Madariaga, *Anthology of Apologists and Detractors of the Basque Language*. —Ed. note

and civil disobedience were common and generalized occurrences, to which the government responded with indiscriminate repression by the police. In this climate of resistance, ETA's terrorism was viewed positively by broad swathes of the population, especially Basque nationalists, even if it was also justified by many non–nationalist opponents of Franco. The prudence of the majority of the political leaders of the "transition" (the name given to the period between Franco's death and the attempted military coup in 1981), among whom I will mention as examples only the prime minister, Adolfo Suárez, and the secretary of the Communist Party, Santiago Carrillo—representatives of the two antagonistic worlds that arose out of the war—succeeded in giving birth to a democratic constitution (1978) that guaranteed extensive autonomy to the Basque Country, detailed in its Statute of Autonomy, with the rank of constitutional law (1979). Nonetheless, a constitutional text, however important and necessary, could not solve on its own problems built up over decades, even centuries, and exacerbated in recent years by the extreme attitudes of certain sectors of Spanish society. Another element working against calm was ETA's terrorist activity, one of the objectives of which was to provoke the intervention of Franco's numerous military supporters still in control of the army, and which almost achieved that goal with the mentioned coup attempt of February 23, 1981. There was a need for actors with a sincere desire to understand the ideas and aspirations of the opposing sides, broad-minded and generous openness when it came to revising their own decades-old views, and perceptive intelligence for building connections with the proponents of other ideologies on the basis of shared humanist values. Tovar was one of these men.

The Author: His Academic Career

Antonio Tovar was born on May 17, 1911, in Valladolid, to a bourgeois family of traditionalist leanings: his father was a notary, and a maternal uncle, Daniel Llorente, would become bishop of Segovia. Because the family moved frequently for his father's career, Tovar received his secondary education at home, studying on his own and taking the official examinations to obtain a diploma. From a young age, he was inclined to the study of languages, perhaps aware of the linguistic differences between the Spanish that his family spoke and the languages used in the places where his father practiced his profession, whether that was Basque in Elorrio or Catalan in Morella de Castellón. As a teenager, he learned not only Latin, Greek, and French, part of the usual school curriculum, but also English and German on his own. He initially studied law at university, on his father's recommendation, but once he had completed that degree, he made up his mind to devote himself to his true vocation and enrolled in the Faculty of Philosophy and Letters at the University of Valladolid, subsequently continuing his studies at the Center for Historical Studies (Centro de Estudios Históricos) in Madrid. At that prestigious institution, Tovar met two of the greatest Spanish scholars of the time, who exercised a profound influence on him: Ramón Menéndez Pidal, who laid the foundation for the history of the Spanish language, and Manuel Gómez Moreno, who revolutionized the study of the Iberian Peninsula's prehistory by deciphering the mysterious Iberian script.

In 1935, with the aim of furthering his study of classical philology, Tovar obtained a government scholarship to study in Berlin, where the world's best classicists were teaching. There, he had the opportunity to attend the classes of the Hellenist Eduard Schwyzer, although he was unable to make the acquaintance of either Eduard Norden or Julius Pokorny, despite his great desire to do so, because both had been removed from their university posts, the former due to disagreements with the Nazi regime and the latter due to his Jewish origin. Nevertheless, he did meet Werner Jaeger, who was in a similarly delicate political situation.

The young Tovar, who had experienced the radicalization of Spanish politics under the Second Republic during his student years in Valladolid and Madrid, from the conservative and anticommunist side, was fascinated in Berlin by the Nazi regime's achievements and organization. The force, vitality, organization, and cohesion displayed by German society under the Nazi Party's leadership, so different from the internal division of the Spanish Republic, put him under its spell. At the age of twenty-four, he was unable to see the malign germ of horror and inhumanity that hid beneath the glittering cloak of the regime's excellences, to which he attributed Germany's innovative industry, well-equipped universities, and scholarly vitality. When General Franco rebelled against the Republic's legitimate government in July 1936, Tovar did not hesitate to place himself at the rebels' service in order to install in Spain a society similar to the one he knew in

Berlin, becoming a member of the Spanish Falange, a political organization with a fascist or national-syndicalist ideology. During the years
of the Spanish Civil War (1936–39), he was the first director of Radio
Nacional, a communication and propaganda organ in Franco's camp.
Once the war had ended, in his capacity as a member of the Falange,
he accepted the position of undersecretary of state for press and propaganda, which he held for only five months, from December 1940 to
April 1941.

Tovar never held any other strictly political positions for the rest
of his life. At the age of thirty, he abandoned his political career in
order to devote himself entirely to academic life. He obtained a professorship in Latin at the University of Salamanca and dedicated himself body and soul to a complete renewal of classical studies at that
university, which was deeply mired in intellectual mediocrity, like all
Spain's universities. It is clear, in any event, that Tovar was not just
any professor: his acknowledged political authority, which allowed
him to act much more expeditiously than others, came united with
undeniable intellectual ability. He had not obtained his chair, as so
many colleagues newly arrived in the universities under Franco had,
by putting his pistol on the table during his appearance before the
search committee. He was a cultured man, a polyglot, truly aware of
the demands of research and good teaching, and personally familiar
with the academic ideals of German *Altertumswissenschaft* (classical
studies). In addition, he was a man of bold spirit, not afraid of large
enterprises, and at the same time endowed with both extraordinary
capabilities and a great capacity for work.

All this explains why during the 1940s, in his Salamanca post,
Tovar began an ambitious research program that encompassed not
only the study of the classical languages but also new fields unex-
plored until then, prominent among them the study of the pre-Roman
languages of the Iberian Peninsula.

Manuel Gómez Moreno, whom Tovar came to know during his student days at the Center for Historical Studies, had deciphered the
original Iberian script in which many ancient, pre-Roman inscriptions
from extensive regions of the Iberian Peninsula were written. However, this discovery, which its author had noted in passing in 1925,
had no impact until after the Spanish Civil War. Tovar was one of the

first scholars, along with the Basque-German linguist Gerhard Bähr and the Spanish archeologist Pío Beltrán, to confirm the accuracy of Gómez Moreno's decipherment, giving plausible readings of the legends on many Iberian coins and of some inscriptions. An immense field of research on the pre-Roman languages of the Iberian Peninsula, which could now be studied directly through their texts, opened up before him. In addition, there was a great deal of secondary material, especially the names of indigenous individuals documented in Latin inscriptions of the Roman period, which had not been adequately collected or studied.

Tovar's training as a classicist with knowledge of Indo-European languages qualified him to study Celtiberian and Indo-European linguistic remains. To study Iberian, he saw no other path than by way of Basque. In the midst of the Spanish Civil War, in Burgos in his role at the head of Radio Nacional, he began to study Basque on his own with dictionaries and grammars; in his university position in Salamanca, he continued his self-taught study, corresponding with the president of the Academy of the Basque Language (Euskaltzaindia, Academia de la Lengua Vasca), Resurrección M. Azkue, and taking advantage of his summer vacation to practice the language in Orio. Although it is true that many native speakers of Basque were traditionalist in politics and religion, the majority of the Basque-speaking regions in the Basque Country at that time—the provinces of Bizkaia and Gipuzkoa—had supported the Republic, under the orders of the Basque autonomous government and its nationalist majority. It was at least somewhat unusual that an outsider to the region and a Falangist would devote himself to the study of Basque, a supreme symbol of identity for all those who had been defeated in the civil conflict.

However, Tovar had a true appreciation for the Basque language, above and beyond its utility as a hermeneutic tool for the study of Iberian. He became interested in its linguistic structure, its history, and its literature, to the point that in 1950 he published a brief volume introducing the language to a general audience (*La lengua vasca* [The Basque language]), along the lines that another linguist, the Frenchman René Lafon, would imitate somewhat later. In this first essay, Tovar already confronted a good part of the material that would be the object of the current book. His comparative studies of Basque and other languages, especially Iberian, and the various etymological studies he carried out during the 1940s and 1950s were collected in *El Euskera y sus parientes* (Euskara and its relatives, 1959), which brought together the results of his research activity in Spain, before his departure from the country led to a change in his line of research.

Tovar acquired international prominence thanks to his appointment as rector of the University of Salamanca (1951–56). Franco's alliance with the Axis Powers during World War II and his nonparticipation in the Marshall Plan for European recovery after the war led to the regime's international political and economic isolation, which only began to ease after 1953 as a result of a set of accords with the Holy See and a bilateral treaty with the United States, which was looking under Dwight D. Eisenhower for allies in the anticommunist struggle. Tovar had the brilliant idea of taking advantage of the 1954 celebration of the seventh centenary of the University of Salamanca's foundation—although the correct date for the anniversary had been in 1918—to attract the attention of numerous European universities. He gave new energy to the university press, creating a monographic section that published not only the best Spanish scholars, such as the ethnologist Julio Caro Baroja, nephew of the famous novelist Pío Baroja and a specialist in Basque language and history, but also famous foreign linguists who worked on topics of Hispanic interest, including Karl Bouda, Johannes Hubschmid, René Lafon, and Michel Lejeune, with Basque topics maintaining a privileged position.

The creation of the Manuel de Larramendi Chair of Basque Language and Literature was one of Tovar's most original and inspired actions as rector of the university. This was a foundation belonging to the University of Salamanca, sustained by its own funds, the primary objective of which was to provide a space at the university for studies of the Basque language. Since it was not an ordinary chair and had a limited budget, its activities were restricted to organizing specialized courses and lectures given by experts in a variety of fields, especially Basques, who were invited for the purpose. The inaugural course was given by José Miguel de Barandiarán, a well-known anthropologist and historian of prehistory, who had engaged in extensive scholarly activity before the war in partnership with a professor at the University of Barcelona, Telesforo de Aranzadi. He was followed by other prominent Basques such as Juan Gorostiaga, a member of the Academy of the Basque Language. Finally, the Basque linguist Luis Michelena (Koldo Mitxelena) was invited with increasing frequency, until he became practically a visiting professor in residence.

The creation, preservation, and development of the Larramendi Chair clearly shows the kind of man Tovar was. Creating a chair of the Basque language was not the same as creating a chair in any other discipline. For Franco's regime, any language other than Spanish was almost a taboo topic, even though many of his supporters were native speakers of Basque or Catalan. Politically, they defended the complete supremacy of Spanish as the language of the state, and they viewed other languages, especially Basque and Catalan, as subverting the unity of the fatherland. In addition, the scholars first invited to teach, like Barandiarán, even if they were not declared enemies of the regime, were suspected of Basque nationalism. Luis Michelena, only four years younger than Tovar himself, was not merely suspected of Basque nationalism but a declared activist; he had participated in the Spanish Civil War as a *gudari*, or soldier of the Basque government, in defense of the Republic's rule of law and the Basque Statute of Autonomy, and had been taken prisoner and sentenced to death, although this was subsequently commuted to several years in prison.

It is not surprising that a prominent figure characterized by this kind of liberality of spirit, inclined to recognize personal and scholarly merits even in ideological opponents and to act accordingly in the public sphere, would arouse a certain discomfort among traditionalist and reactionary sectors of the regime who defended the privileges won on the battlefield and a clear division between victors and vanquished. At the same time, the new economic winds favored the ascent of a new class of politicians with ties to the conservative Catholic organization Opus Dei, who pushed the preceding Falangist generation out of government. As a consequence, Tovar not only resigned from his position as rector in 1956, but in view of the regime's inability to evolve in the direction of greater reconciliation, chose to leave Spain and begin his New World adventure.

During the 1948–49 academic year, Tovar had been a visiting professor of classical languages at the University of Buenos Aires. At that time, he had the opportunity to gain a very superficial acquaintance with South America's linguistic riches, which aroused his great interest. Consequently, in 1958 he accepted an invitation from the University of Tucumán (Argentina)—where an old acquaintance of his from his time as secretary of the journal *Emerita* was teaching, Cl. Hernando Balmori—with the intention of dedicating himself to the study of the region's indigenous languages. In Tucumán, far from political intrigues and administrative chores, accompanied by his wife and his five children, he applied himself with his characteristic enthusiasm to the study of the languages of El Chaco, especially Wichí (known in the Spanish tradition under the name of *mataco*), Chulupí, and Chorote. A classicist by training and hence used to the study of languages attested in corpora of ancient documents, he now had to devote himself to fieldwork, recording indigenous phrases and stories on a tape recorder in order to subsequently describe a language without a written tradition. Tovar did not stop merely with an academic description of the languages studied, but as a born humanist, he concerned himself with the cultures transmitted in these languages and especially with their uncertain future in a globalized world in which they had to compete with major languages of culture such as Spanish.

Language contact, particular situations of equilibrium or inequality between languages, and the processes leading in some cases to language extinction were phenomena that he saw in front of him in relatively clear and well-defined forms and that he could transfer by analogy to past situations in the Iberian Peninsula's linguistic history that could not be observed directly. The result of these reflections was his well-known essay *Lo que sabemos de la lucha de lenguas en la Península Ibérica* (What we know about language conflict in the Iberian Peninsula, 1968). During this period he also pursued the study of methods especially designed for the linguistic comparison of languages without a written tradition, in particular the lexicostatistical method developed by the American linguist Morris Swadesh, who was persecuted as a communist and went into exile in Mexico, where he became a citizen. As a classicist and an Indo-Europeanist—he had begun in Spain the *Manual de Lingüística Indoeuropea* (Manual of Indo-European linguistics), to which he contributed the grammars of Gothic and Old Slavic—Tovar was familiar with the comparative method applied to Indo-European languages from the beginning of historical comparative linguistics. Swadesh's method consisted in comparing a hundred or two hundred basic words in the languages being studied, in order to observe the percentage of similarities and consequently establish the degree of kinship between them. The results were not as reliable or as fine-grained as those obtained by the traditional comparative method, but they served on occasion as a suggestive indicator of a probable relationship, to which the traditional method could then be applied. Tovar had a great deal of confidence in the new method and proposed to apply it to Basque as well, in collaboration with the inventor of the Swadesh method himself and Luis Michelena. The results were inconclusive, since the outcome of the comparisons was that Basque showed weak indicators of kinship with both Berber and Caucasian languages. For a genetic classification, in which the same language cannot be ascribed to different families, this obviously represented a significant problem, but in Tovar's view, alongside genetic kinship due to a common origin, there was another kind of relationship among languages that he called "progressive kinship through coexistence," according to which languages contained in their basic lexicon, and probably in other areas of their grammar, strata derived from different linguistic families, as a consequence of historical contact at some point in the past. This is an underlying idea in some of his publications on Basque and the pre-Roman Hispanic languages, as when he accepts a single origin for the Basque locative genitive suffix -*ko* and the Indo-European suffix -*ko*-, highly productive in Celtiberian for the formation of derived family names of the *Urdinocum* type.

In 1961, he accepted the University of Illinois's offer of a professorship in classical languages. He continued his research on Amerindian languages, without abandoning the pre-Roman languages of the Iberian Peninsula. His studies on the languages of El Chaco had made him aware of the need for a general introduction to the indigenous languages, so that he rapidly composed a useful *Catálogo de las lenguas de América del Sur* (Catalog of the languages of South America), the title of which recalls the venerable work by Lorenzo Hervás y Panduro discussed in this volume. He also took advantage of his time in America to publish in English a survey of current thinking on the Iberian Peninsula's pre-Roman languages, *The Ancient Languages of Spain and Portugal* (1961), which would be the standard work on the topic for many years.

As enriching as his New World experience was for him, he wanted to be in Madrid, where his now-elderly mother lived and where his children could attend university. He had always wanted a professorship at the Complutense University of Madrid, which he finally obtained in 1965. However, his dream did not last long. In that same year, serious student revolts against the policies of Franco's government took place, with the support of some prominent university professors, including the philosopher José Luis López Aranguren, the legal historian Enrique Tierno Galván, and the philologist Agustín García Calvo, who were definitively removed from their posts by the regime. Putting his intellectual integrity and his ideals of a better university above his personal convenience, Tovar resigned his recently obtained chair in solidarity with those expelled and went into voluntary exile. He returned to Illinois, where he taught classical languages for two years, until in 1967 he accepted an invitation from the University of Tubingen (Germany) to occupy the Chair of Indo-European Linguistics that had been left vacant on the death of Hans Krahe.

In Illinois he had found an academic institution that offered him every advantage for research, with extensive bibliographical resources and excellent personal contacts with prominent researchers, but he was far from Spain. Consequently, the offer from Germany allowed him to return to Europe and be closer to cultural and political affairs in his homeland, at a historical moment in which Franco's regime was showing evident signs of exhaustion.

During his time in Tubingen (1967–79), he continued working in all the fields he had cultivated over the course of his life, although he devoted more time to Indo-European studies. He thus took up again with vigor the study of new indigenous inscriptions that had recently been discovered, such as the Lusitanian inscription from Cabeço das Fraguas (Portugal), and proposed the existence of a distinct Indo-European language in the western part of the Iberian Peninsula, different from Celtiberian, itself now enriched by the appearance of the extraordinary inscription from Botorrita (Zaragoza, Spain), which he edited and studied together with Antonio Beltrán. He took an interest in the arduous subject of the Indo-Europeanization of Europe, making his own contribution to the study of the ancient names of European bodies of water—a primary topic of his predecessor Krahe—with an explanation based on the accumulation of materials of different origins. He set out to update the *Iberische Landeskunde* (Iberian geography), a work begun years before by Adolf Schulten, which he was able to complete in three volumes (*Baetica*, 1974, *Lusi-*

tanien [Lusitania], 1976, and *Tarraconensis*, posthumously in 1989); published updated editions of his histories of Greece and the Near East; worked on Latin, Celtic, and Mycenaean topics; and multiplied his numerous reviews, notes, and commentaries on Spanish literary and cultural publications. During these years in Germany, he changed the methodology of much of his linguistic research, adopting a typological perspective that demonstrated his reception of the proposals made by Joseph Greenberg starting in 1966. Along these lines, his work on Basque abandoned the etymological perspective that had characterized his years in Salamanca, focused on compiling the *Diccionario Etimológico de la Lengua Vasca* (Etymological dictionary of the Basque language), in favor of this new typological approach.

The pauses in academic activity between semesters allowed him to travel to Spain, where he followed the course of political and cultural events closely. He also took advantage of these trips to visit prominent members of the Spanish political opposition living in exile in various European cities, especially Paris. Discreetly but firmly, Tovar had been moving in the direction of the democratic opposition to Franco, which encompassed a broad spectrum of political views at this time.

When he retired from the University of Tubingen (1979), Spain was immersed in a political transition to democracy. In only a few years, and in something of a surprise to everyone, the formal transition had taken place, with the dismantling of the former regime's political laws and the creation of a state, in the form of a constitutional monarchy, that acknowledged the existence of autonomous regions such as the Basque Country and Catalonia, the official status of the Basque language, and the *ikurriña* (the Basque flag), for which so much blood had been shed in earlier years. However, all this had not yet pacified the Basque Country: ETA radicalized its attack on the democratic monarchy, which it considered the previous regime's heir, while diehard supporters of Franco, especially in the military, saw themselves attacked with impunity by terrorists, whom they considered beneficiaries of the political liberalization. It was necessary to build up a broad democratic political space within which the different positions could acknowledge a shared set of norms, bringing together opposing attitudes as much as possible. Tovar used his intellectual and moral authority to assist in this effort, especially in the cultural sphere. The linguistic issue posed by Basque and Catalan was among the most pressing problems of the day. The official recognition of these languages within the framework of the recently approved Statutes of Autonomy was one thing, and the coexistence of languages, the concrete application of the rights of speakers of Basque or Catalan, and the development of the languages themselves were something else again, all these being issues that aroused the disdain, when not the hostility, of many monolingual Spanish speakers. Typical of those years was the polemic frequently stirred up in the communications media, pseudointellectual circles, and conversational gatherings of all kinds regarding the suitability of Basque for scientific communication, for intellectual essays, and even as a vehicle for teaching and public administration. Motivated in most cases by ignorance and prejudice, many thought that Basque would never serve these purposes. It had long been clear that it was a language that could be written and that even had a complicated grammar, as Bernard Dechepare had demonstrated in the sixteenth century and Manuel de Larramendi in the eighteenth, in response to similar prejudices of the time. Now the attacks were directed at Basque's alleged capacity to serve as a language of culture.

In 1968, the Royal Academy of the Basque Language, Euskaltzaindia in Basque, had agreed on the basic norms for the language's unification. Literature of one kind or another existed in some eight different dialects, with major differences in production, and although three of them (Bizkaian, Gipuzkoan, and the Lower Navarrese–Lapurdian variety) had greater prominence than the others, none of them was sufficiently strong to impose itself naturally as the common variety, so that it was necessary to agree to choose among various options. The result of these decisions was *Euskara Batua* or Unified Basque,[2] the primary purpose of which was to serve as a written language for general needs, especially in teaching, the communications media, and public administration. Although the Basque-speaking community, especially the younger generation, accepted the proposal with enthu-

---

2. These topics are discussed in two books published by the Center for Basque Studies: *Koldo Mitxelena: Selected Writings of a Basque Scholar* (compiled by Pello Salaburu) and Salaburu and Alberdi, eds., *The Challenge of a Bilingual Society in the Basque Country*. —Ed. note

siasm, there was resistance on the part of some sectors nostalgic for the supposed richness and naturalness of the dialects.[3]

Through publications and lectures, Tovar participated in creating a climate of opinion favorable to the existence of a unified linguistic variety, which in turn implied—a fundamental issue—a position in favor of official status and the use of Basque for high-level cultural pursuits. The current book is indirectly related to this objective.

Over the course of his life, Tovar received numerous honors and awards. He was a full member (*académico de número*) of the Royal Spanish Academy of Language (Real Academia Española de la Lengua) (1968) and a corresponding member of Euskaltzaindia, and he belonged to numerous other institutes and academies. He was awarded honorary doctorates by the universities of Buenos Aires, Munich, Seville, and Dublin, and three Festschrifts were dedicated to him, published in Madrid (1972), in Tubingen (1984), and posthumously in Salamanca, with a joint dedication to Tovar and Luis Michelena (1990).

Despite his numerous activities, the Basque language always had a place on the horizon of his interests and his efforts: Through all his moves, whether to Salamanca, Tucumán, Illinois, or Tubingen, he carried with him the numerous entry slips for his Basque etymological dictionary, which he completed and corrected when he had the time. Above all, he filled for the time in which he lived, a century and a half after Wilhelm von Humboldt, the role of ambassador of the Basque language in the international academic world, whether with his works on the linguistic situation of the Old World or through the diffusion of his publications on Basque, such as the translation of his *Lengua Vasca* (1954; English translation: *The Basque Language*, 1957) into Georgian (1980).

Tovar died at the age of seventy-four, in Madrid, fully active to the end, reveling in his enormous capacity for work—he had more than two thousand publications of all kinds—and widely known and respected among his Spanish and European colleagues, as demonstrated by the award of the 1981 Goethe Prize given by the F. V. S. Foundation in Hamburg, in recognition of "his efforts in favor of

---

3. On the Basque dialects, see Zuazo, *The Dialects of Basque*.

rapprochement between peoples and for his defense of freedom of research and teaching in his country, preferring exile to adaption."

The Book

Tovar's aim in this book is to offer a survey with commentary of the ideas about the origin of the Basque language that circulated from the first medieval and Renaissance opinions up to the early twentieth century. This is not exclusively a story about the origins of Basque, however, but in fact discusses along the way the linguistic roots of the entire Iberian Peninsula and especially of Spanish. What is more, since the origins of the two languages are closely linked in this narrative, the ideas discussed are the source of a long-lasting polemic that, as Tovar himself says at the beginning of the book, has frequently been a source of conflict in Spanish political life. The author aims to give an objective account of these ideas, contextualizing them in the state of knowledge at the time and pointing out the extent to which they make innovative contributions or repeat the tradition in an uncritical and self-interested way, in the hope that real knowledge of history will help to solve the old problem of the mutual incomprehension of opposing views. Nevertheless, the account remains the product of a Spanish linguist, fundamentally interested in Spanish culture and for whom the Basque language is an integral part of that culture. This is why he organizes his prologue as a reflection on the strengths and weaknesses of Spanish scholarship from the Renaissance to the present, viewing the problem of the origins of Basque as just one example of this general theme, even if perhaps one of the most significant ones.

Although the Basque language is and was spoken, going back to the first witnesses to its history, on both sides of the western Pyrenees, it has been considered more "Spanish" than "French." Various historical factors have undoubtedly contributed to this perception: first of all, the French Basque Country was distant from the French crown's territorial center of power, and during the Middle Ages, its provinces belonged to non-French political entities, including the Kingdom of Navarre, the Kingdom of Aragon, and the Duchy of Aquitaine and Kingdom of England, while the Spanish Basque Country was centrally located in relation to or bordered on the original territories of the Kingdoms of Navarre and Castile in the crucial moments of the Reconquest against the Arabs of al-Andalus. Arnauld Oihenart already commented at the beginning of his *Notitia utriusque Vasco-niae* (Notice of both Gasconies, 1638, 2) that "soli [Vascones] vnà cum Cantabris atque Asturibus ... liberatae Hispaniae authores dici possint" (they [the Basques] alone, together with the Cantabrians and the Asturians . . . can be called the authors of the liberation of Spain). The French looked back to their Frankish origins and before that to the Gauls. At the same time, the French Revolution brought with it the abolition of the institutional idiosyncrasies of the French Basque provinces, while the *fueros* (norms of self-government) continued in force in the Spanish crown's Basque provinces, garnering Humboldt's enthusiastic praise during his 1801 trip to the Basque Country. A modern author from outside the country, Rodney Gallop, expands on the same idea in his entertaining *A Book of the Basques*: "Scarcely a single Basque name of any importance is to be found in the annals of the French history, with the one notable exception of Marshal Harispe. In Spain, on the other hand, from the earliest days . . . the Basques have played a great part in history."[4]

Even if this is true in general terms, and acknowledging the great abundance of Spanish authors who discussed the topic, in comparison with those of French origin, Tovar's survey fails to mention a number of individuals who wrote in French or strictly in Basque and who expressed opinions no less interesting or developed on some aspect of the subject. The Abbé D'Iharce de Bidassouet, who defended Basque's universal status and pre-Flood origin in his *Histoire des Cantabres* (History of the Cantabri, 1825), is no less radical and forceful in his views than Pablo P. Astarloa or other Hispanic defenders of Basque; in addition to maintaining point by point all of the traditional arguments, he dares to explain French place names and even offers as proof of Basque's primordial nature the use of Basque to explain words from the Austronesian languages, new to Western scholars in his day.[5] On the opposite side of the debate, it would be necessary to include the Gascon historian Jean-François Bladé, author of the *Étude sur les origines des Basques* (Study on the origins of the Basques, 1869), as

4. Gallop, *A Book of the Basques*, 24.

5. D'Iharce de Bidassouet, *Histoire des Cantabres ou des premiers colons de toute l'Europe*, 405.

one of the most determined detractors of Humboldt's theory about the universality of Basque in the Iberian Peninsula and one of the most biting critics of attempts to read the Iberian scripts by way of Basque, proposed with exaggerations and lapses in rigor of all kinds not only by Juan Bautista de Erro—mentioned by Tovar in this book—but also by the Frenchman Pierre-André Boudard in his *Numismatique ibérienne* (Iberian numismatics, 1859).

In the same way, the Basque authors who appear in Tovar's account are those who expressed their ideas in Spanish (from Esteban de Garibay to Astarloa, by way of Andrés de Poza and Larramendi) or even in Latin, like the ever-original Oihenart. Mentions of Basque-speaking authors who promoted the same ideas in Basque are rare or nonexistent: for example, Juan Ignacio de Iztueta summarizes in the first part of his *Guipuzcoaco provinciaren condaira edo historia* (History of the province of Gipuzkoa, 1847) the traditional arguments already expressed by Astarloa and Larramendi, both of whom he admires. More notable is the absence of any reference to the Bizkaian Pedro de Madariaga, the author of *Honra de escribanos* (Honor of scribes, 1565), who closes his book with a chapter on the elegance and antiquity of the Bizkaian language, meaning Basque. Original and novel in his systematization of the art of writing, Madariaga also precedes even Garibay and Poza in his discussion of the Basque language.

Tovar offers us a survey in chronological order of works that discuss the nature and origin of the Basque language. Here, we find alongside authors of recognized talent and care in the formulation or organization of their arguments—both among those who defended the antiquity of Basque, such as Poza, Larramendi, Astarloa, and Humboldt, and among their critics, among whom Bernardo de Aldrete, Gregorio Mayans, and Miguel de Unamuno stand out—others who were no more than popularizers of received ideas or who discussed the subject only in passing.

The debate, which began with a few references to the peculiarity of the Basque language in the context of other European languages, became immensely polemical in the late eighteenth and nineteenth centuries, because linguistic observations and theories were closely linked to historical justifications of the peculiarity and autonomy of the system of Basque traditional law and privileges (the *fueros*) in the context of the Spanish crown.

There is no doubt that from a strictly linguistic point of view, the Basque language was a strange phenomenon for medieval scholars well versed in Latin and in Romance and Germanic languages, as we will soon see in the observations of Rodrigo Ximénez de Rada, echoed by the humanists who had direct knowledge of Basque, from Lucio Marineo Sículo to Julius Caesar Scaliger. This peculiar nature of Basque was evaluated by foreign eyes in different ways from the beginning, since while for some it was an unpolished, almost unpronounceable language—a topos going back to the writers of antiquity—for others it was just as worthy and deserving of record as any other. The famous accounts of late-medieval travelers are an example of the former attitude, while an example of the latter is an episode in François Rabelais's *Pantagruel* (1552) in which Panurge responds to Pantagruel's questions, without succeeding in making himself understood, in German, Arabic, Italian, and English, continuing in Basque, Dutch, Spanish, Danish, Greek, Breton, and Latin. Similarly, rather than disdaining Basque, the humanist Nicolao Landuchio, a native of Lucca in Tuscany, left a manuscript of 328 folios containing three bilingual vocabularies, the *Dictionarium Lingue Toscane* (Dictionary of the Tuscan language), listing Spanish words with their Italian equivalents; the *Dictionarium Lingue Franconie* (Dictionary of the Franconian language), with French equivalents; and finally the *Dictionarium Lingue Cantabrice* (Dictionary of the Cantabrian language), with the Basque equivalents of the Spanish entries (1562). Joseph Justus Scaliger (1612, 122) expressed an explicit positive judgment when he said that Basque "[n]ihil barbari, aut stridoris, aut anhelitus habet: lenissima est, et suauissima" (has nothing that is barbarous or grating or panting; it is extremely smooth and pleasant).

The Tubalic origin of the Basque language, that is, the theory that it originated in the confusion of tongues at Babel (Genesis 11) and was brought to the peninsula by a grandson of Noah named Tubal, was a rather ordinary way of explaining this language's unusual characteristics in the paradigm of the time, which on the one hand accepted the veracity of the Biblical account, and on the other hand conceived of linguistic change only as the corruption of an original state of perfection, resulting from the mixture of peoples, and not as an essential aspect of every natural language. This scholarly paradigm flourished until the early-nineteenth-century revolution in comparative and historical linguistics—personified by the founders of Indo-European linguistics, Rasmus Rask, Franz Bopp, and Jacob Grimm—and could still be found in the influential *Catálogo de las lenguas de las naciones conocidas* (Catalog of the languages of the known nations) by Hervás y Panduro (1800–1805).

Basque's origin at Babel was quickly combined, as a necessary historical condition to explain its preservation, with the idea of isolation and the absence of subjection to the control of foreign powers, especially Rome, giving rise to the notion of "Cantabrianism," the theory that Rome never really conquered the Basque Country, henceforward identified with the Cantabria of Roman times.

Along with a variety of others, these ideas, which might have appeared reasonable to the majority of Renaissance scholars—and which appear reasonable to many even today, reformulated in modern terms to characterize a pre-Indo-European language in Europe and a certain relative isolation of the region with respect to the centers of cultural innovation—were used by Basque writers as arguments for the exaltation of their own language. The Renaissance brought with it the ascension of many vernacular languages to the category of written languages of culture and administration, to the relative detriment of Latin, on the one hand, and other dialects and languages that did not attain this status, on the other. In these years, in which both the new monarchies and the regions and cities enriched by trade competed with one another for greater prestige on the world stage, the literary genre of apologias for vernacular languages arose. Examples include Juan de Valdés's well-known *Diálogo de la Lengua* (Dialogue on language, 1535 [1737]) in favor of Spanish, João Barros's *Dialogo em louror da nossa linguagem* (Dialogue in praise of our language, 1540) in favor of Portuguese, and Martín de Viciana's *Alabanza de las lenguas hebrea, griega, latina, castellana y valenciana* (Praise of the Hebrew, Greek, Latin, Spanish, and Valencian languages, 1574). Our Garibay, Echave, and Poza were not doing anything different.

One of the arguments these writers most often used to elevate their respective vernaculars was to compare them to Latin and Greek and try to find the most similarities with the classical languages, thereby justifying claims for their lexical wealth, harmonious elegance, and minimal corruption. The Basques could not deploy this argument, but they exploited to the hilt the notion of a language of Babel or mother language that, by the very fact of being such, was also presumed to be "philosophical," that is, such that its words provided a rational explanation of the objects to which they referred. This resource was also not invented by the Basque authors, since Goropius Becanus had already used it in his *Origines Antwerpianae* (Antwerp origins, 1559), which Poza read, to defend the primordial and Edenic character of the Dutch dialect of Brabant. Even before Poza, Pedro de Madariaga, in his *Honra de escribanos* mentioned above, used the argument of brevity as grounds for praise, as when he says that 'A' by itself means 'that one' and 'I' means 'you'.

If all these considerations acquired a more intense polemical tone in the Basque Country over the course of time, while elsewhere they came to be seen as more or less arcane erudite theories, this was due to their utilization in defense of the Basques' nobility of origin, uncontaminated by Jewish or Muslim ancestry, which was a source of great prestige in inward-looking Habsburg Spain and which was subsequently applied to the defense of the *fueros*. In this way, a series of mutually dependent ideas became amalgamated into a single complex: the Tubalic origin of Basque; its antiquity and universality in the Iberian Peninsula; its uncorrupted purity, which explained its philosophical nature; its provision of loanwords to many other languages, especially Spanish, understood as derived from it; the never-lost freedom of the Basques, identified with Cantabria (the reason for the habit, widespread starting in the Renaissance, of referring to a native of the Basque Country as *Cantaber*); the origin of the *fueros* as a consequence of this freedom and simultaneously as an expression of the truest essence of Spanish national character; and so on.

Evidently, some of these views included quite a bit of exaggeration. Many of these arguments were lucidly criticized by their contemporaries, including by Basques such as Oihenart. On the most basic level, they were reactions to two deeply rooted phenomena that any interested Basque could observe quite clearly: the decadence and abandonment of the language, on the one hand, and the continuous centralizing pressure exerted by the Bourbon regime, on the other.

The first theme, a sensitive matter exclusive to Basque speakers, appears quite early in Basque literature: the first book printed in Basque, *Linguae Vasconum Primitiae*, by Bernard Dechepare (1545), can be described as a demonstration that despite what some thought—"*eta bertze nazione orok uste dute ezin deus ere skriba daiteyela lenguaje hartan, nola bertze orok baitute skribatzen berian*" (and all other nations think that nothing can be written in that language, as all others write in theirs)—Basque was a suitable language for writing books.[6]

Pedro de Madariaga complained, in Spanish this time, "I cannot refrain from becoming a little angry with my Bizkaians, because they do not use it in letters and business and give many people occasion to think that it cannot be written, when there are books printed in this language."[7] The topic was taken up again in the masterpiece of classic Basque literature, Pedro de Axular's *Guero* (Later). The focus of debate shifted from the impossibility of Basque being a written language to that of it being a language without a grammar, a lack remedied by Larramendi when he wrote the first grammar of Basque, which he published with the significant title of *Impossible vencido* (The impossible conquered, 1729). In the prologue to the work, which he dedicated to the province of Gipuzkoa, he observed, with the rhetorical flourishes customary in dedications, that he had completed a work "that envy has always reckoned to belong in the land of chimeras and impossible things." Later, in the nineteenth century, when the *fueros* and the use of Spanish in the schools became central, it is interesting to read what Basque-speaking authors like Iztueta, already mentioned, thought about attitudes interested only in the fiscal advantages of the *fueros* and not so much in the cultivation and preservation of the language.[8]

---

6. See Etxepare, *Linguae Vasconum Primitiae: The First Fruits of the Basque Language, 1545*.

7. Madariaga, *Arte de escribir ortografía de la pluma*, 252.

8. "Euscara ill ezquero Fueroac ez dira bicico; bañan Euscara bici bada, Fueroac piztuco dira. Fueroac nai dituanac, maite izan bear du Euscara; eta Euscara maite dabenac, Euscaldunai Euscaraz bear die itzeguin ta adierazo, berai dagozquioten gauza guzti guztiac. Bestela, zapuztuco da Euscara, muishinduco dira Euscaldunac, eta igues-eguingo dute Fueroac."

Even if some aspects of the traditional theory, such as the equation of the Basque Country with ancient Roman Cantabria and the identification of Basque loanwords in Spanish and even in Latin, had been questioned by more rigorous research, such as that of Henrique Flórez, Mayans, and Joaquín Traggia, the nineteenth century saw the high point of the Basque-Iberian linguistic hypothesis, which in part continued the traditional vision of the universality and antiquity of Basque in the Iberian Peninsula. Humboldt, in his famous brief study of 1821, *Prüfung* (Examination), is usually credited with introducing the theory, which was well received in European academic circles, especially in Germany.[9] Tovar clearly saw the weak points of Humboldt's text, due principally to an excessive dependence on traditional ideas drawn from the writings of Basque scholars, and its strengths, located chiefly in the methodological rigor applied to the arduous problem of ancient Hispanic place names. However, Humboldt did not succeed in conveying in his final conclusions, which would be what his followers would use, the uncertainties and methodological precautions he made a point of displaying in his text. Although he succeeded in identifying, with sound methodology, the existence of Celts in the interior of the Iberian Peninsula and attributed a series of specific toponyms to them, including *-briga,* this fact was overshadowed by his presumption that Basque was the direct descendant of the peninsula's Iberian language, extended generally throughout the region and older than the Celtic one. His prudence led him not to take into account the Iberian coin legends and inscriptions, the interpretations of which appeared entirely fantastical to him, but many of his followers, convinced of the basic idea that Basque was the modern successor of Iberian, insisted throughout the nineteenth and early twentieth centuries on reading Iberian inscriptions by way of Basque, including not only Basque grammarians like Arturo Campión but also great epigraphers like Emil Hübner and linguists like Hugo Schuchardt. This was the majority opinion until Gómez Moreno deciphered the

---

"If Euskara dies, the *fueros* will not live, but if Euskara lives, the *fueros* will revive. The defender of the *fueros* should love Euskara, and the lover of Euskara should speak to the Basques in Euskara and express in it everything that concerns them. Otherwise, Euskara will be ruined, the Basques will be weakened, and the *fueros* will vanish like smoke."

9. In English, see Humboldt, *Selected Basque Writings*.

script between 1925 and 1943. Tovar was able to confirm in his own research that knowledge of Basque was not useful in understanding Iberian inscriptions.

Some authors are only mentioned, but others receive a more detailed discussion. In some cases, such as that of Hervás y Panduro, there is an interest in recovering the figure of this highly erudite Jesuit, who was able to compile a vast amount of data about numerous languages of the world, although on the basis of scholarly assumptions that would become outdated only a few years later. The reader has the impression that the elaboration of Tovar's own catalog of Amerindian languages made him sympathetic to someone who had engaged in a similar task.

The second author who merits a more detailed treatment is Larramendi. There is no doubt that this Jesuit's vigorous personality, the enormous capacity for work that went into the composition of his *Diccionario Trilingüe* (Trilingual dictionary), and his achievements in the grammatical description of Basque attracted Tovar. Although he criticized Larramendi's extreme "ideological and mythological" approach to the central topic of Basque's antiquity, on which much more nuanced and empirically more solid opinions could be found already in Larramendi's own day, Tovar nevertheless observed in the etymological proposals of Larramendi's dictionary some fragments of truth or plausibility that he took into account in his own etymological study of Basque.

One of the prominent figures to whom Tovar dedicates more attention in this history is Miguel de Unamuno, a professor of Greek, a philosopher, an influential thinker, and the rector of the University of Salamanca in the years prior to the Spanish Civil War. Perceptible in the account is the author's sense of kinship with the Basque philosopher who, like him, initially supported Franco's rebels but was quickly disillusioned and fell dramatically into disgrace, removed from his post by those who could not endure his famous "you will conquer, but you will not convince" (*venceréis pero no convenceréis*). There are some similarities between Tovar and Unamuno in their approach to the Basque language: both learned it as adults out of scholarly interest and were much better trained in linguistics than the defenders of the mythical traditional ideas, as is evident in Unamuno's discussion of Latin loanwords in Basque, for example. There is also a substantial difference, however, in the practical attitude that each one adopted in view of the language's uncertain future. While the venerable Basque language appeared to Unamuno to be a treasure of the past, an archeological asset, a fossil not easily reconciled with the demands of a language of culture, Tovar had a broader conception of culture and knew that any language can acquire the expressive resources necessary to function in its environment, if its speakers decide accordingly.

This is the basic idea with which the book ends, in sharp contrast to Unamuno's opinion, maintained by a significant number of people in Spain, some for reasons of political centralization, others out of ignorance of the social behavior of languages. In the crucial days of the Spanish transition, when the foundations were being laid for a new coexistence in the Basque Country, Tovar's brief book served to legitimate the aspirations of those who were fighting for the language's unification and for its future: "a language cannot subsist today without schools and modern communications media, and a unified form of language is necessary . . . Depriving a language of this today is the same as condemning it to death."

Bibliography

Barros, João de. "Dialogo em louror da nossa linguagem." In *Grammatica da lingua Portuguesa*, 50r–60r. Olyssipone [Lisbon]: L. Rodrigues, 1540.

Bladé, Jean-François. *Étude sur les origines des Basques*. Paris: A. Franck, 1869.

Boudard, P. André. *Essai sur la Numismatique Ibérienne: Précédé de recherches sur l'alphabet et la langue des Ibères*. Paris, 1859.

D'Iharce de Bidassouet, Pierre, Abbé. *Histoire des Cantabres ou des premiers colons de toute l'Europe*. Paris: J. Didot Aîné, 1825.

Etxepare, Bernard. *Linguae Vasconum Primitiae*. Bordeaux, 1545.

———. *Linguae Vasconum Primitiae: The First Fruits of the Basque Language, 1545*. Translated by Mikel Morris Pagoeta. Foreword by Pello Salaburu. Preface by Paxti Altuna. Introduction by Beñat Oyharçabal. Reno: Center for Basque Studies, 2013.

Gallop, Rodney. *A Book of the Basques*. London: Macmillan, 1930. Reprint, Reno: University of Nevada Press, 1970.

Goropius Becanus, Johannes. *Origines Antwerpianae sive Cimmeriorum Becceselana*. Antwerp: Chr. Pantinus, 1569.

Hervás y Panduro, Lorenzo. *Catálogo de las lenguas de las naciones conocidas, y numeracion, division, y clases de estas segun la diversidad de sus idiomas y dialectos*. Madrid: Imprenta de la Administración del Real Arbitrio de Beneficiencia, 1800–1805.

Humboldt, Wilhelm von. *Prüfung der Untersuchungen über die Urbewohner Hispaniens vermittelst der Vaskischen Sprache*. Berlin: F. Dümmler, 1821.

———. *Selected Basque Writings: The Basques and Announcement of a Publication*. Translated by Andreas Corcoran. Introduction by Iñaki Zabaleta-Gorrotxategi. Reno: Center for Basque Studies, 2013.

Iztueta, Juan Ignacio de. *Guipuzcoaco Provinciaren Condaira edo Historia*. San Sebastián: Imprenta R. Baroja, 1847.

Landuchio, Nicolao. *Dictionarium Lingue Cantabrice*. Edited by Manuel Agud and Luis Michelena. San Sebastián: Diputación de Guipuzcoa, 1958.

———. *Dictionarium Lingue Toscane, Dictionarium Lingue Franconie, Dictionarium Lingue Cantabrice*. Manuscript in the Biblioteca Real de Madrid, 1562.

Larramendi, Manuel de. *Diccionario Trilingüe del castellano, bascuence y latín*. San Sebastián: Bartholomè Riesgo y Montero, 1745.

———. *Impossible vencido: Arte de la lengua vascongada*. Salamanca: Antonio Joseph Villargordo Alcaráz, 1729.

Madariaga, Pedro de. *Honra de escribanos: ò arte de escribir bien presto; orthographia de la pluma*. Valencia: J. de Mey, 1565. 2nd ed., *Arte de escribir ortografía de la pluma, y honra de los profesores de este magisterio*. Madrid: Antonio de Sancha, 1777.

Madariaga Orbea, Juan. *Anthology of Apologists and Detractors of the Basque Language*. Translated by Frederick H. Fornoff, Cristina Saavedra, Amaia Gabantxo, and Cameron J. Watson. Reno: Center for Basque Studies, 2006.

Mitxelena, Koldo. *Selected Writings of a Basque Scholar.* Translated by Linda White and M. Dean Johnson. Compiled and with an introduction by Pello Salaburu. Reno: Center for Basque Studies, 2008.

Oihénart, Arnauld. *Notitia utriusque Vasconiae, tum ibericae, tum aquitanicae, qua, praeter situm regionis et alia scitû digna, Navarrae regum caeterarumque, in iis, insignium vetustate et dignitate familiarum stemmata ex probatis authoribus et vetustis monumentis exhibentur: Accedunt catalogi pontificum Vasconiae aquitanicae, hactenus editis pleniores.* Paris: Sebastian Cramoisy, 1638.

Rabelais, François. *Le Tiers Livre des faicts et dicts heroïques du bon Pantagruel.* Paris: M. Fezandat, 1552.

Salaburu, Pello, and Xabier Alberdi, eds. *The Challenge of a Bilingual Society in the Basque Country.* Reno: Center for Basque Studies, 2012.

Scaliger, Joseph Justus. "Diatriba de hodiernis Francorum linguis." In *Opuscula Varia.* Frankfurt: J. Fischer, 1612.

Tovar, Antonio. *The Ancient Languages of Spain and Portugal.* New York: S. F. Vanni, 1961.

———. *Baskuli ena.* Tbilisi, 1980.

———. *The Basque Language.* Philadelphia: University of Pennsylvania Press, 1957.

———. *Catálogo de las lenguas de América del Sur.* Madrid: Gredos, 1984.

———. *El Euskera y sus parientes.* Madrid: Minotauro, 1959.

———. *Iberische Landeskunde: Baetica.* Baden-Baden: V. Koerner, 1974.

———. *Iberische Landeskunde: Lusitanien.* Baden-Baden: V. Koerner, 1976.

———. *Iberische Landeskunde: Tarraconensis.* Baden-Baden: V. Koerner, 1989.

———. *La lengua vasca.* San Sebastián: Icharopena, 1950.

———. *Lo que sabemos de la lucha de lenguas en la Península Ibérica.* Madrid: Gregorio del Toro, 1968. German translation:

Einführung in die Sprachgeschichte der Iberischen Halbinsel.
Tubingen: G. Narr, 1977.

————. *Manual de Lingüística Indoeuropea.* Madrid: Nueva Epoca,
1946–1958.

Tovar, Antonio, and Manuel Agud Querol. *Diccionario Etimológico
Vasco.* Anejos del Anuario del Seminario de Filología Vasca
"Julio de Urquijo." San Sebastián: Diputación de Guipúzcoa,
1989.

Valdés, Juan de. *Diálogo de las lenguas* (1535). In Gregorio Mayans,
Orígenes de la lengua española. Madrid: J. de Zúñiga, 1737.

Viciana, Martín de. *Libro de alabanças de las lenguas hebrea, griega,
latina, castellana y valenciana.* Valencia: J. Navarro, 1754.

Zuazo, Koldo. *The Dialects of Basque.* Translated by Aritz Branton.
Reno: Center for Basque Studies, University of Nevada, Reno,
2013.

Mythology and Ideology of the Basque Language: A History of Scholarship

Antonio Tovar

Translated by Jennifer R. Ottman

To the memory of my friend Francisco Echevarria,
a native of Durango like Astarloa

Prologue

The culture of scholarship in a country can be measured by comparing
the number of works of synthesis, theory, and systematization
published to the number of works of information. The more theory
and the less research, the weaker the scholarly culture.

— Unamuno (1893, 251)

This book is an attempt at the objective presentation of a lengthy
debate, sometimes more than a debate. A problem that complicates
our country's political life—with the insistence of many Basques,
sometimes beyond all political and moral limits, and the resistance
of many non-Basques, sometimes also without any sense of politics
or morality—originates in the lack of clear ideas about these issues.
We will restrict ourselves to their linguistic aspect, since I believe that
an uncritical attitude to the always-incomplete information available
and the belated arrival and spread of objective ideas and standards of
scholarship have contributed to aggravating the political situation.

The desire to contribute to the understanding of reality led me
long ago to devote no small part of my work to the study of Basque,
or Euskara.

A lecture I was invited to give at the Fundación Universitaria
de Madrid (University Foundation of Madrid) last year revealed to
me the current relevance and richness of the topic. I would like to
begin by thanking the event's learned sponsor, Pedro Sáinz Rodríguez,
who as an enthusiastic cultivator of the fields of study pioneered by
Menéndez Pelayo suggested the title of "Basque Studies in Spain since
the Sixteenth Century."

After reviewing a series of books with which I was already familiar
and reading others I had not previously seen, however, it became clear
what scholarship was like in past centuries. In the sixteenth century,
and even in the seventeenth, it was unthinkable that there could be a

university professorship or research institute or what we would call a seminar for the study of a language considered primitive and rustic, like Basque. The books that we can read are studies and explications by learned individuals, especially historians, who tried to answer the question posed by a mysterious language, so different from the rest. In addition, alongside the concerns of historians and scholars from outside the Basque Country, there are the works of Basque scholars, going back to the sixteenth century itself, who reflected on their language and who later set out to describe it, starting with Larramendi, the author of the first Basque grammar and dictionary.

Nonetheless, what we consider scientific scholarship arrived in our country late. Menéndez Pidal's foundation of the modern discipline of linguistics in Spain coincided with the appearance of the generation of Basque scholars represented by the two great names of Resurrección María de Azkue and Julio de Urquijo. Yet even so, truly scholarly works on Basque topics were slow to become known in Spain. H. Schuchardt, H. Gavel, G. Lacombe, C. C. Uhlenbeck, and R. Lafon were not widely read, although we knew of them thanks to the *Revista Internacional de Estudios Vascos* (International review of Basque studies). Basque was not studied at any university, and the appearance of appropriate institutions in the Basque Country, beginning with the Basque Academy, Euskaltzaindia (1919), was somewhat belated, while the abnormal political circumstances, exacerbated starting with Primo de Rivera's dictatorship, did not permit an untroubled and continuous development.

For this reason, we find ourselves in this book, to gloss Unamuno's words quoted in this prologue's epigraph, with more attempts at synthesis and especially theory-building than efforts at research and information. At first, this was what the scholarship of the time was like; later on, scholarly approaches arrived late, and their results did not become general knowledge.

Our topic is an illustrious example for that long debate, which reached its peak with Menéndez Pelayo, about "Spanish scholarship" and the scholarly achievements Spain has offered to the world.

What are we calling scholarship, then? If it is scholarship, as in one sense it is, to know facts and become acquainted with an issue in depth, then there is evidently scholarship contained in the writings we discuss here, at least those of the most important authors. Larramendi, for example, is comparable in our field to the great grammarians who described other languages. On the other hand, if we demand that scholarship be characterized by a skeptical and critical attitude, a more rigorous examination of the data, and an elimination of irrational elements, then the reader will find that it scarcely existed before Prince Bonaparte, W. J. van Eys, Arturo Campión, and Miguel de Unamuno. Precisely as a consequence of his dependence on Spanish sources, a writer as significant in the history of modern thought as W. von Humboldt maintained quite unscientific views on our topic, such as the presence of Basques in Italy and its islands, and the problem was that he was still infected by the mythology of Tubal and the histories of the forger Annius of Viterbo.

Modern scholarship, meaning critical scholarship, began all too late in Spain, and as a result, the rancor of the disputes originating in this book's topic has never been corrected by knowledge of the objective data. Mythology ended up becoming ideology, routine, and ignorance, in unfavorable and dangerous circumstances.

The reader will also be able to observe the absence of a continuous line of development in these studies. Even if it has to be acknowledged that some learned men of the sixteenth century achieved quite respectable results in determining the identity of Spain's primordial languages, it is also the case that they were unable to recognize where Basque fit in. Spanish linguistic studies, which reached great heights in that period, were able to produce, for example, the collection of "Hispanic" words that Ambrosio de Morales gathered from classical sources, and to formulate in Bernardo de Aldrete's writings the historical, that is, evolving, nature of all languages, while groping toward the sound correspondences that would make it possible to trace this process of change securely.

The Basque authors, in their apologias, are not distinguished by the rigor of their critical approach. Humiliated by the characterization of Basque as uncultured and rude, they aimed primarily to defend their language and to find in its antiquity a patent of nobility. They enthusiastically accepted the idea that it was the ancient single language of Spain, and Poza initiated a copious flow of arguments on this subject, utilizing place names. The Biblical and Christian idea of the seventy-two languages of Babel and Tubal's bringing of one of them to the Iberian Peninsula were put to use by the Basque writ-

ers as they had been before and would be later by the champions of
Spanish.

In the seventeenth century, the climate of fanaticism and religios-
ity, of which the false chronicles were symptoms, impeded any progress. Except for the special case of Henao, we know of no non-Basque
author after Aldrete who took up the subject. On the other hand, two
writers, one a French Basque and the other Navarrese, represented a
high point: Oihenart and Moret. The latter had a critical sense that
perhaps flourished better in distant provinces and in the New World
than in the fantastical Madrid of the last Habsburgs.

The eighteenth century was a period of great progress for Basque
studies. Larramendi, despite his theory-building, was the author of
the language's first grammar and its first dictionary. Unfortunately, the
latter was composed in order to demonstrate the richness of Basque
and that it was the source of a great deal of Spanish and . . . Latin. In
Larramendi, alongside a positive effort of information and, for example, a statistical study of etymology for which we have so far found
no precursors and which looks forward to mathematical linguistics,
there is a great deal of false synthesis. On these issues, Larramendi's
influence misled a scholar as diligent and alert as Hervás: it is incredible that a forerunner of comparative linguistics, as he was, who had
a mastery of the panorama of world languages unmatched by anyone else in his time, should accept, for example, that Latin was not a
mother language, but a mere mixture of Greek, Celtic, and . . . Cantabrian, that is, Basque, or that he should likewise trace the toponymy
of Spain and of Italy itself back to Basque origins. Surprisingly, the
great linguist Wilhelm von Humboldt, at the moment of his contribution to the foundation of modern linguistics, relied all too much on
theories not his own, due to his contacts with Moguel and Astarloa
and with Hervás himself.

Astarloa as well, amid the ingenuousness that led him to consider his native language to be the native language of all humanity,
did meritorious work in the analysis of Basque and even anticipated
structuralism in some ways in his account of the possibilities and
developments of the Basque verb.

It is evident, then, that the topic of Basque can serve as an indica-
tive example of the history of Spanish scholarship. The significant
achievements of the sixteenth century were followed by the sterility of

the seventeenth century, and the nineteenth century in turn saw little of value to follow the eighteenth, in which Mayans made a respectable contribution to the history of Spanish and at the same time attained a certain level of information about Basque, and in which Flórez methodically untangled the old conflation of Cantabri and Basques while Larramendi traced the outlines of the description of Euskara.

It was in the nineteenth century, moreover, when it became possible to approach the study of Basque scientifically, with the development of the comparative and historical grammar of the Indo-European languages and of Romance linguistics—not to mention Humboldt's own leadership of general linguistics, continued first by Steinthal and then by E. Lewry.

However, we have refrained from attempting to present a complete history of Basque studies during the nineteenth century in this book, because they were affected by unfavorable conditions. One of these was the influence of the fiery French Basque writer Agustín Chaho (1811–58), who on the one hand developed an entirely unfounded theory about the relationship between Euskara and Sanskrit, and on the other hand invented a mythology that had undeserved success. For Chaho's invention of the thesis that the Carlist War was a kind of Basque war of independence, see Corcuera (1979, 53–56).[1] Another unfortunate influence on Basque studies was the prestigious tradition based on Humboldt. The Basque-Iberian thesis sterilized a large part of the work done on the Iberian Peninsula's primordial languages, both in E. Hübner's (1893) careful collection of materials and in the works of the always-brilliant H. Schuchardt.

It is only at the end of the century that we finally find studies, instead of theories and theses. We have refrained from examining them in the way we have done for previous periods and for some examples from nineteenth-century Spain, including Cejador, instead limiting ourselves to summarizing at the end of this book the most reliable results that have been obtained.

---

1. This work was translated by Albert Bork and Cameron J. Watson and published as *The Origins, Ideology, and Organization of Basque Nationalism, 1876–1903* (Reno: Center for Basque Studies, 2006).

I would like to end by thanking those who have helped me in this book with their work: librarians and assistants at the Biblioteca Nacional (National Library) in Madrid, to whose efficiency and kindness I testify with gratitude, and the librarians of the Real Academia Española (Royal Spanish Academy), Cecilia López-Aranda, and the Real Academia de la Historia (Royal Academy of History), Pilar López Brea.

The Subject of Basque in the Middle Ages

The Biblical tradition about the world's repopulation after the Flood served as a foundation for the dominant ideas about the origin of Basque, as it did for other languages. The famous tenth chapter of Genesis was commented on a thousand times, and it was where the founders of peoples and languages were sought. We need not go into many details, and we will limit ourselves to recalling some of the ancient commentaries that played a dominant role in medieval culture.

Flavius Josephus, the famous Romanized Jewish historian, discusses the sons of Japheth in his *Jewish Antiquities* (I, 6, 124), where after enumerating Javan and Madai, the progenitors of the Ionians or Greeks and the Medes, respectively, he says:

Theobel founded the Theobelians, nowadays called Iberians.[1]

As he goes on to mention Meshech, the ancestor of the Moschi or Cappadocians, it is evident that these Iberians are the Caucasian or Georgian Iberians.

Leaving aside for now the Greek Christian commentaries, we are interested in saying something about the Western tradition, in which this mention of the Iberians turned out to be very significant and complicated matters.

In effect, Saint Jerome, in his commentaries on sacred texts, was clearly dependent on what Josephus had said, but also had the other, western, Iberia in mind. Thus, in *In Isaiam* (On Isaiah) XVIII, 66 (Migne, *PL* XXIV, 694), he says:

---

1. Josephus, *Jewish Antiquities*, book 1, v, 1 (124). From Loeb Classics Library, vol. 4. Translated by H. St. J. Thackeray (London: Heinemann, 1961).

Thubal autem siue Thobel aut Italia interpretatur aut Iberia, hoc est Hispania, ab Ibero flumine, unde et hodie Hispaniarum regio appellatur Celtiberia. De quibus pulchre Lucanus
Gallorum Celtae miscentes nomen Iberis;
quos nos possumus Gallohispanos dicere.

[However, Tubal or Tobel is interpreted either as Italy or as Iberia, that is, Spain, from the river Iber, for which reason the region of Spain is also today called Celtiberia. Lucan beautifully says in this regard,
The Celts of Gaul mixing their name with the Iberians,
whom we can call Gallo-Hispani.]

Jerome not only places the reference to the western Iberia alongside the earlier interpretation, but with his etymology of the name of the Ebro River, he seems to incline to the former, and with his reference to Gallo-Hispani, it would appear that he would accept the same origin for the Gauls.

This hesitation between the eastern and western Iberians, with the same etymological connection to the Ebro, is repeated in his *Comment. in Ezechielem* (Commentary on Ezekiel) VIII, 27 (Migne, *PL* XXV, 253).

The reference to Italy made by this scriptural expert, also repeated in the following passage, served as support for a very long tradition that would last until Humboldt: *Liber Hebraicarum questionum in Genesim* (Book of Hebrew questions on Genesis), commenting on chapter ten, verse three:

Thubal Iberi, qui et Hispani, a quibus Celtiberi, licet quidam Italos suspicentur.

[Tubal: the Iberians, who are also called Hispani, hence Celtiberians, although some conjecture the Italians.]

As we will see, Hervás (1784, 62) calls Tubal's descendants Iberians and refers to this passage, and it is very possible that he was also thinking of it when he found so many "Cantabrian" elements in Italy.

In a work as basic to medieval culture as the *Etymologies* of Saint Isidore of Seville, we find (IX, 2, 28f) the same opinion originating with Josephus and transmitted by Jerome:

Madai, a quo Medos existere putant. Iauan a quo Iones, qui et Graeci. Unde et mare Ionium. Thubal, a quo Iberi, qui et Hispani; licet quidem ex eo et Italos suspicentur. Mosoch ex quo Cappadoces . . .

[Madai, from whom they suppose the Medes to exist. Javan, from whom the Ionians, who are also called Greeks; hence also the Ionian Sea. Tubal, from whom the Iberians, who are also called Hispani, although some conjecture that the Italians also come from him. Meshech, from whom the Cappadocians . . .]

The same is true of a medieval author who especially interests us because his native language was very probably Basque: Archbishop Rodrigo Ximénez de Rada of Toledo.

Rodrigo was born (around 1175) in Puente de la Reina, previously named Cares, a town that we can presume to have been located within the Basque-speaking area in the twelfth century, since according to data from 1587 cited by J. Caro Baroja (1945, 13 and map facing p. 36), it was on the linguistic border at that time.[2] Ximénez de Rada, who came from a noble family, studied in Bologna and Paris and became bishop of Osma and in 1210 archbishop of Toledo. He took part in the battle of Las Navas de Tolosa and died in 1247.

At the beginning of his chronicle (1545, fol. I^v), he discusses Japheth's descendants in Europe and, in agreement with the Biblical commentators, describes Gomer as the ancestor of the Celts, while he considers Magog the ancestor of the Germans and Scythians. Subsequently (chap. III), he says that Japheth's fifth son, Tubal, was the ancestor of the

Iberi, qui et Hispani, ut dicunt Isidorus et Hieronymus.

[Iberians, who are also called Hispani, as Isidore and Jerome say.]

Tubal's sons, he continues,

diuersis prouincijs peragratis curiositate vigili occidentis vltima petierunt, qui in Hispaniam venientes, et Pyrenaei iuga primitus

---

2. Unamuno (1902, 558) says that in Rodrigo's birthplace, "Basque was spoken until the last century." I believe that this reference has to be understood as applying to the eighteenth century. Undoubtedly, Unamuno did not correct notes that he had written some years before publication.

habitantes in populos excreuere, et primo Cetubeles sunt vocati, quasi cetus Tubal.

[having passed through various provinces, roused by curiosity, sought out the farthest west. Arriving in Spain and becoming the first to inhabit the heights of the Pyrenees, they grew to form peoples and were at first called Cetubales, as if to say 'the company of Tubal' (*cetus Tubal*).]

For the Toledan archbishop, this first dispersion of peoples is not yet the separation of tongues, since Genesis evidently speaks of the latter in the following chapter, containing the story of the Tower of Babel, and it is at the latter point that Rodrigo presents a picture of the languages of Europe that bears witness to his travels and his extensive knowledge of the world of his day. G. Bonfante (1954, 680–92; 1973, 284ff) has rightly pointed out the importance of this "splendid linguistic description of Europe in his time," since almost all the linguistic families appear in it: Latin, Greek, Slavic, the Germanic languages, Hungarian, the Gallic-Breton and Irish-Scottish branches of the Celtic group, even perhaps Finnish, and of course, "Basque and Navarrese."

This is what he says (1545, fol. II, erroneously numbered IIII):

Dicitur autem Europa a quadam filia Regis Agenoris sic vocata, quam Iupiter rapiens tertiae parti mundi ex eius nomine nomen dedit. Hi post diuisionem li[n]guarum, vt regiones adirent, et vt Nemrod tyrannidem euitarent, diuisi sunt in linguas, et nationes, et linguam, quae nunc Latina dicitur, obseruarunt, alij et filij Iaphet, qui in Europae partibus resederunt, linguas alias habuere, Greci aliam, Blaci, et Bulgari aliam. Cumani aliam. Sclavi, Boemi, Poleni aliam. Vngari aliam. Insulae etiam Hibernia, et Scotia specialibus linguis vtuntur. Teutonia vero, Dacia, Noruegia, Suecia, quae a Sueuis, et Scytis nomen accepit. Flandria, et Anglia unicam habent linguam, licet idiomatibus dignoscantur. Scantia, et aliae Septentrionales Oceani insulae, quae Europae annumerantur, alijs linguis vtuntur. Valia contigua Angliae, et britannia minor circa littus Britannicum linguas proprias sunt sortitae, similiter Vascones, et Nauarrij.

[Europe is named after a certain daughter of King Agenor who had this name and was carried off by Jupiter, who gave a name derived from her name to the third part of the world. After the division of languages, so that they would go into the regions and escape Nimrod's tyranny, they were divided into languages and nations and maintained the language that is now called Latin. Others among the sons of Japheth, who settled in the districts of Europe, had other languages. The Greeks had one, the Vlachs and Bulgars another, the Cumans another, the Slavs, Bohemians, and Poles another, and the Hungarians another. The islands of Ireland and Scotland also use particular languages. On the other hand, Germany, Denmark, Norway, Sweden (which took its name from the Suevi and the Scythians), Flanders, and England have a single language, although dialects are recognized. Scandinavia and the other northern islands in the ocean, which are counted as belonging to Europe, use other languages. Wales, which is next to England, and Less Britain, near the British coast, have their own languages assigned to them, as do the Vascones and the Navarrese.]

We interrupt the text of the learned Navarrese archbishop, who locates Basque within his quite accurate survey of the European languages of his time (cf. Coseriu, 1972, 199f), because what follows, without any transition, does not refer to the situation of his time, but rather is taken from the patristic tradition we have seen represented in Jerome:

Cetubeles, itaque in populos dilatati ad plana Hispaniae descenderunt, et iuxta fluuium, qui nunc Iberus dicitur, villas et, pagos, et oppida construxerunt, et inibi remanentes, qui prius Cetubales ab Ibero fluuio, corrupto vocabulo Celtiberes se vocarunt.

[So the Cetubales, having expanded into peoples, descended to the Spanish plains and built country houses, villages, and towns along the river now called the Ebro. Remaining there, those who had previously called themselves Cetubales corrupted the term and called themselves Celtiberians after the Ebro River.]

It seems that it cannot be deduced from these passages that the archbishop thought that Basque was brought to the Pyrenees by the Tubalians. He attributes that migration of Tubal's descendants to the previous period, before Babel. Of course, we have to ask whether he was not thinking about the language of the Vascones and Navarrese in situating them precisely in the mountain range where this language has been preserved, but he never says that such a language spoken by Tubal's descendants, subsequently the Celtiberians, was the only one in the Iberian Peninsula. In his history, he immediately goes on to speak about very different regions, such as the one where Geryon was born. It has to be kept in mind that according to his chronology, 1,263 years passed between the confusion of tongues at Babel and the birth of Hercules, who killed Geryon in Andalusia, 455 years before the foundation of Rome.

We do not know how awareness of Euskara spread during the following centuries, although the language was undoubtedly coming into increasing contact with its neighbors as the late Middle Ages progressed. Permit us to note the following text of Enrique de Villena in the prologue to his translation of the *Aeneid*:

> Some say that the language that the kingdoms of Castile first had was Bizkaian, but I never saw it anywhere authoritative.[3]

The tone of the reference suggests that it was an idea held by ordinary people, inspired by facts like the presence of Basque in areas of La Rioja and what is now the province of Burgos.

In the Biblical commentaries of Alonso de Madrigal, known as "El Tostado" (circa 1400–1455) and proverbially prolific, we find a review of the patristic ideas on the origin of languages.

He takes up our topic in his commentaries on Genesis 10 and 1 Chronicles 1, following the doctors of the Church. On Tubal, he says:

> *Tubal.* A quo Hispani; iste sedem posuit in descensu montis Pirenei apud locum, qui dicitur Pampilona. Deinde cum isti se multiplicassent in multos populos ad plana Hispaniae se extenderunt, et tunc illa terra primum à coetu idest comitiva Tubal Latina lingua Coetubalia dicta est. (*In Gen.* 10, q. 1, OO I, 154)
>
> [*Tubal*, from whom the Spaniards come. He established himself on the slopes of the Pyrenean mountains at the place called Iruñea [Pamplona]. Subsequently, when they had multiplied into many peoples, they spread out into the Spanish plains, and then that land was first called Coetubalia in Latin, from 'coetus', that is, the company, 'of Tubal'.]

As can be seen, the older tradition is combined here with that of Archbishop Ximénez de Rada of Toledo. Madrigal thus goes on at once to speak about the change of the name Cetubalia to Celtibe-

---

3. This quotation is found in J. Amador de los Ríos (1862, 362).

ria in connection with the Ebro River. The name of Hesperia allows El Tostado to explain the Latin commentators' double reference to Spain and Italy as Tubal's destination.

Simplifying Saint Augustine's somewhat more complicated calculations, El Tostado then accounts for the seventy-two primordial languages:

> Et quia Japheth quindecim habuisse nominatur filios mediatè, et immediatè, ut patet in littera; ideò quindecim idiomata ab eo descenderunt. Et quia Cham triginta filios habuit, triginta idiomata habuit. Et quia Sem viginti septem filios habuit, viginti septem idiomata orta sunt, quae simul faciunt idiomata 72. (Ibid., OO I, 155)

> [And because Japheth is said to have had fifteen sons, directly or in the next generation, as is clear in the text, fifteen languages descended from him. And because Ham had thirty sons, he had thirty languages. And because Shem had twenty-seven sons, twenty-seven languages came into being, making seventy-two languages all together.]

For this purpose, Alonso de Madrigal notes that some languages took their origin from the sons of Japheth, and others from his grandsons (see *In Paralip.* [On Chronicles] I, 1, q. 6, OO [Opera omnia (Collected works)] XVI, 42).

He also mentions the topic of the population of Spain by Tubal, with the same sources in the church fathers and the archbishop of Toledo, in his *Comment. ad epist. Hieronymi ad Paulinam* (Commentary on Jerome's letter to Paulina) 1 (OO I, 4), where he shows the same interest in the name of Hesperia, which he considers the primordial name of the Iberian Peninsula.

The most interesting passage in El Tostado's Latin works is in his *Comment. in lib. Paralip.* (Commentary on the books of Chronicles) I, 1, q. 5 (OO XVI, 40).

> *Thubal.* Quintus filius est Japheth, à quo nominati sunt Hispani, sic ait communis positio Historiographorum, sic etiam Josephus cap. primo Antiquitatum, ait, quòd Thubal condidit primò Jobelos, qui nostris temporibus Hiberi appellantur, et tamen Hiberia Hispania est: non est tamen credendum, quòd tota Hispania à Thubal populata sit, nisi postea magnae mutationes factae fuerint propter bella, vel aliàs; quia Thubal unicum idioma habuit, et unicam gentem nominavit cùm dicatur de omnibus istis Genes. cap. decimo, quòd omnes in suis linguis

fuerunt, idest, quilibet habuit unum idioma distinctum ab alio: et tamen in Hispania fuerunt multae linguae à principio, et sunt; ideò non solus Thubal terram istam habitaret, sed aliae gentes cum eo venirent; verum tamen est, quòd Thubal fuit princeps habitatorum Hispaniae: nam, ut referunt Isidorus, et Lucas Todensis, et Joannes Aegidii Zamorensis post divisionem linguarum in Babylonem dispersis omnibus, qui ibi erant, quibuslibet cum similibus linguae suae Thubal cum multis aliis, usque ad montes Pyrenaeos, qui sunt claustra Hispaniae, pervenit: habitavitque ibi in terra, que nunc Navarra dicitur.

[*Tubal*. He is the fifth son of Japheth, from whom the Spaniards take their name according to the historians' common position. Josephus also likewise says in the first chapter of the *Antiquities* that Tubal first founded the Iobeli, who in our times are called the Iberians, and nevertheless Iberia is Spain. It is not to be believed, however, that all of Spain was populated by Tubal, unless great changes occurred later on account of wars or otherwise, because Tubal had a single language and gave his name to a single people, since it is said about all these in Genesis 10 that they were all in their languages, that is, each one had a language that was different from the others. Yet there are and were from the beginning many languages in Spain, so it would not have been only Tubal who lived in this land, but other peoples would have come with him. It is nonetheless true that Tubal was the chief of the inhabitants of Spain, since, as Isidore, Lucas de Tuy, and Juan Gil de Zamora recount, after the division of languages at Babel, when all those who were there were scattered, each with those of his own language, Tubal came with many others to the Pyrenean mountains, which close Spain in, and lived there in the land that is now called Navarre.]

El Tostado's account continues with the story of the Cetubelians and Celtiberia until it joins up with that of the presence of Hercules in Spain, as was usual in medieval historiography.

In this passage, we find El Tostado, for reasons we will soon better understand, convinced that various languages existed in ancient Hispania, as in the Spain of his own time. Aldrete, as we will see, made use of the passage that we have quoted in his well-founded study of the plurality of primordial languages in Spain.

In his Spanish commentary on the *Chronicle* of Eusebius, in the version expanded by Saint Jerome, El Tostado was more decisive on this issue and surprisingly lacking in a sense of history. In this work, he devotes chapter twenty-five to "The root and foundation of the population of Spain, how and why it was populated, and its names." He begins by referring to Tubal, as mentioned in the familiar passage from Josephus, and then says, "This is the common opinion, that Tubal was the captain of the people and language of Spain. Isidore says this . . ." After substantially repeating what we have already seen in the Latin texts, he insists on the confusion between Spain and Italy as the place where Tubal established himself and explains it by way of an argument based on place names:

> because Italy and Spain have a single name in Latin, since both are called Hesperia. Nevertheless, it has to be considered in this regard that, as reliable authors say, Spain was populated by Tubal, the fifth son of Japheth, who in the scattering of peoples when the languages were divided came with many people of his language, which is ours now, although much polished and altered from that first condition . . .

He goes on to affirm that Tubal's people settled "along the Pyrenean Mountains, as they are called in Latin, which we call the mountains of Aspa in the vernacular." The explanations of the names Cetubalia and Celtiberia follow (1506-7, II, fols. XV and XVᵛ).

As Alarcos (1934, 221, n. 2) has rightly pointed out, El Tostado preceded López Madero in his theory of Spanish as the primordial and Tubalic language of Spain. He did not realize that to make Noah's son arrive precisely in the Pyrenees and Navarre and on the banks of the Ebro was to place him in relation with Euskara more than with Spanish. What is more, Archbishop Rodrigo perhaps had Euskara in mind, although the truth is that he did not say so.

These medieval ideas continued to hold sway among the traditional and largely uncritical chroniclers who presented the history of Spain in the wake of Alfonso the Wise's *Crónica general de España* (General chronicle of Spain). We will turn, then, to a few such chroniclers in order to conclude this chapter.

Pero Antón Beuter

This chronicler (born in Valencia at the end of the fifteenth century) accepted the thesis that Tubal came to Spain and was the one who populated it (1604, 24).

Josephus called him Iobel and said that those who were later called
Iberians were called Iobelians from him . . . Noah wanted to give his
grandson Tubal this garden of nature, because Tubal was very valiant.

The old patriarch then came to Spain and founded cities (1604,
25).

Beuter accepts the theory that Tubal arrived in the north, and it
is curious that we find the same argument used by Garibay, that the
fruit trees of the Pyrenees made the area especially favorable for those
first settlements (1604, 26).

> And the old doctors, like Berossus himself and others, say that it was
> previously called Celtubalia or Cetubalia, as if to say "Celts of Tubal."
> (1604, 25)

Beuter also gives the Tubalic etymology of Tudela and Tafalla
(1604, 27), and later on he identifies the Navarrese with the Cantabri
(1604, 134). With regard to Basque, Beuter recounts some opinions
that, as we will see, would arouse the protest of the Basque Garibay.

In the controversial passage, he says (1604, 173):

> In the parts of the Pyrenees that are closer to the greater sea, which are
> the valley of Roncal and of Salazar, the valley of Esqua, the valley of San
> Estevan, and the surrounding areas, which descend into Gipuzkoa and
> extend along the coast in Araba and Bizkaia, the Christians remained as
> free from the Moors as they had once been from the Romans, preserv-
> ing until today the language that they had before—not that I believe
> that it was the language of Spain that the sons of Tubal used, the first
> inhabitants of Spain after the Flood, since it is neither Aramaic, which
> they spoke before the Flood, nor Chaldean, nor similar to them.

Beuter supposed that over such a span of time, Basque must have
received influence from other languages, and

> there is reason to think that the language is not as pure as what they
> spoke then. However, the principal part and foundation of that lan-
> guage is the language that was first spoken in Spain, taking into itself
> some words of newcomers who came to that coast from England and
> Germany, and so, according to their greater or lesser interaction with
> these newcomers, more or less different ways of speaking developed in

Bizkaia, Araba, Gipuzkoa, and Ruconia, which we call Navarre, so that they came to seem almost to be foreign languages . . .

Beuter is making a dialectological argument, it seems, in order to prove that Basque changed over time, and it is surely for the same reason that he immediately goes on (1604, 174) to say that the Romans imposed their language in that region as well.

Pedro de Medina

The famous cosmographer Pedro de Medina (born in Seville circa 1493) wrote a popular book on the *Grandezas y cosas notables de España* (Great and notable things of Spain). In this work, he compiled the ideas then current about the Iberian Peninsula's ancient population, basing himself on Josephus for the knowledge that Tubal, a great civilizing hero who taught geometry and the calculation of the length of the year, arrived in Spain by sea. The stories of Setúbal, Tafalla, and Tubela as Tubalic place names are included, along with all the rest (1595, fol. 21ᵛ). We find the various themes of this legendary history: Medina gets from Strabo the idea that the Andalusians were the first to have writing after the Flood (1595, fol. 24), and from fantasists like Annius the conquests of Spaniards such as Siculus in Italy (1595, fol. 28).

On the formation of Spanish and on Spain's primordial language, he presents the most widespread and generally accepted idea:

These same Romans sought to introduce their Latin or Roman language among the Spaniards, making them abandon their own barbarous language that they had until then, which some say was Basque, a language that the Bizkaians speak now, in the same way that they also introduced the use of other things . . . This is why the Latin language that the Romans introduced is called "Romance," which appears to mean "language of Rome." (1595, fol. 189).

Florián Docampo

We have selected this compiler, who lived between approximately 1449 and 1556, as a representative of the opinions current among the chroniclers.

He reports (1541, fol. 3) the history of the sons of Japheth and then (fol. 4) turns to Tubal, from whom

> came great peoples; they called them Cetubales, which means the equivalent of "the companies of Tubal."

From this name, as usual, he derives that of Celtiberia. He also refers (1541, fol. 4ᵛ) to the division of tongues at Babel, but he does not mention Basque. There is no trace of the equation of Cantabri and Basques in the mention of the Cantabrian Wars (1541, fol. 70). The Vascones appear under the name of "Gascons" in the wars of King Wamba (1541, fol. 188).

Later on, he repeats the history of the sons of Japheth (1541, fol. 287ᵛ) and their arrival (fol. 288) "straightaway to populate Spain; and as soon as they arrived, they settled in the Pyrenean Mountains." Once they were sure that there would not be another flood, "they descended from the Pyrenean Mountains and the Mountains of Aspa to settle in the plains along the banks of the Ebro."

We have seen quoted as coming from Docampo a passage in which it is supposed that the language brought by Tubal was Chaldean, until with the passage of time and the arrival of other peoples, that language gradually became corrupted, but not so much that

> we do not still find some Chaldean words mixed in with our vernacular Romance.

This text, which we have not been able to find anywhere, is not from Florián Docampo.

We end our medieval chapter with this chronicler, since in reality, he did no more than partially rework the famous chronicle of Alfonso the Wise.

Lights and Shadows of the Golden Age

> . . . but when Spaniards once begin with Tubal, the
> best plan is to shut up the book.
>
> — Richard Ford, *The Spaniards and Their
> Country* (New York, 1852), 16

Lucio Marineo Sículo

The Italian humanist Lucio Marineo Sículo (1460–1533), who was a
chronicler of the great events of the reign of Ferdinand and Isabella
and recounted them in Latin for an audience abroad, took up the question of "Which language was that of Spain in ancient times" in the
fourth book of his *Cosas memorables de España* (Memorable things
of Spain). He accepted the medieval tradition and began by affirming
(1539, fol. XXVIII^v) that

> the first inhabitants of Spain, according to what some say, all used the
> Bizkaian language, until the arrival of the Romans and Carthaginians.
> Then they all spoke Latin, although through all these centuries and
> changes of era, the Bizkaians never changed their language or customs,
> and still less the way they dress, and that way of speaking did not come
> from the Iberians or Sagii [?], still less from the Phoenicians, who once
> lived in Spain, according to what some write, but from those first inhab-
> itants of Spain, who were exiled from their native place by the great
> diversity of languages, because whoever it may have been who first came
> to Spain after the building of the Tower of Babel, that person truly
> brought one way of speaking from among the seventy-two into which
> Our Lord divided those who built the Tower at the beginning of that
> new city. Since that way of speaking has been changed or corrupted by
> the arrival of foreign peoples in Spain, it remained entirely unchanged
> only among the Bizkaians and the people of the surrounding areas, due

to the loneliness of those regions and their scant contact and interaction with foreigners, two things that, as we have said above, commonly lead to change in language as well as in customs.

He explains the spread of Latin at the expense of the original language with the help of an example from his own experience, the establishment of the Christians in the kingdom of Granada, where Arabic was preserved only in the remote and inaccessible Alpujarras. The only interesting novelty that this Sicilian humanist contributes (already noted by J. de Urquijo; cf. Michelena 1964, 146f) is a list of words "of that ancient language of Spain," Basque, with their translation.

Another chapter (fol. XXX) is dedicated to Spain's Romance language, which according to him is spoken well "from the city of Seville to Burgos and Zaragoza in Aragón." He makes no mention of either Catalan or Portuguese. Spanish appears to him to be a Roman language, but he adds that "it also has a share in Greek," and he gives as examples of Graecisms in its vocabulary *río* 'river', from the verb *rhéo* 'to flow', *artesa* 'kneading trough' from *ártos* 'bread' (an etymology that some would still defend for the Basque *arto* 'millet, maize' as well), *cara* 'face' from *kára* 'head' (it seems that there is still no better etymology), and *tío* 'uncle' from *theîos* 'uncle' (a late but certain borrowing).

He begins the sixth book of his work (fol. XLIII^v) with an account of the primordial inhabitants of Spain, in which Tubal is mentioned and ancient place names such as Noela and Noega, from Pliny, are explained as derived from the Biblical Noah. There also appear a son of Javan, Tarshish, the founder of Tarsus in Cilicia, and a son of Tubal, Iberus (1539, fol. XLIV^v). We will continue to find genealogies of this kind, which come more or less directly from the false Berossus, even in Mariana (1950, 7f).

Juan de Valdés

The idea that Basque was the ancient language of Spain is found in other authors, but we are interested in what Juan de Valdés has to say in his *Diálogo de la lengua* (Dialogue on language), part of the literature of the time on Latin and the vernacular languages. Valdés (1969, 53) says:

The language spoken today in Castile . . . has part of the language that was used in Spain before the Romans made themselves lords of it, and it also has a part from the Goths . . . and a great deal from the language of the Moors.

Slightly further on, he adds (ibid.):

although the principal part [of Spanish] is from the language that the Romans introduced, which is the Latin language, it will be well to first examine what language was that ancient one that was used in Spain before the Romans came to it. What the majority of those who inquire about these things hold and believe is that the language that the Bizkaians use today is that ancient one of Spain. They confirm this opinion with two sufficiently plausible reasons. One is that, just as the Romans' arms, when they conquered Spain, were unable to pass into that part that we call Bizkaia, so neither could their language pass into it at the time when, after having made themselves lords of Spain, they wanted the Roman language to be spoken throughout the country. The other reason is the lack of conformity between the Bizkaian language and all the other languages used in Spain today. Hence it is considered almost certain that this nation preserved its first language together with its freedom.

We will see these ideas reappear many times. They are based on the identification of the Cantabri with the Basques and attribute the possibility of saving their language to the last defenders of indigenous liberty against the Romans. With little knowledge of history, it was imagined that the Cantabri were never tamed, and Basque scholars would uphold this patriotic idea. When Strabo and Mela say that the names of the Cantabrian territory are horrible and impossible to pronounce, this is seen as evidence that such names were specifically Basque. A great deal of time would have to pass before eighteenth-century historians would correct this identification of Cantabri and Basques.

Valdés goes on in his *Diálogo* to maintain that the Iberian Peninsula's primordial language,

although it had a mixture of others, was in its largest and most principal part derived from Greek. (1969, 53)

He believed that Greek colonies and trade, the significance of which he misjudged, had spread the Greek language, as the Romans spread Latin later.

Very sensibly, Valdés's interlocutor Pacheco objects that historical sources sometimes tell us that Roman generals spoke with Turdetani, Iberians, Celtiberians, and so on, by way of interpreters, which would not have been necessary if Greek had been the language generally spoken. Valdés, although he has attempted to provide a basis for his Greek thesis with some more or less improvised etymologies, shows himself willing to give way, since

> it is better to be considered to be stupid than to be held to be stubborn. Look, however, if anyone wants to say that the Bizkaian language is even more ancient in Spain than Greek, I will not be very concerned to argue the contrary, but will rather say that it could well be . . . (1969, 56f)

Without accepting that Basque was the ancient language of the entire Iberian Peninsula, Valdés points out the contrast between Basque and the Romance languages and does not fail to recognize the entrance of Latin elements into it.

Although it cannot be said that the *Diálogo* was influential, since it remained unpublished for almost two centuries, its ideas are found in other authors, no doubt as the reflection of quite generally held opinions, except for the unusual one of a period of Greek predominance.

Antonio Agustín

Antonio Agustín (Zaragoza, 1517–Tarragona, 1586) studied in Alcalá, Bologna, and Padua. A lawyer and papal nuncio, he then became a bishop and finally archbishop of Tarragona; in that capacity, he took part in the Council of Trent. He shone not only in the legal field but also as a philologist, historian, epigrapher, and numismatist. Among his works, we are interested here in his *Diálogos de medallas, inscripciones y otras antigüedades* (Dialogues on medals, inscriptions, and other antiquities).

In the sixth dialogue (1744, 241ff), he acknowledges that

> medals in Spain are found in two kinds, some in a known language, such as Latin and Greek, others in an unknown language, which I imagine

to be the ancient language that was spoken in Spain when the Romans came to live or trade in it.

Precisely in Ampurias, he discovered, in confirmation of the well-known passage in Livy, coins with inscriptions in three languages: Greek, Latin, and correctly localized, although still without a good identification of the letters, Iberian, reading $u - n - ti - ce - s - ce - n$. Slightly further on, he is more successful in identifying on coins from Celsa the Iberian sign that we now read as *ce* and that he believes represents *c*, without a vowel, as scholars would continue to believe all the way until Hübner.

When discussing French coins in the fifth dialogue, Agustín identifies as foreign languages in the neighboring country those of the Bretons and the Basques.

> The language of the Bretons must be a foreign one that came from England, which was anciently called Britain, and that of the Basques is the Basque language of Navarre and Bizkaia. (1744, 237)

He asks (1744, 238), "Is Basque the ancient language of Spain, or of France, or that of Tubal when he came to populate Spain and France?" His interlocutor responds:

> Who can affirm either the one or the other? It is enough to know that those people of France and Spain understand one another in that barbarous language, and since they do not have books or other memorials written in that language, it is difficult to know the truth about where it came from.

This is all that we have found about Basque in this learned antiquarian. His prudence led him to not prematurely entangle the problem of Basque with that of the Iberian coins, which he also discusses in the seventh and eighth dialogues of this work.

Ambrosio de Morales

Ambrosio de Morales (1513–91) was a conscientious scholar whose primary activity was as a historian and antiquarian. His *Discurso sobre la lengua castellana* (Discourse on the Spanish language) is a panegyric that does not interest us here (1793, II, 135–53), but in his historical work, in which he continued Florián Docampo's (1541) reworking of the *Crónica general,* we find an interest in the problem of Spain's primordial language and the implantation of Latin following the Roman conquest.

The generalized identification of Cantabri and Bizkaians, that is, Basques, comes up several times in his narration of the Roman conquest. Thus, in reference to Luculus's campaign on the Duero plateau, he warns about Cantabria that

> the borders of that province were very different in ancient times from what Bizkaia is now. (1573, 109)

However, he repeatedly accepts the identification of Cantabri and Bizkaians (1573, 125, 160, 195, 196ff).

His historical sense enables him to understand the replacement of the primordial languages by Latin. Referring to the age of Augustus, he takes it that "everything that was anciently Spanish" had been lost.

> The native language had also been almost entirely lost, and everyone already spoke Latin like Romans. (1573, 196)

An especially important contribution by Morales to the study of this problem is the chapter (IX, 3) he devotes to "The various languages that the Spaniards had at this time, and the traces found of them" (1574, 221^v-222^v).

He correctly points out that in this period, that of Tiberius, Latin had become widespread, even if

> in each province of Spain, the particular language that it had was preserved.

He denies that there was one single primordial language for the entire Iberian Peninsula, just as there was no single language in his time. He bases this affirmation on his study of the classical sources, finding in Strabo the well-known passage (III, 1, 6) on the diversity of languages and scripts, in addition to the one in which he speaks (III, 3, 7) of the difficulty of transcribing the geographical names of the Cantabrian coast, which Morales does not hesitate to interpret as a reference to "the coast of Bizkaia." Likewise, he takes Mela's passage

(III, 15) on the difficulty of the same region's names as a reference to the language of the Bizkaians.

Morales compiles in these brief pages all the important texts, including Tacitus on the Termestine who spoke in his language in the time of Tiberius (*Ann.* [Annals] IV, 45) and Seneca on more or less Hispanic ethnographic elements on the island of Corsica (*Ad Heluiam* [To Helvia] 7, 8f).

He also gives a very complete list of the words that ancient authors identify as "Spanish." Quintilian, Pliny, Varro, Gelius, and Livy supply him with a list that we will encounter in the debates of the following centuries: to start with, Mariana and Aldrete will use these words in the same way, and as we will see, Larramendi will confront the same list. Words such as *gurdus* and *lancea, caelia* and *palacra, cusculia* and *cuniculus* were invoked as testimony of the Iberian Peninsula's ancient languages, even sometimes being taken up as such into the dictionary of the Spanish Academy, and for many, the fact that they do not reappear in Basque signified what Morales formulates in resolute terms:

> And from what has been said it can be understood how they lack a good foundation who want to say that the language that the Bizkaians have now and call Basque was the ancient common one of all Spain. (1574, 222^v)

Juan de Mariana

Juan de Mariana (1536–1623) can serve us very well as an example of how the Basque issue can be posed with an absence of tact. For the rest, Mariana, like his model Livy, accepts what tradition provides him, and even if he does not refrain from offering criticism, this critique often remains covert and dissimulated.

In his epic and grandiose way of presenting the origins of the nation's history, he accepts (1950, 1a) the view that Tubal, "the son of Japheth, was the first man who came to Spain." He was "finally sent to the lands where the sun sets, that is, to Spain" and "founded there, fortunately and forever, in that rude and unpolished beginning of the world, not without Heaven's providence and favor, the Spanish people and their valiant empire."

In his description of Spain, Mariana (1950, 5b) notes that Cantabria, "anciently a small region and one that did not reach the Pyrenees" was later

> more extensive, an argument for which is the city anciently called Can-
> tabriga, which was located, as is believed, between Logroño and Viana
> on the banks of the Ebro, on a steep hill that is still today called Canta-
> bria by the common people . . .; all of which demonstrates that Canta-
> bria was at one time larger than what Ptolemy indicates and even than
> what we call Bizkaia today.

Mariana is well aware that Bizkaia is only one part of the district
"divided into Bizkaia, Gipuzkoa, Araba, and the mountains," but he
uses the name in the broad sense, as was common at the time.

On surveying the languages of the Iberian Peninsula and noting
their Latin origin, he mentions Spanish, Portuguese, and Catalan-
Valencian, after which he adds:

> Only the Bizkaians preserve until today their rude and barbarous lan-
> guage, which does not receive elegance and is very different from the oth-
> ers and the most ancient in Spain, and which was common throughout
> Spain in ancient times, as some think; and it is said that all Spain used
> the Bizkaian language before Roman arms entered these provinces, with
> which their language took root. They add that since that people were of
> their nature rude, ferocious, and uncouth, like trees that are mellowed
> and improved by the goodness of the soil when they are transplanted,
> and since the mountains where they dwelled were inaccessible, they
> either never entirely received the foreign empire's yoke or else shook it
> off very quickly. It is also not improbable that the ancient and common
> language of the entire province of Spain was preserved there along with
> its ancient liberty. Others think otherwise and say on the contrary that
> the Bizkaian language was always particular to that area and not com-
> mon throughout Spain. They are moved to say this by the testimony of
> ancient authors who say that Bizkaian words, especially those for places
> and peoples, were harsher and more barbarous than those of the rest of
> Spain and could not be adapted to a Latin declination. (1950, 6)

It is clear that Mariana was familiar with the development of
these topics in the previous literature and with the famous passages
from Strabo and Mela on the Cantabrian names that we have repeatedly heard mentioned.

Mariana later uses the list of indigenous words that Morales had taken from classical authors, and like Morales, whom he does not cite, he says that

> no trace of any of these words is found in the Bizkaian language, which demonstrates that the Bizkaian language was not the one commonly used in Spain. Nevertheless, we do not deny that it may have been one of the many languages that were anciently used and possessed in Spain; we only mean to say that it was not common throughout Spain, which opinion we do not want to confirm at greater length, nor would it be relevant to our purpose here to spend more time on it. (1950, 6b)

Mariana based himself on Morales, and after considering the various possibilities, he inclined toward the latter's opinion.

Gregorio López Madera

We find a true step backward in the ideas about the life of languages held by this magistrate, who played a role in the polemic about the false relics of Granada. The famous parchment supposedly written in Spanish by Saint Caecilius in apostolic times posed no difficulty to this official of the Royal Treasury Council, since he was sure that our language was spoken at the time of the Apostles and was one of the seventy-two instituted by God at Babel (cf. Alarcos, 1934).

In his *Historia y discursos* (History and discourses), he dedicates various chapters to the issue of the language of the forgeries and attacks those who maintained that Spanish is a corruption of Latin consequent on contact with the Cimbrian language "brought by the northern nations" and then with Arabic, such that, according to him, our language is reduced to "a perpetual cento sewn and patched together from these three languages" (1602, fol. 57).

His thesis, by contrast, is that Spanish has always been spoken in Spain: "Latin was never the vernacular in Spain" (1602, fol. 58), and when the Romans conquered Spain, Spanish and Latin coexisted, since "it was impossible to take their native language away from them."

López Madera already knows that many have maintained that Spain's primordial language was Basque, and he opposes them, citing Garibay and Alonso Venero (to whom Alarcos adds as defenders of the antiquity of Basque Marineo Sículo, Martín de Viciana, and

Poza). The principal argument, in his view, is the one often put forward about the multiplicity of languages in Spain, with the famous
passages from Pliny and Mela on the unpronouncability of Cantabrian names, that is, of a Basque language that already had distinct
existence in that region.

Using passages of Saint Augustine (*De ciu. Dei* [On the city of
God], XVI, 3), who in fact only mentions Tubal, he maintains as a
great argument "the dignity of our language," which

> was one of the original ones into which the languages were divided in
> the confusion of Babel, because he says that the number of original
> languages agreed with that of the sons and grandsons of Noah who are
> recorded in Genesis and of whom there are seventy-two, and that each
> one ended up with his own language, and so one came to belong to
> Tubal, the son of Japheth and the founder of our Spain. (1602, fol. 61)

He shuts his eyes to language change in history and asserts the
thesis (in the margin of fol. 68ᵛ) that "a nation's vernacular language
is never presumed to change." Unlike the clear-sighted Aldrete, who
acquired his information from the Inca Garcilaso, López Madera
maintains that only Spanish was now spoken in the New World.

The explanation López Madera gives for the obvious similarity
between Latin and Spanish is sufficiently absurd, but the truth is that
it formed part of the repertory of received ideas in his age, and curiously, we will see it survive into the nineteenth century, still used by
Hervás and by Humboldt himself. Annius of Viterbo's famous kings,
"Atlas, Italus, and Hesperus" and all the rest, held dominion in Spain,
and in addition,

> all the land of the aborigines, where Rome was founded and the Latins
> first resided, was full of colonies and settlements of Spaniards, Sicilians,
> and Sycanians. (1602, fol. 61)

Thus the Latins, like "the Etruscan that Noah brought to Tuscany, had no language closer at hand than Spanish." Although we do
not recall that Hervás cites López Madera, this is perhaps the root of
the strange idea that Latin was not a mother language, but rather a
mixture.

For this reason, Saint Caecilius could write in Spanish in ancient
times, and this explains why Latin

always had great concordance and similarity with Spanish. (1602, fol. 62)

López Madera has no doubts. In one chapter, he demonstrates "how the language today called Spanish was always spoken in Spain," and in addition

it would result from many arguments that our language of today is the same as a thousand and fifteen hundred years ago. (1602, fol. 68ᵛ)

Further on, López Madera asserts the thesis that Arabic also could have been spoken in Spain or neighboring regions in ancient times, since he is in fact aware of the kinship among the Semitic languages (fol. 116), to the point of wanting to prove that the Carthaginians spoke a language very close to Arabic (fol. 119). Aldrete would oppose this thesis with great erudition.

For the rest, the idea that modern languages could have coexisted with ancient ones, however nonsensical it may seem to us, did not lack its partisans. Our magistrate, López Madera, could thus cite (1602, fol. 74ᵛ) the authority of the French Benedictine Génébrard, who was archbishop of Aix-en-Provence and had studied with the great humanist Turnebus, and who believed that the French language was the same in antiquity as now.

López Madera did not lack followers for antihistorical ideas of this kind in seventeenth-century Spain. Alarcos (1934, 221ff; cf. Bahner 1956, 66ff) cites authors as well-known as Gonzalo de Correas and Pellicer y Ossau as partisans of the theory that Spanish was already Spain's primordial language. *Non ragioniam di lor . . .* (Let us not speak of them . . .)

Bernardo de Aldrete

A canon of the cathedral of Córdoba, Bernardo de Aldrete (1560–1641) published two very important works related to our topic. As Amado Alonso has said, Aldrete

had a powerful scholarly mind, and in his book [1606], we admire the foundations and the first realization of historical and comparative grammar, only further developed in the nineteenth century. (quoted in Nieto Jiménez 1975, 33)

In both his works, Aldrete insistently defends the idea that the origin of Spanish was "in corrupted Latin" (Nieto Jiménez 1975, 35). Without entering here into an evaluation of his indisputable merits, as Gauger (1967) and Nieto Jiménez (1975) have done, what we are interested in noting is that this scholarly activity of Aldrete's was a reaction to the unfortunate triumph of the false chronicles. His clear sense of history led him to confront the nonsensical ideas of the miracle-mongering defenders of the lead tablets and texts that claimed to be authentic works of the apostolic age written in Spanish. Yet nevertheless . . .

In 1588, a lead casket was found during the construction of the cathedral of Granada. It contained a number of prophecies in Arabic and in a Hispanized Latin, of millenarian content and possibly referring to the end of the world. As the historian Godoy Alcántara (1868, 15) put it in his narrative of the events, it was a "pious fraud," one that gave rise to a great deal of confusion at the time and led to a long history in which Aldrete and his two books would play a role.

Once the initial forgers had met with great success, the favorable circumstances of the waning years of Philip II's reign would give rise to new forgeries. The Jesuit Román de la Higuera at once invented in Toledo a clumsy Latin chronicle that he attributed to a personage mentioned in ecclesiastical literature, Dexter, the son of Bishop Pacianus of Barcelona.

It was in vain that the bishop of Segorbe, Juan Bautista Pérez, a serious and scrupulous scholar, pointed out the poor quality of these forgeries. Fanatics clamored that criticism of these apocryphal histories endangered traditions that the forgeries sought to confirm, such as Saint James's voyage to Spain, and even—when Granadan Moriscos fighting to forestall their imminent expulsion became involved later on—fantastical arguments in Arabic texts in defense of Mary's Immaculate Conception, a topic of passionate interest at the time.

It is in this atmosphere that we have to situate Aldrete's activity. Studying the prologue of his *Origen y principio* (Origin and beginning, 1606), we have to note his desire, on the one hand, to exalt Latin and, on the other hand, without neglecting the Romance vernacular, Spanish, to oppose the nonsense that aimed to make the latter already nothing less than the language of Tubal, Spain's first inhabitant. It is the cultivation of a language by writing well in it that exalts it, not such nonsensical pretensions as those of the defenders of a Tubalic origin:

> Similar trappings and ornaments of antiquity do not beautify or honor a language that has its own rich and lustrous and unfeigned adornments.

However, it concerned Aldrete that among the parchments and lead tablets of Granada "there were writings in Spanish that claimed to go back to the time of Saint Caecilius" (Martínez Ruiz 1970, 103; cf. Godoy 1868, 101f), for after the first texts found in the Granadan cathedral's Turpiana Tower, the discoveries had continued. On the hill of the Sacromonte, with the intervention of Moriscos, whom we must suppose to have been fearful of the hostile environment that surrounded them, relics had appeared, accompanied by miracles and strange texts (Godoy 1868, 75ff).

We have no right to remove Aldrete from his time, nor to suspect him of hypocrisy, but on the one hand, his historical sense enabled him to demonstrate—with an arsenal of arguments that foreshadowed the Romance philology of the nineteenth century—that Spanish, like Italian, comes from Latin. On the other hand, it seems that he did not doubt the authenticity of the alleged documents by Saint Caecilius, one of the seven apostolic men who were supposed to have founded the Spanish Church. In his work (1606, 4), he resolves the contradiction in a way that is for us difficult to understand:

> I do not write against anyone, I do not contradict or oppose anyone, I only try to say truthfully what I think; it would be more than discourtesy to judge or affirm the contrary, because I esteem and reverence all, and still more the sacred things, on account of which this work has passed many years in silence and would be buried in oblivion if I were not obligated to express what I should in this matter. So let no one oppose me by saying that the things of the saints are not to be judged by the ordinary rules about which I write and which I discuss: what is supernatural makes its way beyond those rules . . . If the holy Apostles and those on whom they laid their hands received the gift of speaking different languages and prophesied, it was no more difficult for the same power to give them those languages that did not exist and would exist at some future time than to give them those that existed in the world and that they did not know.

With these caveats, Aldrete begins to present a history of the Romanization of the Iberian Peninsula. He devotes a dozen chapters to demonstrating that Latin was spoken in antiquity both in Rome and in the western provinces and that Latin was a vernacular language in all regions. He turns to the list of Hispanic words compiled by Ambrosio de Morales and correctly determines that some of them are really Latin, the *aues tardae* or 'avutardas' of which Pliny speaks, or the name of *canalicium* for gold extracted from pools, or the class of cave-raised snails called *cauaticae* in the Balearics (1606, 108ff). The entire first book is dedicated to explaining how a conquest like that carried out by Rome brings with it the imposition of the conquerors' language in the provinces, and Aldrete invokes the example, familiar to him, of the imposition of Spanish in the New World.

The second book demonstrates that Romance vernaculars succeeded Latin. Time brought corruption, which the barbarian invasion accentuated (Bahner 1956, 49f). Undoubtedly, the atmosphere in which the false chronicles and the fantastic theories of a López Madera arose forced Aldrete to spend too many pages on something that was obvious and had been defended by the most current and authoritative opinion. It is interesting how he is able to make use of certain forms mentioned by Saint Isidore, as when the author of the *Etymologies* speaks of the pronunciation of *hodie* as *hozie* by the Italians of his time. However, he has to waste time demonstrating that the translation of the *Fuero Juzgo,* the Visigothic law code, is relatively recent, later than the Latin original. In chapter five, he reduces to absurdity the theory that Spanish or Romance was Spain's primordial language, and he notes in the following chapter that "languages change over time," something not as generally accepted in his day as we might believe. Using examples from older Spanish, he shows change in a specific language, and in examining etymologies, he appeals to non-literary forms of Latin.

> Latin words have been reduced to only the written ones, which are undoubtedly not all of them, especially when so many books of Marcus Varro have been lost and Festus has been so mutilated, and others of Pliny and many others, in which there was a great treasury of the language, and so I am convinced that many words are Latin that we consider barbarous. (1606, 198)

He goes on (1606, 205ff) to establish the changes in vowels and replacements of consonants, a field in which Aldrete is considered, with reason, a precursor of the phonetic laws of modern linguistics (cf. Gauger 1967, 224ff). At the end of this well-founded examination, he is able to affirm that

> at the time that the Romans held the monarchy of the world, the Spaniards spoke Latin, from which the Romance that we speak now comes,

and that in maintaining this, he is following "the common sentiment of the learned men of our times" (1606, 224).

He then raises the topic that interests us in this book, that of the primordial language or languages of the Iberian Peninsula. Aldrete is resolutely in favor of the plural: "it is shown that there were many," he says in the chapter title (1606, 227). The theory of unity, along with Basque, had been defended by Garibay, he says, and in opposition to other hypotheses, El Tostado, as we have seen, had supposed that this Tubalic language had been nothing other than "ours, although much polished and altered from that first one." Faced with these theories, Aldrete turns to the classical tradition, which speaks of different languages, as we have already seen.

After affirming that Latin comes from Greek, he turns his attention to the long history of the Sycanians, a "Spanish people" who crossed to Sicily (1606, 235ff), and then, on more reliable foundations, traces the history of Latin in Spain to the Mozarabic period. The comparison of Spanish to Italian (1606, 255ff) helps him to confirm his ideas.

Like the learned authors of his age, he grants Greek a somewhat exaggerated importance in its lexical contribution to Spanish, and even, forcing somewhat a passage of Strabo in which the latter is talking about Cantabria (III, 4, 3), says (1606, 267) that "in Bizkaia, the Spartans . . . founded a city," as if he wanted to forestall the Basque authors who maintained that their homeland had always been entirely isolated.

We will not continue making extracts from Aldrete's book, since it is not of interest for our topic, but the reader can find in it extensive and critical erudition on classical texts referring to geography and toponymy, as well as on Gothic, Hebrew, and other influences.

Godoy Alcántara (1868, 163) supposes that Aldrete,

> due to a weakness of character, had allowed himself to be recruited for
> the defense of the lead tablets.

In reality, the times were changing, and no one dared confront the
propagandistic current dominant at court. Arias Montano himself
refused to speak publicly (Godoy Alcántara 1868, 163), and

> the captain of this entire host was López Madera, an ascetic magistrate
> of a type profoundly marked with the stamp of his age, who wrote
> about bonds and other legal matters just as he wrote in defense of the
> discoveries of the Sacromonte and the excellences of Spain or of Saint
> John the Baptist. (ibid.)

Aldrete at that time came into contact with an individual who
would further entangle him in this unfortunate matter of the forgeries: Archbishop Pedro (Vaca) de Castro y Quiñones, the son of the
victor over Diego de Almagro the Younger and the pacifier of Peru,
who had become the great defender of the lead tablets from his archi-
episcopal seat in Seville (Godoy 1868, 105). In March 1608, a correspondence began between the canon of Córdoba and the archbishop,
published by Martínez Ruiz (1970). The archbishop was not content
merely to protect the movement and to look everywhere for scholars
who could shed light on so many problems (Arabists were lacking
in Spain, and it was necessary to seek them abroad, in order not to
be at the mercy of deceitful and ignorant Moriscos), but also took it
upon himself to formulate his own opinion. He had his own ideas, on
which he consulted Aldrete, daring to compete with him. It could be,
he said, that

> upon the corruption of Latin, and with the vulgar language of Spain,
> the barbarous Spanish language came into being, a mixture of the two.
> (in Martínez Ruiz, 100; cf. 282)

All the same, the relationship between the erudite canon and the
arrogant prelate was not an easy one. Aldrete wrote (Martínez Ruiz
1970, 85) that he was afraid of informers; he flattered the archbishop,
saying that "our prelate is made for religious withdrawal from the

world" (Martínez Ruiz 1970, 85), something that does not appear true of that fanatic.

In 1614, Aldrete published his book on the *Antigüedades de España, África y otras provincias* (Antiquities of Spain, Africa, and other provinces). In order to understand this book, we must recall the following paragraph from a letter by Archbishop Castro to Aldrete:

> In sum, there are these two difficulties, one in the introduction of Arabic, the other in the introduction of Spanish. You place Arabic with the arrival of the Muslim Moors and Spanish with the arrival of the Goths, as there is more reason for it to have been introduced in these times than in the ancient ones, when the Carthaginians entered Spain the first time and when the Romans did.[1] (Martínez Ruiz 1970, 282f)

Aldrete comes to the archbishop's aid, addresses him with the words of a Psalm, "The Lord is my rock [*Pedro*] and my fortress [*Castro*]" (*Dominus petra mea et arx mea,* in the margin, 1614, fol. *3ᵛ), and concedes the authenticity of the writings of Caecilius and Tesiphon, expressing the hope that the Arabic in which they are written will finally be deciphered.

The new book, much more extensive than the previous one, discusses many erudite issues, motivated in part by the debate with which the earlier book had been received (1614, 2): Spain's geography and ancient history, sacred and profane, and a new examination (I, 11) of the origin of Spanish, without the corruption of Latin entering into the picture prior to "the arrival of the Goths" (1614, 85), and with great erudition but without confronting López Madera by name. In this book, we see how Aldrete had devoted himself in these years to studying Hebrew, as can also be seen in the correspondence published by Martínez Ruiz, and with these Eastern studies, he was able to discuss the true relationship of Arabic to the language of the ancient Phoenicians and Carthaginians (1614, 107ff). When we find a chapter (I, 30) titled, "There were no Arabs in Spain until the arrival of the Muslims," we already know what is at stake.

Book two's erudition in Eastern languages unfortunately ends in the defense of the "Holy Parchment and . . . the books and the rest

---

1. It seems clear that the last lines should be punctuated as a question, reading "What more reason is there for it to have been introduced in these times . . . ?"

that have been found on the Sacred Mount of Granada" (1614, 269).
Since "Saint Caecilius had the gift of tongues and of prophecy" (1614,
295), his letter in Spanish is explained accordingly:

> Saint Caecilius spoke a language that did not exist, but that would exist
> in the future . . . This new miracle, the like of which has never been
> heard or read of and which has been manifested and discovered in our
> days, deserves to be considered and paid great attention . . . The parch-
> ment's language also gives us to understand and proves what I have been
> saying, since it is very much in the manner of the court and of what is
> most used today; going word by word, it can be seen that they are all
> new words of this age, without any whiff or mixture, I do not say of
> what is very old, but not even of a hundred years ago . . . (1614, 299f)

Books three and four contain the geography and ancient history
of North Africa, with great classical erudition and use of Aldrete's
studies in Eastern languages, especially his Biblical studies.

Archbishop Castro was not satisfied with Aldrete's book, which
their correspondence reveals that he read in manuscript. With reference precisely to Caecilius's parchment, he wrote to Aldrete,

> You defend this fact as being entirely prophetic . . . I would be glad for
> you with your erudition to see your way to defend it without miracle
> and prophecy. (in Martínez Ruiz 1970, 288)

We have already seen, however, that Aldrete was unable to please
the archbishop. In the published book, he continued to say that in the
parchment written in the Spanish of his day, Caecilius had performed
an extraordinary miracle.

Was it a concession to the archbishop that in the copies of the
Antigüedades that I have seen, pages 97 to 104 are missing,[2] including
the passage that the index tells us discussed "what the language of
Spain was before the Romans came . . . 99"? Was it an imposition by

---

2. I have verified this in a copy that I possess and in another belonging to the Royal
Spanish Academy, as well as in another in the National Library in Madrid. Since my copy
has notes in French, demonstrating that it was used in France in the seventeenth century,
it has to be supposed that the suppression of these pages was carried out not only in the
copies brought into Spain, but at the press itself where the work was published.

López Madera's partisans? Did Alderete say anything more precise than in his previous work? There (1606, 227) he had said:

> I understand that the language spoken in Spain before the Romans came cannot be known with certainty or even with probability.

In any event, the religious and political climate, in which it would still take years before, by an intervention from Rome, the forgeries lost their authority (the materials were not turned over to Rome until 1641), embittered the subsequent years of Aldrete's life. He continued studying the books of the Sacromonte, even after Archbishop Castro's death. In their correspondence, we read a sad summary of the entire history from his hand (Martínez Ruiz 1970, 88):

> Would that neither the first nor the second book had come out, and that I had not done other things, which have done me much harm and destroyed me, and more so the second book, which has cost me quite a few hundreds of ducats, and I have not received even a "God give you health" for it! It does not matter; divine providence will have to remedy it.

We lament the sufferings of a scholar who had to live and work in so unfavorable an environment, and with respect to our topic, we note as a positive result his awareness that

> when the Romans came to Spain, there were various languages there, of which it is not recorded which ones or how many there were (1606, 87f)

and that from the same passages of Seneca and Mela on the Cantabri in Corsica and on Cantabria's difficult geographical names, so often cited, he deduced the plurality of languages in Spain, since those natives of Hispania pointed it out. The advocates of the universality of Basque themselves recognized as much:

> those who say that it was a general language well acknowledge this, because this was also the case at the time when Tubal came, and that with the arrivals of other nations it was gradually lost and was preserved in Bizkaia, and that this was one of the seventy-two. If this is a comfort to them, may they never lose it on my account, for I am not now trying to take it away from them. (1606, 229)

Perhaps he vented against the Tubalists the anger he had to repress against López Madera, who maintained that the Tubalic language, one of the seventy-two inspired by God, was Spanish.

Fray Jacinto de Ledesma y Mansilla

The count of La Viñaza (1893, no. 11) mentions an unpublished work of this Dominican friar from the Toledo convent of San Pedro Mártir, *Dos libros de la lengua primitiva de España* (Two books on Spain's primordial language), found in two manuscripts in the Royal Spanish Academy and in the National Library in Madrid and dated 1626.

What is of most interest to us is a paragraph that Viñaza transcribes from the dedication to the reader:

> Finally, I beg all the Basques to deal piously with this book, and that they do not discharge against it the fury of their cutlasses and darts, considering the great deal of reason it has in what it proves, and the little reason they have in usurping what was not theirs; and if perhaps they do so, let it be at a time at which I am able to respond to them, because I inform them that I have kept the best still to write.

We have not considered it worth the trouble to read the entire original, since Viñaza gives us the table of contents of the work, and its first book discusses Hebrew as the original language of all humanity. Fray Jacinto de Ledesma accepts that "the language that Tubal introduced in Spain would be called Tubalea or Tubalina," and what he is sure of, in contrast to Poza, whom he debates, is that "Basque is not the language that Tubal brought to Spain."

Ledesma supposes that this language of Tubal was preserved longest not among the Basques, but rather in Cantabria and Asturias. However, it was overlaid by other languages carried by Greeks and Phoenicians, Carthaginians and Celts.

> The Celts greatly depraved the language of Tubal in a large part of Spain, although not as lords, but rather as companions and neighbors. (fol. 215)

It is a curious idea, and I do not know where the author might have gotten it. It was the Roman conquest, according to him, that definitively wiped out Tubal's language, and after that, the Latin brought by the Romans was overlaid in its turn by the language of the Goths and that of the Arabs. Moreover, we find that Ledesma was certainly influenced by Aldrete, for he says:

> Due to these changes, notable to such a degree, it cannot be determinately known which was the first language of Spain, although numerous nouns and verbs are found that are held by the learned to belong to Spain's primordial language.

Beginning with the list of words of ancient Hispania collected by Ambrosio de Morales, he continues with others from Aldrete, and perhaps others of his own harvest, without neglecting to make use of some Basque ones from Poza.

3.

Basques Write about Their Land

> We, *euskaldunes,* the last Iberians.
>
> — G. Celaya, *Iberia sumergida* (Sunken Iberia, 1978)

Esteban de Garibay

This Basque historian (1533–99), the first native to take up the history of Basque origins since Archbishop Ximénez de Rada, reshaped in more modern form the material that the chronicles repeated. He traveled in Spain and Portugal to gather information, and in Arrasate [Mondragón] he wrote not only his *Compendio* (Compendium) but also other genealogical works, in large part unpublished. He went to Flanders to see his great chronicle through the press, and Philip II named him a royal chronicler.

Garibay has a place in Basque literature not only as a collector of proverbs but also for having transmitted in their original language some of the most significant fragments of the epic and lyric poetry of the age of the factional wars (see Villasante 1961, 61ff).

In his work, he includes "the arrival in Spain of the patriarch Tubal, Spain's first king" (1571, 81) and notes his "settlement and habitation in the region of Cantabria and lands of Navarre."

He rejects the opinion, which he reads in Docampo, that Tubal founded Setúbal in Portugal, and he puts forward an interesting argument to defend the theory that it was in Navarre and Cantabria that these original immigrants established themselves. The spontaneous products of the earth, such as mushrooms and fungi, chestnuts, and so on, as well as millet, would have made the region of the Pyrenees and Cantabria attractive prior to the cultivation of wheat, which, Garibay says (1571, 84), basing himself on Justin, was the invention of Habis. Nor could Tubal have arrived by way of Catalonia, as others claim, Master Esquivel of Alcalá for example (1571, 88), since that region was not as appropriate for the primordial way of life.

Garibay is the first to use the argument of place names to prove the Eastern origins of Basque. Thus he brings in (1571, 86) the name of the Caucasian Araxes, comparing it to that of the Araiça or Orio River, and that of Armenia's Ararat, comparing it to that of Mount Aralar, and so on.

In opposition to those who allege that Setúbal in Portugal demonstrates that Tubal was there, he triumphantly cites Tudela = Tubela.

Tubal brought order, a calendar, and elements of civilization. The language that he brought is believed by many to be Chaldean, but according to Garibay, the latter language arrived in Andalusia later, brought by Nebuchadnezzar.

> The majority of our authors write that Spain's first language was the one commonly called Basque, which is the same spoken until our day in the regions of the majority of Cantabria, especially in the provinces of Gipuzkoa, Araba, Bizkaia, and in a great part of the kingdom of Navarre, and in particular in the whole district of the *merindad* [rural policing district] of Iruñea [Pamplona], with the city itself, the *merindad* of which is the largest of the five into which the whole kingdom is divided. This language extends further to France, in the regions that border on Gipuzkoa and Navarre, because it is spoken in the city of Baiona [Bayonne] and in its diocese and on all the Pyrenean slopes as far as the lordship of Bearn. (1571, 90f)

Of this language, Garibay says that "the natives themselves call it *Enusquera*" (1571, 91), where the *n* must be a typographical error.

He criticizes Beuter, who says that Basque is "a composition of various languages," and he denies that the Valencian chronicler has the authority to speak about mixtures of Aramaic or Chaldean, since he knows neither those languages nor Cantabrian (1571, 91).

Garibay affirms (1571, 92) that "it has been verified that the Cantabrian language is pure and perfect," and that it must have some relationship with that of Armenia, which he confuses with Aramaic, but it has no mixture of Latin or Greek, "and much less Hebrew."

A curious piece of information is that the natives of Newfoundland learned Basque from Basque fishermen (1571, 92).

Andrés de Poça

Andrés de Poza (†1595) was from Lendaño de Abajo (Urduña [Orduña]), and after lengthy studies in Louvain and Salamanca and residence in Flanders, he established himself in Bilbao as a lawyer. He was also a teacher of navigation and cosmography and wrote an important work in this field. He knew various European languages, not only Latin ones, but also Flemish.

Coseriu (1972) has discussed Poza's knowledge of the distribution and classification of the languages of Europe, highlighting the Bizkaian scholar's superiority on various points over those who took up the question at the time with greater authority: Conrad Gener (1555) before Poza, and after him, Hieronymus Megiser (1603) and the famous J. J. Scaliger (1599–1605). This chapter on the languages of Europe is the sixth in the work Poza published (1587) on the ancient languages of Spain and on Cantabria, and in it he mentions the seventy-two languages that resulted from the confusion of tongues at Babel.

Our interest here is in laying out Poza's ideas about Euskara in ancient Hispania. In opposition to the critical hesitations of Ambrosio de Morales, who accepts the existence of various languages, Poza inclines to the traditional opinion that we have also found in Garibay: Basque was the primordial general language of the Iberian Peninsula (1587, fol. 4ᵛ). Poza counters the testimony of Seneca and Quintilian cited by Morales by arguing that they can be admitted for the Roman period, when different peoples well known to history had already arrived in Spain. The "great salad of words" (fol. 6ᵛ) that Morales collected from Roman sources belongs to that period and is not applicable to the primordial ages.

After Hebrew, which was by general consensus the language of Adam, Basque was the general language in Hispania before the historical colonizations. Poza calls this language "Babylonian," because it came directly from the confusion of tongues at Babel. Thus he says:

> In our Spain, besides Hebrew, the general language of the world, there then entered Basque, as a purely Babylonian language, and third there entered Greek, and fourth Phoenician, fifth African, sixth Roman, and seventh we picked up some Gothic words; last, the Arabs naturalized their language as far as the mountains.

Poza's method is the etymological one, which made its first appearance in Garibay. With his knowledge of Basque, he sets out to interpret place names from the entire Iberian Peninsula. Alongside Greek and Hebrew, he posits Basque as a source of etymologies. Already on the first folio, he explains Asturias as *asturiá* 'province or district of forgotten villas' (that is, without syntax, *aztu* 'to forget' and *uri* 'settlement'), and slightly further on, he interprets Cantabria as having the element *–briga,* which is similar to a variant of the same *uri.* He continues with similarly nonsensical etymologies, in which he will have illustrious followers, such as Larramendi and Hervás, and does not forget "the eastern Iberia" (chapter eight), "inhabited by the ancient Spanish nations." Poza concludes his work with a dictionary of place names with Basque etymologies, something in which we can consider him Humboldt's first precursor, as Unamuno has previously noted (1902, 578).

Poza was convinced of the ties between Cantabria and the ancient East. In chapter thirteen, he explains the Assyrian and Babylonian origin of the famous horn-shaped headdress of Bizkaian women; Queen Semiramis, no less, was the model, and this would explain the spread of that headdress by way of Scythia and Muscovy.

Poza lays out in complete form the topics of the lengthy debate we will review: the general diffusion of Basque in the Iberian Peninsula with abundant etymological evidence, a connection with the Caucasian Iberia, and the identification of Cantabri and Basques. On this last issue, nevertheless, Poza (chapter fourteen) is more prudent than Garibay, since he has already realized that neither the Vascones nor the Varduli could be included within the borders of the Cantabri according to the most reliable sources.

Confirming Poza's pioneering role in all areas of our topic, we also note that he is the first in whom we find (chapter twelve) Euskara characterized as a "substantial and philosophical" language.

Baltasar de Echave

In 1607, Baltasar de Echave published his *Discursos* (Discourses) in Mexico. He dedicated this book to the count of Lemos, to whom Cervantes had dedicated the first part of *Don Quixote* two years earlier, with famously little success, and who was at the time president of the Council of the Indies.

Echave took up the defense of Basque, that is, "the ancient language of Spain," against its detractors, and he affirmed that it is "as ample and elegant as the Romance that is used."

The Dominican Fray Hernando de Ojea wrote some words of praise for the front matter of Echave's book and thanked the author for having provided, by means of his knowledge of Basque, "information on the understanding and signification of many names of towns, mountains, rivers, and valleys, both of Galicia and of other provinces." We see, then, Echave applying Poza's method.

With reason, Echave made use of his New World experience to support the use of place names as a historical source, since he saw that in Mexico, place names could be understood by way of the indigenous languages.

Naturally, Echave was convinced of Basque's Tubalic origin. "One hundred forty-three years after the universal Flood," at the Tower of Babel, Basque was chosen by Tubal and his family (1607, fol. 5). For Echave, the Basque interpretation of the Biblical Senaar is undoubted: 'field of the male'. There, Basque was called *gueuzera,* "which means the same as 'ours' in Romance."

Echave is rooted in the Basque tradition, which we have already seen, that affirms this Eastern origin of Basque, finding its confirmation in Caucasian names more or less accurately repeated: Armenia, Gordeya (from *igordeya* 'the one who guards or who is made responsible for guarding'), Arage (*sic,* instead of Araxes), and Ararat demonstrate Basque's presence in the Caucasus (1607, fol. 7).

Echave references all the familiar explanations of Hispanic place names by means of Basque, without forgetting Setúbal, nor Celtiberia from *çaldia*[1] 'horse' and *ybarra*[2] 'valley', nor *–briga* from *Uriaga,* and adding, apparently on his own inspiration, the comparison of the ancient personal name Indibil to the modern surname Mendiuil (1607, fol. 31). He considers a disaster the revolution that occurred in Spain with the defeat of the Carthaginians and the Roman conquest,

---

1. In Unified Basque *zaldia.* —Ed. note
2. In Unified Basque *ibarra.* —Ed. note

1,961 years after Spain's population by the patriarch Tubal, followed
by the definitive ruin of "sad Cantabria" in the campaigns of Augustus, a misfortune originating in the envy of "the Vaccei of Old Castile" (1607, fol. 47^v).

Nevertheless, Echave notes that the Cantabri or Basques man-
aged to remain free and exempt, "as perpetual confederates of the
Roman Empire, as they were before the uprisings about which I have
told you."

He subsequently takes up the task of demonstrating the deep relationship that exists, according to him, between Basque and Spanish.

> If the promoters of the Romance called Spanish want to heed in this
> point the Basque language personified, they will find that in their courtly
> language that they esteem so much, they speak many of my words with
> the same letters and meaning with which I understand, speak, and pro-
> nounce them, and when it was introduced in Spain, in order to warn
> my children of the harm that had come to them, so that they would
> keep away from it, I called it *berbera*, which means 'foreigner'. (1607,
> fol. 58)

As the conclusion of his book, he presents a list of words common
to Euskara and Spanish, prefiguring Larramendi's work on a smaller
scale and without distinguishing between Latinisms or Romance borrowings in Basque and Basque elements in Spanish.

Arnauld Oihenart

This French lawyer, born in Maule [Mauléon], on the border of Gas-
cony and Lower Navarre (1592–1668), wrote a book on the Basque
Country in Latin, the *Notitia utriusque Vasconiae* (Notice of Both
Gasconies).

In the literature written by Basques about their homeland, the
book is original and represents the reaction of a Navarrese to the
identification of Basques with Cantabri that Gipuzkoans and Bizkaians had generalized, no doubt with earlier precedents. He explicitly opposes this confusion, spread by Paolo Giovio, the Scaligers, and
Mariana, and previously by Peter Martyr d'Anghiera. He notes the
contradictions of Fray Prudencio de Sandoval himself on this point
(1656, 4) and rejects the false descriptions of Cantabria on which
Garibay and Poza relied.

Well-informed about ancient geography, Oihenart consequently provides a description of Cantabria (1656, 8ff) and of the geography of Augustus's war. Despite the good critical sense with which he makes use of classical sources, he allows himself to be persuaded by Nebrija's authority to find traces of the Cantabrian War in Gipuzkoa, with mention of Mount Hernio.

With his excellent knowledge of the historical sources, he knows that Cantabria was called La Rioja in the time of the Goths and the Saracens (1656, 16ff).

Oihenart is the source of the idea, which has persisted to our own time, that the ancient Vascones were the authentic speakers of the Basque language. The Spanish name *Provincias Vascongadas* (Basque provinces) has been interpreted along these lines, as *vasconizadas* 'Vascon-ized'. For Oihenart, the region of the Varduli, Caristii, and Autrigones was occupied already in ancient times by the Vascones, who defeated the Cantabri, that is, those three tribes (1656, 18ff).

Opposing the dominant doctrine among Basque writers, Oihenart defends the theory that the Romans occupied the land of the Cantabri and supports it with his excellent knowledge of the ancient sources.

In his theory of the westward expansion of the Vascones, that is, the Navarrese, he notes that the Cantabri who appear as victorious in the chronicles of the Goths are none other than the Vascones,

> namque illos tres populos Biscainos inquam, Alauenses et Ipuzcuates Galli uno nomine Bascos appellant, quae uox solo declinandi et pronuntiandi modo a nomine Vasconum discrepat, Hispani autem ipsos Vascongados, eorum autem linguam Vascuence nominant, ab iisdem Vasconibus ducta utraque denominatione. (1656, 21)

> [for the French call those three peoples (the Bizkaians, Arabans, and Gipuzkoans) by the single name *bascos*, which differs only in the manner of declination and pronunciation from the name of the Vascones. The Spaniards call them *vascongados* and their language *vascuence*, both names derived from the same Vascones.]

That is, the Euskara-speaking community is for him the area where the ancient Vascones predominated. Along the same lines, he goes on at once to take advantage of the testimony of medieval chronicles, for example, that of Sebastián of Salamanca, according to whom King Fruela I of León fought against the Basques.

Oihenart then (1656, 35–37) turns to the topic of the Basque language and reports J. J. Scaliger's praise:

> nihil barbari aut stridoris aut anhelitus habet, lenissima est et suauissima, estque sine dubio uetustissima et ante tempora Romanorum illis finibus in usu erat.

> [It has nothing that is barbarous or grating or panting. It is extremely smooth and pleasant and without doubt extremely old, and it was used in that region before the time of the Romans.]

He corrects Marineo Sículo's idea that *a* and *ac* at the end of nouns are singular and plural markers, recognizing them as the article, and in passing he reproaches Garibay for having followed Marineo in this (1656, 37). He then rejects Mariana's insults to Basque and corrects his confusion of it with the language of the Cantabri, although not without praising the Jesuit's Latin style.

Afterward, he opposes Morales on the topic of the plurality of languages in the Iberian Peninsula and on his argument that his collection of Hispanic words is evidence of other languages than Basque (1656, 38). One of them, *gaesum* 'dart', he recognizes as Basque *gezi*. Oihenart shares with the Basque writers the thesis of the universality of Basque in Spain.

On the original extension of Basque, nonetheless, he does not fail to contradict himself. Swept along by Strabo's famous description of all the peoples of the northern part of the Iberian Peninsula as a group, he thinks that Basque was their primordial language:

> hanc uniuersis illis montanis populis, qui Septentrionale latus Hispaniae incolebant, communem fuisse existimo, Vasconibus scilicet, Vardulis, Autrigonibus, Caristis, Asturibus, Cantabris, Gallaecis ac Lusitanis. (1656, 44)

> [I consider that this language was common to all those mountain peoples who inhabited the northern part of Spain, namely the Vascones, Varduli, Autrigones, Caristii, Astures, Cantabri, Gallaeci, and Lusitani.]

On the same grounds, he thinks that it is in modern Spanish that remnants of that language survive. He explains this with the image of such lexical remains as ruins fitted to one another in Spanish by means of a cement that is also similar to Basque:

in hac hodiernae Hispanicae linguae compage reliquiae seu rudera deprenduntur, cum caementis Vasconicae admodum congruentia. (1656, 44)

[in this structure of today's Spanish language, remnants or rubble that correspond quite well to Basque are detected, along with unworked stones.][3]

As proof of this affirmation, he goes on to present a series of Basque-Spanish comparisons in which, alongside etymological problems for which solutions have repeatedly been sought in Basque (*asco, ascua, bizarro* . . .), we have elemental words like Spanish *ama* 'mistress of the house' and Basque *ama* 'mother', Spanish *buz* 'lip' and Basque *musu* 'snout'; shared Latinisms, like Basque *apostu* and Spanish *apuesto, apuesta* 'wager'; Arabisms like Spanish *alcalde* and Basque *alkate* and *alcandora*,[4] Spanish *zaragüelles* and Basque *çaragollac*; and finally fantasies and errors like Spanish *arriate* 'causeway' and Basque *arri* 'stone' and *ate* 'door', and derivations of Spanish *ahilarse* 'to become faint' from Basque *hila* 'dead' and Spanish *ancho* 'wide' from Basque *andicho*, the diminutive of *andi* 'large', or Spanish *burujón* 'bump on the head (caused by a blow)' from Basque *buru* 'head' and *jo* 'to hit'. He recognizes the Basque origins of Spanish *bruzes* 'face downwards' and *çatico* 'small bit of bread', but he explains (1656, 54) Spanish *hijodalgo* 'gentleman (literally 'son of something')' as a translated concept, the equivalent of Basque "*aitoren seme,* which means the son of a certain father, as if you were to say *ait'joren seme,* and which is likewise applied among the Basques to a nobleman."

---

3. Tovar seems to have misread Oihenart's rather involved seventeenth-century Latin. "Caementa" (ablative plural "caementis") are blocks of unworked stone, not cement (Spanish "cemento"), and what is similar to Basque ("Vasconicae admodum congruentia") has to be the "remnants or rubble" ("reliquiae seu rudera"), not the "caementa." —Trans. note

4. In Unified Basque, *alkandora*. —Ed. note

With a particular sense of his own authority as a collector of proverbs, he finds a similar identity between Basque and Spanish proverbs, the latter being clumsy reproductions of what he finds to be metrically and more fittingly expressed in Basque.

His knowledge of Basque allows him to be more precise in top-onymical matters that had often been addressed with less seriousness, such as, for example, the question of Basque *iri* and *ili* (1656, 55).

After this, he sets out an explanation of Basque grammar, for the first time in a work of history. It is easy to find mistakes in it, as a first attempt, but Oihenart's acumen is also evident in many points.

The third book of the *Notitia* deals with the Basques north of the Pyrenees (1656, 383ff). Scaliger had thought that they established themselves there as a consequence of Messalla's campaigns, but Oihenart refutes him very effectively, as well as rejecting the idea that it was Pompey who established the Vascones north of the Pyrenees with the colony of Convenae. Studying later texts, he finds references to the movements of the Vascones in Ausonius's poetry and above all in the well-known passage by Gregory of Tours, *Histor.* (History) IX, 7:

> Wascones uero de montibus prorrumpentes, in plana descendunt, agrosque depopulantes, domus tradentes incendio . . .

> [Bursting forth from the mountains, the Vascones descend to the plains, depopulating the countryside, setting houses on fire . . .]

In reality, however, the Merovingian chronicler does not mention colonizations or settlements of the Vascones, but simply an incursion. As in the case of the Caristii and Autrigones, whom he supposes to have been conquered by the Vascones, here also the identification of Euskara with the nation of the Vascones leads Oihenart to develop an entire theory that enables him to trace the French Basque Country back to an invasion from Navarre.

Joseph de Moret

Joseph de Moret was born and died in Iruñea [Pamplona] (1615–87). He served as rector of the Jesuit school in Palencia and, after having written a Latin account of the siege of Hondarribia [Fuenterrabía] by the French, he was named a chronicler of the kingdom of Navarre.

Prior to his great historical work, which he was unable to complete and which would be continued by a fellow Jesuit in its last volumes, he wrote *Investigaciones históricas* (Historical inquiries) (1665) for special discussions of some points. Of particular interest to us are the first six chapters of book one, which deal in particular with the ancient Vascones.

Moret, a conscientious historian with a much more critical spirit than the majority of Basque scholars, begins with an excellent historical geography of the region of the Vascones, which approximately coincides with Navarre (1665, 1). Their mention with reference to the territory of Araba in Visigothic times is explained, according to Moret (1665, 61ff), by their raiding expeditions, which extended even as far as La Bureba (Burgos). This also explains the references to the Vascones early in the Reconquest. He likewise interprets in terms of Vasconian expeditions the mentions of their penetration into Aquitaine around 581.

When he takes up the original population of Spain in chapter four, he is faced with the topic of Tubal. He places alongside the "tradition from time immemorial of the entire Spanish nation" (1665, 73) the authority derived from the Bible, with its interpreters Flavius Josephus and Jerome. In this part of his work, Moret is much more erudite and careful than others who discuss the subject, both in his compilation of Biblical passages (Genesis 10: 2, Ezekiel 27: 13, and even the non-canonical IV Maccabees 1) and in his exact references to the commentators.

He is also quite critical when it comes to etymologies, dismissing, for example, the widely accepted derivation of Setúbal, which he correctly points out is a modern fishing town (1665, 81), and the nonsensical derivations of Tudela[5] and Tafalla from Tubela and Tubala (ibid.). He at times gives way on Navarrese matters and so accepts the famous link between the Armenian Ararat and Aralar, in addition to believing that Araxes is the same name as Araitz [Araiz] (1665, 85).

---

5. Moret discussed this widespread and nonsensical etymology of Tudela from Tubela in a separate pamphlet that I have not seen, published under a pseudonym and with a false imprint: *El Bodoque contra el propugnáculo histórico y jurídico del licenciado Conchillos* (The pellet missile against Licentiate Conchillos's historical and legal bulwark), by Fabio Silvio y Marcelo, Cologne, 1667.

In the following chapter, he discusses the language of the Vascones, Basque, "over which so many centuries have passed" (1665,
90), and says:

> it appears that it can be proved not only by plausible and prudent con-
> jectures, but even more efficaciously, that the Basque language, which
> the northern mountains of Spain retain today, Navarre, Gipuzkoa,
> Bizkaia, and Araba, is immemorial, primordial, and original to these
> regions from the first population of Spain,

going on (1665, 91) to cite the testimony of Basque words in medieval
Navarrese documents.

Note Moret's critical prudence, with which he insists on Basque's
antiquity only in the area where it is preserved and does not insist on
identifying the Cantabri with the Basques, although without opposing the common belief that the Basque-speaking region was never
dominated by the Romans.

For the rest, Moret follows common opinion as far as the Basque
etymologies of geographical names are concerned. He insists on the
explanation of the name Ebro as *ur-bero,* and although he is familiar
with its possible relationship to the Basque *ibai* 'river', he prefers the
more widely accepted interpretation as *ur bero* 'hot water', which he
reinforces with the existence of an Ibero River in Leitza [Leiza] with
two hot springs (1665, 95f).

He concludes this argument:

> The Vascon origin, then, of the Ibero River, which gave its name to all
> of Spain at such an ancient date, is an argument that this language, at
> least in the regions where it is spoken today, is original and primordial
> from its first population and one of those that are called "mother lan-
> guages" and one of the seventy-two from the first division at Babel.
> (1665, 96)

Faced with the Basque place names also found in other regions
of the Iberian Peninsula, on which Moret will comment, his critical
spirit imposes some reservations. He begins:

> Proving whether it was common to all the Spaniards is a more difficult
> matter. (1665, 97)

He goes on to recall Iliberis and other classical toponyms and adopts Morales's accurate observations on the Celts and Strabo's testimony on the Turdetani.

He is unable to respond very well to Morales's argument about the words from ancient Hispania preserved in various authors and incapable of explanation by way of Basque, and he risks a few fantastic etymologies, such as *baluce* 'nugget of gold' from Basque *baliz luce* 'if it were long' (1665, 104).[6]

In response to Mariana's accusation that the language is rude and barbarous, Moret says (1665, 108):

> If it was original and common to all of Spain and was preserved as a witness to Spain's freedom, why mock having it?

He falls into the temptation, to which Larramendi and Astarloa will succumb later, of considering Basque as a language of marvelous and profound etymologies, and so he gives as examples some that are accurate and others that are fantastical: *Jaungoikoa* 'God', that is, 'Lord of what is above', *eguzkia* 'sun', 'day maker', *gizon* 'man', *gauz-on* 'good thing'. That the *euskaldunes* (Basque speakers) have preserved their language is a source of pride for him, and he says as much (1665, 109):

> If in this necessity of fortune other peoples are not mocked for having lost their language entirely, why is it cast up to this one that it has retained it, although in a somewhat diminished and less cultivated form?

On the subject of the identification of Cantabri with Basques, to which Bizkaian and Gipuzkoan authors were and would remain so resolutely inclined, Moret (1665, 110ff), persuaded by Oihenart's work and by his own perfect knowledge of the classical sources, affirms the correspondence of the territory of the Vascones with Navarre and does not refuse to recognize the separate existence of Caristii, Varduli, and Autrigones between Navarre and ancient Cantabria. He analyzes the opinions of the Spanish historians, noting, for example, Fray Prudencio de Sandoval's vacillations and Morales's concession to

---

6. In Unified Basque *balitz luze*. —Ed. note

the commonly held idea, even if he may have realized that the identification was false. He does acknowledge that during the Middle Ages,
the name of Cantabria was used less precisely than in the classical
sources. We should note here once again Moret's excellent knowledge
of ancient geography and his analysis of the campaigns of Augustus's
war against the Cantabri.

In his *Anales del Reyno de Navarra* (Annals of the Kingdom of
Navarre), of which we will examine only the section on the ancient
period, he begins (1684, 3ff) by summarizing his work on the Vascones.
He accepts the etymology of *vasco* 'Basque' from *baso-ko* and interprets *Navarra* 'Navarre' as a compound of *nava* 'plain surrounded by
mountains' and *erri* 'land or region'. He says (1684, 3ff):

> The Navarrese, like their Gipuzkoan, Araban, and Bizkaian neighbors
> as well, take pride in tracing their origin to the primordial and original
> Spaniards and in the population of Spain by Tubal having begun in this
> region of theirs in the Pyrenees and their flanks and on the banks of the
> Ebro . . .

For further information, he refers the reader to the Navarrese
historian Rodrigo Ximénez de Rada, with whom we can observe his
coincidence of views.

Moret goes on to note that Basque has lost territory (1684, 4),
although there are Basque names throughout the Iberian Peninsula
that

> are an argument for its first origin and that it was a common language
> throughout Spain before late-coming peoples entered, as the Navarrese
> Doctor (that is, Martín de Azpilicueta) thought, along with other seri-
> ous writers.

He turns once more to the Basque place names that he had presented with more critical safeguards in his *Investigaciones*. In confirmation of his etymology of *Ebro* from *ur bero*, he claims that in
Fontibre (Cantabria), at the river's source, the water never freezes,
despite the rigor of the climate.

The first part of the appendix of this first volume of the *Anales* is
devoted to a discussion "Of the population and primordial language
of Spain" (1684, 1–30).

The motive of this review of a topic that had already been discussed in the *Investigaciones,* as we have seen, was to engage in polemic against a work, the author of which he does not name, that aimed to exclude Tubal from any participation in Spain's primordial population,

> substituting in his place as Spain's first inhabitant his nephew Tarshish, the son of his brother Javan, and wanting to insist that the original and primordial language of the ancient Spaniards was in substance the same one that we speak today and that we popularly call Romance . . .

This is the thesis, which we have already mentioned, of the defenders of the chronicles of Maximus and the rest. Against this view, Moret insists on his arguments founded on the Tubalic tradition, just as in his *Investigaciones.* The point at issue in these alliances was to demonstrate that

> the Spanish language that we commonly use in Spain today was one of the seventy-two mother languages infused by God in the division of peoples. (1684, 30 of the appendix)

The conclusion of this whole part is the defense, as in Moret's earlier work, of the antiquity of Basque (1684, 30 of the appendix):

> And so at the time of the Romans, as before and since, the provinces and peoples of the Basque language have preserved their Spanish blood and origin more purely and without admixture of late-coming nations, something that helped to preserve the primordial language.

What ancient prejudices survive in Moret's critical spirit to defend the purity of blood that Larramendi and Arana-Goiri will invoke, and against which Unamuno will still speak two centuries later!

Gabriel de Henao

Henao (1611–1704), although a native of Valladolid, may serve to close this chapter on Basque authors. His work on the *Antigüedades de Cantabria* (Antiquities of Cantabria) (1689–91), which first appeared in Latin in Zaragoza in 1637 (*De Vizcaya illustranda* [On illustrious Bizkaia]), is a homage "to Saint Ignatius of Loyola, a Cantabrian, the founder and patriarch of the Society of Jesus, a son

of the three Cantabrian provinces, Gipuzkoa, Bizkaia, and Araba."
The motive of his great publication, a compilation of exhaustive
erudition, is the cession of the founder's ancestral home by the mar-
quises of Alcañizas y de Oropesa de Indias, lords of Loyola, to
Queen Mariana, and then by her to the Society for the foundation
of a school.

Henao spent some time in Iruñea [Pamplona], where he became
familiar with the Basque regions, and then spent the majority of his
life in Salamanca, where he wrote a large number of religious and
theological works.

His study of the Basque provinces as a homage to the founder
of the Society also belongs to this genre. Ignatius's genealogy, which
opens the work, and the saint's relationship to Azpeitia, which concludes the two folio volumes, bookend issues that are in part of interest to us, since they represent a viewpoint widespread among Basques
at the time.

Naturally, Henao defends Tubal as Spain's first inhabitant and
attacks Alonso de Cartagena, who had maintained that our country
had already been inhabited before the Flood (1689, 2ff). He then discusses at length the conquests of the Cantabri: in Ireland, in England,
in the Asian Iberia, in Corsica, in India . . . Such conquests or the
possibility of them are examined with quantities of citations. Basing himself on the real importance of Basque sailors in his day, he
defends the "expertise, valor, and conquests of the Cantabri by sea.
They discovered," he says, referring to those primitive ages (22ff), "the
Canaries and the Americas."

He studies the Cantabrian War and once more takes up its geography in detail in order to try to situate it in the Basque regions. He
does not lightly accept the identifications of Arracilium, Vinium, and
so on proposed by Basque scholars, but even so, he cannot resist the
temptation to provide more evidence for the thesis that the Basque-
Cantabri were never pagans. Chapter twenty-eight of this first part is
titled, "Augustus imitates on his banners the device of the cross used
by the Cantabri on theirs." We find, as well, that the Christian interpretation of the Cantabrian standard goes back to very ancient times,
to Minucius Felix and Tertullian. What we find for the first time in

Henao, who takes it from Juan Cortés,[7] is the Basque etymology *lau buru* for the Constantinian labarum.

The pious Henao takes the opportunity to ask whether his Cantabri were really idolaters before receiving Christianity (1689, 154), and he supports Garibay and Echave with new arguments.

Henao's real erudition does not allow him to rest content with this, and in various chapters (1689, 270ff), he examines the identity of the Varduli, Caristii, and Autrigones and their relationship with the Cantabri. He also opposes the opinions of the Navarrese who want to make Vascones out of the Arabans.

The second volume of the work is of less interest to us, but the nobility of Saint Ignatius's line is linked for Henao with the independence and non-contamination claimed for the ancient Cantabri. There we read that not even Leovigild entered Cantabria; that if Suintila did enter, it was in order to take the Bizkaians under a kind of pact of protection; and that Pelayo, the first king of the Reconquest, was a Goth on one side of his family and a Cantabrian, that is, a Basque, on the other. The last book primarily argues that the most important locations in the Basque provinces were never occupied by the Moors: neither Urduña [Orduña] nor Gernika [Guernica] nor others.

From Henao we may turn to Larramendi, his inferior in erudition, but his superior in knowledge and study of Basque.

---

7. This is the authority Henao cites, in the work *De la constancia de la fe* (On the constancy of the faith), book III, chapter V. The Espasa dictionary lists a seventeenth-century writer by the name of Juan Cortés, from Tolosa, but I have so far been unable to find more information.

4

The Polemic between Larramendi and Mayans

> . . . the mysterious paths of Euskara, which has, I know
> not why, the rare privilege of causing everyone who takes an
> interest in the interpretation of its enigmas to stumble.
>
> — Menéndez Pelayo (1941, 198)

Larramendi: His First Works in Basque Studies

Manuel de Larramendi, who was born in 1690 in Andoain (Gipuzkoa)
and died in 1766 in Loiola [Loyola], is one of the most important figures in the history of scholarship on the Basque language. We owe to
him Basque's first grammar and its first published dictionary.

Larramendi, who used his mother's surname in place of his
father's, Garagorri, entered the Society of Jesus in 1707 and studied
at the Villagarcía de Campos novitiate. On the title page of his grammar, he identifies himself as holding a master's degree in theology
from the Royal College of Salamanca. Forgetting this, the biographi-
cal notice that accompanied the republication of his *Diccionario* (Dictionary, 1853, XVI) says that it was during the period when he served
as confessor to Charles II's widow, the dowager queen Maria Anna
of Neuburg, in Baiona [Bayonne] (1730–33) that he occupied himself
with "making a study of his native language, Basque, comparing it to
an infinity of living languages and many dead ones, an arduous task"
with which he desired "to do an important service to his country,
which he wanted above all, as well as to philological scholarship."

The same source indicates that when he left his post at the dowager queen's court, "he returned to his native region, where he continued working more enthusiastically than ever in demonstrating the
antiquity of Basque, a language that, as can be seen in the luminous

prologue of this dictionary . . ., he aimed to prove was one of the primordial ones." In effect, Larramendi spent the rest of his days in Loiola [Loyola]. He was undoubtedly a great preacher, and the censor of his *Diccionario*, the Augustinian Fray Bartolomé de Galarza, praised him by saying that "the language of his fathers has not been heard with greater exquisiteness for many years in Gipuzkoa." One of these sermons has been published (Villasante 1961, 135).

Larramendi wanted to continue the tradition, strongly rooted among the Basques, that their language was the primordial one of Spain, and as such, one of the primordial or mother languages that arose from the confusion of tongues at Babel itself.

Motivated by patriotic enthusiasm for his native language, and preparing the publication of his grammar, he began by publishing a brief work *De la antigüedad y universalidad del bascuence en España* (On the antiquity and universality of Basque in Spain), dedicated to the count of Salazar, Juan de Ydiáquez (at the time governor of the Prince of Asturias), a fellow countryman and hence convinced of the excellences of Basque proclaimed in the book. In the note to the reader that follows the dedication, Larramendi justifies the "bold, heated, and brusque tone of his language" and immediately goes on to explain the motivation for his work.

Considering the Spanish Academy "a very respectable guild, both on other grounds that make it worthy of all attention and because it is made up of individuals of well-known letters and exquisite erudition," and judging the dictionary that we commonly call the *Diccionario de Autoridades* (Dictionary of authorities, 1726–39) "to be a work of the greatest erudition, full of select specimens, maturity of judgment," and so on, he describes at the same time "the just sentiment aroused in us Basques by the scant use made of Basque, the knowledge of which, even in the view of impartial scholars, appears indispensable for success in their enterprise."

Larramendi's anger demonstrates that he already held at that time the etymological ideas that he would later apply in his *Diccionario*, but on the other hand, the Madrid academicians who compiled the *Diccionario de Autoridades* had no documentation available to them in order to research the possible Basque etymologies of Spanish.

Larramendi thus begins his treatise by declaring that he well knows that I have to do battle with strangers and kin, with the learned and with the ignorant, since even the mute commoner wants to take an interest in this joust. (1728, 1)

He boasts that he has been able to compose a grammar of Basque and that (1728, 4f)

I have overcome difficulties they called impossible, and that I do not owe this to fortune and chance, but to work and application, both the general application I have had to these subjects and the particular one of examining with a hundred reflections our most beautiful language.

He goes on to a panegyric of Euskara, already presented almost as a litany in the dedication. Without need of academies like those of Florence, Paris, and Madrid, he says,

without assemblies and at first hand, Basque turns out so exquisite, so well arranged, so harmonious in its declinations, conjugations, syntax with its eight parts of speech, prosody with its accents . . . (1728, 8)

"It is true that the literature is poor," Larramendi acknowledges,

but Basque has not fared so poorly among those peaks that have known how to preserve it so many years, which the plains could not. (1728, 9)

Larramendi organizes his panegyric into sixteen sections, from which we will extract only what interests us for the history of ideas about Basque.

The first three sections present Basque as "the most ancient language of Spain" (1728, 10) and as a "universal language" in Spain (1728, 19). As we have seen, this thesis was very widely accepted, and Larramendi cites (1728, 12) the authority of Mariana and, stretching a point, that of the Academy itself, which said in its prefatory discourse on the origin of Spanish (§ 9), in the front matter of its first dictionary, that the Romans imposed Latin throughout Spain, such that "from the colonies and municipalities it gradually spread to the villages, and only the Bizkaians have tenaciously preserved their language to the present." Larramendi does not fail to correct this widespread use of "Bizkaian" in the general sense of "Basque," and he then makes a syllogistic argument in favor of Basque as the Iberian Peninsula's single primordial language, where the Academy (§ 4) had been very cautious in its pronouncements on the "maternal language" brought by the first inhabitant, "whether that was Tubal, as the majority suppose, or Tarshish, as some think." The Academy said that "this language became buried in oblivion to such a degree that there has remained only the certain memory that it existed, something that naturally could not have happened except through its entire corruption or through the introduction of one or more other different languages."

Larramendi (1728, 28) cites the continuous tradition that this language of Tubal was none other than Basque, as confirmed by the explanation of numerous place names from throughout the Iberian Peninsula.

Against Morales and Mariana, who inclined toward a plurality of languages in the Peninsula, he criticized the very solid argument of the list of "the twenty or thirty words . . . that are not part of Basque today" (1728, 19). He gets around this problem with several somewhat tasteless jokes about "Ambrosio's rifle" (*la carabina de Ambrosio*), playing on this proverbial expression for a useless object and the name of Ambrosio de Morales, the first to compile, with admirable erudition, the references to Hispanic words in classical texts, and with the argument, reasonable for its part, that a language may lose elements of its vocabulary over the course of time, and all the more so when Larramendi believes that the ancient authors may have given us the words in a distorted form. For an etymologist like him (and in general for the etymologists of his time), with a larger or smaller number of hypothesized changes, words such as "*briga, gurdos, cusculia, lancea* clearly have a Basque origin" (1728, 24).

Larramendi sees other evidence that Basque was a "universal language of the ancient Spaniards" in the names of aristocratic families like the Mendozas, the Zúñigas, the Velascos, and so on (1728, 26), which

> have descended through the centuries from the ancient language of Spain, and consequently were imposed in this language and not in another.

He then begins, by way of Spain's various regions, to collect names that can be explained, with more or less violence to the evidence, by way of Euskara. From Catalonia, home of the Aletanos or Laletanos (from "*alá*, a type of large boat"), to Andalusia, with "the famous Eliberri, Eriberri, Yriberri," and Galicia, site of Yria (1728, 28–31), he finds Basque everywhere, like Poza before him and Humboldt almost a century later.

He also accepts the relationship with the Caucasian regions and that "our ancient Spaniards went to populate the Asian Iberia." These Spaniards were not only Gipuzkoans, Bizkaians, and Navarrese, but also from the other provinces of Spain (1728, 35f), in which Euskara was likewise spoken, as proven, in his view, by as many as ten Caucasian place names that he takes from Ptolemy and explains without difficulty by way of Basque. Larramendi concludes (1728, 37f):

> The Basques are the legitimate Spaniards, unmixed, descended from the ancient inhabitants of Spain and their successors, who took refuge in those mountains, either from the general drought recounted in the histories or from the flood of other nations that took control of the other provinces of Spain.

He then confronts the Academy's affirmation that not even a memory of Spain's primordial language had remained (1728, 42ff) and expounds his view that the primordial language, that is, Basque, survives in Spanish words, unrecognized by the Academy's new dictionary. The theory behind his *Diccionario trilingüe* (Trilingual dictionary), which will appear a decade and a half later, is here already present, and ideas of this kind will continue to be promoted by Hervás y Panduro. Here are some examples, among which we have included a larger proportion of successes than of nonsense: *abrevar* is neither Latin nor French, but instead comes in both languages

> from Basque *abere* 'cattle' [a Latinism, from *habere* 'to have'], as if *aberevar* meant 'to take the cattle to water', which is what *abrevar* means. (1728, 53f)

Likewise, *ademán* 'gesture' (a word that indeed has not been explained) must be from Basque "*adi, aditú* 'to understand' and *emanemán* 'to give'" (1728, 55), and so on, as far as *badajo* 'clapper of a bell', supposed to be from *jo, badabadá, jo* 'strike, then, strike', "as said by someone urging the ringing of a bell" (1728, 68) . . . It is true that he has good reason to recognize Basque *chiki, chikitu,*[1] in *achicar,* that there is perhaps no better etymology for *asco* 'disgust' than Basque *asko* 'a great deal and more than enough', and that scholars still speculate about Basque explanations for words such as *bizarría* and *bruces.*

Less interesting for us are the sections that follow, in which (1728, 90f) Larramendi defends Basque from insults like those of Mariana, who called it, as we know, *rudem et barbaram linguam, culturam abhorrentem* (a rude and barbarous language, abhorrent to cultivation), but whom his fellow Jesuit refutes with the words of Joseph Scaliger that we have already seen in Moret.

After citing this great authority on Basque's harmony and antiquity, he lists its perfections one after another.

Filled with enthusiasm for his language, Larramendi asks which language is that of the angels in paradise and hurries to reply to those who might have any doubt on the subject:

> Gentlemen, if you theologians and others knew Basque, you would conclude on the instant that Basque is the angelic speech, and that in order to speak to the angels in their own language, it is necessary to speak to them in Basque. (1728, 101)

Further on:

> Let us grant that there is a language in the world (call it the "language of reason") in which every perfection is found . . . then that language distinguished by the propriety of its words, its distinctness and preciseness in the ways of speaking, its courtesy and discretion, the concord and certainty of its rules, their logicality, the harmony in its arrangement, and its richness and abundance . . . Then I say that according to this rule, Basque is the best language and more perfect than the rest, at least than Latin, Romance, French, Italian. Let us turn to the evidence. (1728, 105f)

There follows a comparison with all these languages in dialogue form, ending with the exaltation of the language of the enthusiastic author.

---

1. In Unified Basque *txiki, txikitu.* —Ed. note

The following year, Larramendi published his grammar (1729). It is a really excellent book, on which we will not comment here. We will merely draw from the panegyric to the province of Gipuzkoa, to which the book is dedicated, the following paragraph:

> Basque was always an adult and perfect language, as one finally suggested by God Himself in the division of tongues, and one of the seventy-two primordial and mother languages. Between Basque and the other languages that pride themselves on being cultured languages today there is the difference that there was between the formation of Adam and that of his descendants. Other languages are formed by human ingenuity and consequently susceptible to weaknesses, errors, and illogicalities, the effects of a sickly origin. Basque was a language formed solely by the ingenuity of God, Who in His infinite perspicacity imprinted it on the first fathers of Basque in a form so beautiful, so ingenious, so philosophical, logical, courteous, most sweet, and with other ornaments proper to so honored a beginning.

In his monograph on Cantabria (1736), the thesis that Larramendi proposes to demonstrate is that the three Basque provinces were included in that ancient region. In this he is replying, as we see in the prologue, to the "most erudite Peruvian author" Pedro de Peralta Barnuevo.

First of all (1736, 47ff), he faces off against Poza, who had interpreted certain Basque names like Gernika [Guernica] as indicating a "foundation by the Greek Hernici," which is, he continues,

> as if he were to say today that Hernani in the province of Gipuzkoa is a foundation of the same Hernici, or of Italians from the city of Narni.

Larramendi's position, far from accepting such intrusions, is that on the contrary, Greek took many words from Basque.

Larramendi opposes the theoreticians of foreign ties for Cantabria, such as the marquis of Mondéjar, who believed (Larramendi 1736, 51ff) that it was Nebuchadnezzar who deported the Hispani to the Asian Iberia, in the Caucasus, and worse still, Alejo de Venegas, who affirmed that "Lycurgus came to Cantabria and that he brought Basque." Larramendi takes the opportunity to say that in Cantabria (and neighboring regions) no such pagans could ever have set foot:

we do not read that in the region of Cantabria there were either oracles or temples for pagan superstition.

The passage in which Strabo affirms that the Gallaeci were atheists according to some authors (III, 4, 16) is interpreted by Larramendi to mean that the Cantabri "were not polytheists and did not adore many gods and idols of those that were adored in the rest of the world" (1736, 56). In the end,

> the Cantabri were of the most pure and noble blood, having so well-known an origin and the most illustrious that Spaniards could have as such, which was Tubal and his companions. (1736, 60)

Hence

> with all this, the nobility and illustriousness of the Cantabri, as descendants of Spain's first inhabitants, is greater and more worthy of esteem for every legitimate Spaniard. (1736, 61)

For Larramendi, the continuity of the Cantabri was uninterrupted, since neither the Romans nor the Goths were able to subject them entirely.

After an extended examination of the texts of ancient geographers, Larramendi turns to an examination of names, and there, with Basque as a key, he finds no insoluble problems: he attributes to Spain, I know not on the basis of what source, the name of Setubalia, which is now not the *coetus Tubalis* (company of Tubal) of Archbishop Ximénez de Rada, but pure Basque: *sein-Tubal-erria* 'country of the children of Tubal', with indisputably strange syntax. Iberia is also pure Basque, however, from *Iber-erria* 'the country of the Ebro' (1736, 104ff), and so on.

For Larramendi, Basque should not be called a *lingua Vasconica* (Vascon language), as Oihenart and Moret first called it, according to him, but rather a Cantabrian language (1736, 116f).

Familiar with Ptolemy, Larramendi makes an effort to overcome the objection that the obvious interpretation of the exact data provided by the Alexandrian geographer poses to his thesis of including the territory of the Autrigones, Caristii, and Varduli in Cantabria. Cantabria's historical importance, according to him (1736, 130ff), demands a more extensive territory, to the extent of including the coast and the territories of the three Basque provinces. Further on, he takes up the ancient geographers again (1736, 199ff), and in the absence of new data, we can admire the Jesuit's facility with the pen and in argumentation. His examination of the texts on the Cantabrian War (1736, 231ff) is based on deductions such as that the setting of that war

> could not be other than that of Bizkaia and Gipuzkoa, principally because it was the coasts that were most damaging to the Romans in that war; so the conflicts of this war took place in Gipuzkoa and Bizkaia, and also in Araba. (1736, 243)

Larramendi's arguments (1736, 145ff) against Zurita and Oihenart, who had opposed the identification of the Basque regions with the ancient Cantabria, are forced, and we can understand Flórez's criticism of them when he faced the same problem half a century later (1786, 8) and said of the Jesuit's argumentation that

> it corresponds to the subtlety with which that learned Bizkaian handled the weapons of the scholastic method, but they are not sufficient to conquer on the historical field, because the subtleties of the schools aim at not descending from the professor's lectern with nothing to say. The subtleties of history sweat over examining things in depth and give precedence to those that are best founded.

Thus Larramendi (1736, 157) proposes to simply emend Ptolemy's text in everything that does not suit him, and he is unable to bring much to bear against Zurita, who analyzes the *conuentus* (assemblies) of Pliny's text and the data of Antoninus's Itinerary, as well as the historians' data on the Cantabrian War. His great argument is nothing more than the tradition that called the Basque region Cantabrian (1736, 184ff), of which he is scarcely able to present examples earlier than the sixteenth century.

Returning to place-name etymologies, he identifies the great settings of the Cantabrian War: Mount Vinium (that is, the *mons Vindius*) is Hernio or Hermio in Gipuzkoa; Aracillum (Aradillos, near Reinosa[2]) is Mount Errecil or Arracil in Gipuzkoa, or if not, Arrazola

---

2. In Cantabria. —Ed. note

in Bizkaia; and Mount Medullium is none other than Mendaria or Madaria in Gipuzkoa (1736, 249f).

With these identifications and a few others, the problem of the Cantabrian War's geography is resolved.

The much-repeated argument of the strangeness of Cantabrian names in the texts of Strabo and Mela is applied to Basque, as is the famous passage of Seneca on the similarity of words and things in Cantabria and Corsica (1736, 294ff).

Even the Vascones, that is, the primordial Navarrese, are considered by Larramendi as belonging to Cantabria, and consequently never dominated by Rome (1736, 323ff). As far as the French Basques are concerned, they are Spanish Cantabri who crossed the Pyrenees "around the fourth and fifth centuries" (1736, 332).

Even the ferocious motto that he reports as current among the Basques in the period of the feuds of the Oñacinos and Gamboínos, "Always at war, never at peace," seems to Larramendi (1736, 343) the only appropriate one for the descendants of those ancient Cantabri with their spirit *pertinax in rebellando* (pertinacious in rebelling), as the rhetorician Lucius Florus said (II, 33, 47).

Gregorio Mayans y Siscar

The great Valencian scholar Gregorio Mayans y Siscar (1699–1781), during his time as royal librarian (1733–40), collected a series of documents on the history of Spanish, beginning with the *Diálogo de la lengua,* unpublished at the time, that would be identified as a work of Juan de Valdés, and published them accompanied by a treatise of his own on the origins of the language.

Among Mayans's various scholarly pursuits, this work, as well as other studies of Spanish literature, have to be seen as part of the same effort in favor of the improvement and restoration of scholarship that led to the foundation and early years of the Royal Spanish Academy. Mayans was not a member of the academy, but upon retiring from his post as librarian, he received a pension from Philip V and founded the Valencian Academy in the capital city of his native region.

In his *Orígenes de la lengua española* (Origins of the Spanish language), Mayans discusses first the primordial language, that of Adam, which he accepts must have been very perfect, and then the languages that resulted from the confusion of tongues at Babel, which, he acknowledges,

> were also most perfect, as infused by God. (1873, 293)

Later on, however, he affirms that languages in history are not free from change, and are

> like rivers, which are considered the same because they preserve their names from very ancient times (ibid.),

when in reality, as a result of this change, no one could (cf. Lázaro Carreter 1949, 94)

> affirm that any language whatsoever of those that are spoken today throughout the world is the same as another that was spoken in ancient times,

so that we have no idea about any of those languages

> that God multiplied at the Tower of Babel. (1873, 293f)

After affirming what a language is in general and defining the Spanish language as "the Castilian or general one spoken today in Spain," which is naturally not the primordial one that might have existed in the Iberian Peninsula (1873, 293), Mayans poses the problem of the latter. He is very skeptical on this point:

> no one can affirm which was the first language of Spain, not even relying on probable conjectures, because the tradition cited by many Spaniards does not have the antiquity required for legitimate proof, even within the limits supposed possible. (1873, 297)

Which tradition this is Mayans reveals a few pages later (1873, 303) upon making reference to Tubal as the first inhabitant and possible carrier of precisely one of the languages that arose at Babel. However, Mayans maintains with good reason, such a language could not have remained without change or differentiation since that time.

With a direct knowledge of the classical authors and a prudent and alert critical spirit, Mayans bases himself on the passages of Strabo that mention the elevated culture of the Tartessians and the

variety of scripts and languages in Iberia in order to defend the plurality of languages in the Peninsula (1873, 298). He subsequently compiles Herodotus's information on the first Greek sailings to Tartessos
and notes that the Greeks' knowledge of the interior of the Iberian
Peninsula and of all of northern and central Europe was incomplete
and only gradually filled in much later.

What can be deduced from the entire classical tradition, as summarized by Mayans, is the linguistic variety of primordial Hispania.
Having established this plurality of languages, even granting that one
of them was that of Tubal, he asks:

> What language was that? What words did it have? What variations?
> How was it pronounced? Is there anyone who has any idea of any of
> these things? Certainly not. (1873, 303)

Mayans goes on to examine the difficulties with the theory that a
primordial language of the region could have survived, given that the
Iberian Peninsula's minerals and other riches attracted a variety of
peoples and

> each of these nations introduced its language in the places it dominated.
> (1873, 305)

He compiles the texts of the different Greek and Latin authors
who indisputably bear witness to the plurality of languages, and he
concludes:

> Let it be established, then, that various languages were spoken in Spain
> even after the Romans took control throughout. (1893, 308)

Granting that Mayans is correct on this point, we will now con-
centrate on his ideas about Basque. He refers first to the passage in
Pomponius Mela (III, 15), so famous and so often commented on, in
which Mela says of the tribes and rivers of Cantabria that they are
"such that their names cannot be articulated in our mouths" (1873,
307), and he goes on to add, accepting the traditional equation of
Cantabri and Basques:

> I well judge that the cause of the difficulty in pronouncing these Basque
> names was nothing other than Mela not being accustomed to hear them,
> and still less to pronounce them, from which it clearly follows that in

Andalusia, where Mela was born, another language very different from that of Cantabria was spoken.

Mayans engages in a very determined debate with those who maintain that Basque was the primordial language of all of Spain. He does not say whom he is attacking, but it is evident that he aims at the two arguments that Mariana confronted less resolutely: he does not accept that Euskara was the primordial language of the entire Iberian Peninsula, and he considers it impossible that Euskara was preserved pure, unchanging, and outside of history.

Hence, leaving aside a further investigation of "the ancient borders of Cantabria" (1873, 331), and even granting for the moment that the Cantabri were the direct ancestors of the Basques, Mayans cites a passage of Strabo (III, 3, 8) in which the ancient writer says that

> those who were most persistent in their pillages, the Cantabri and their neighbors, were conquered by Augustus Caesar, and in place of laying waste the fields of Rome's allies, the Coniaci and the Pentuisii who live near the sources of the Ebro now fight on the side of the Romans. Tiberius, his successor, established in those places the three legions that Augustus Caesar had designated for that purpose and thereby not only pacified them, but made them civilized. (1873, 310; Mayans's translation with some modifications)

With this passage and quite a few others, he finds himself in a position to refute the affirmation of Basque's defenders that the Romans never ruled in Cantabria. He affirms (1873, 311):

> I know well that some have wished to deny that the Romans subjected all of Cantabria, but this is wishing to deny credit to the contemporary authors of the highest authority . . .

With a passage from Horace and another from Orosius (1873, 328), he clinches the long series of witnesses to the complete submission of the conquered Cantabri.

He at once acknowledges that

> both Cantabria and the neighboring peoples always tried to preserve their language, to the extent permitted by that domination and those that followed after.

Referring specifically to the Basques, he continues:

> what most contributed to the preservation of the language was having
> at once returned to their ancient rusticity and scant interaction with
> more cultivated nations, it being certain that where there is no com-
> munication with outsiders, the ancient language is more preserved, and
> much more so if there is no education, because a very great number of
> new words are learned by reading, and a large share of them stay with
> the readers afterwards. The truth is that where people do not study,
> very little is known, and where little is known, the language is very lim-
> ited, and over the course of many centuries, this language cannot fail to
> become corrupted. (1873, 329)

Mayans's arguments are opposed point for point to those that
defended the primordiality and purity of Basque. Language can in no
case be detached from history. Following that history's course, Mayans
recalls the invasions of Goths and Arabs, the flight of the Christians
to the north, and the consequences of contact between Cantabri, that
is, Basques, and these refugees:

> For this same reason, the Cantabri who had dealings with the Span-
> iards who had taken refuge there, who spoke Latin, even if in a corrupt
> form—the Cantabri, I say, in addition to the Latin words that they had
> already received directly from the Romans themselves, received many
> others from the Spaniards, accommodating them to their endings and
> manner of pronunciation, and at the same time they communicated to
> the Spaniards other words of theirs that have lasted until today in Span-
> ish. (1873, 330)

We have to praise in this passage the historical sense with which
Mayans recognizes in Basque two layers of loans: those from ancient
Latin, received "directly from the Romans themselves," and those from
Romance, in the period of the Reconquest. As he continues, however,
in his polemic against the apologists of Basque, Mayans exaggerates,
led astray by the Basque materials that he had available and studied
as well as he could.

We should note that Mayans made the greatest effort made by
a non-Basque up to that time to inform himself about Euskara. He
even turned to the "manuscript vocabulary composed in the year 1532
[that is, 1562] that is found in this Royal Library" (1873, 330). This
manuscript was none other than that of the Italian Nicolao Landu-

chio, first published by Agud and Michelena (1958) and the only one in existence at the time. As preserved in this manuscript, Landuchio wrote Spanish-Italian, Spanish-French, and Spanish-Cantabrian dictionaries. For this last, he used various informants, and Michelena in his prologue (Landuchio 1958, 17ff) has made good use of the different hands and arrived "with reasonable certainty" at the conclusion that

> the [Basque dialectical] variety witnessed in this document has not survived to our day . . . At the same time, it is clear that among the known Basque dialects, it is Bizkaian with which it shows the greatest affinity.

It is possible, then, to arrive at a "southern location, in an area bordering on Romance" (1958, 39), for Landuchio's sources.

This first Basque dictionary, even with the interesting materials that its modern editors have found in it, can well be said to represent, as its many detractors have charged, with Larramendi at their head,

> a Romance-influenced—bastardized—variety of the language,

as Michelena affirms (Landuchio 1958, 9). Hence Mayans made an accurate judgment of the document he had in front of him:

> although it is true that the author of the said vocabulary often did not put the purely Basque words corresponding to the Spanish words, it is also certain that Basque has received from other languages the words for the crafts, their tools and manufactures, and those of the sciences and many of their objects, which are innumerable, those of religion, occupations, and things foreign to the region . . . If this language had a printed dictionary, which I desire a great deal, it seems to me that if it were complete, combining it with others, what I say would be observed and seen. (1873, 330)

Landuchio could only confirm Mayans in his idea of the disappearance and change of Basque vocabulary, leading him to an exaggerated view. If we take at random a page from Agud and Michelena's edition, page 109, we find that all the words without exception are Romanisms of the type

> *dioses* ['gods'], ydoloac; *discorde*, discordea; *dispensar*, dispensadu . . .

The only exceptions in the forty-one entries on the page are the adverbs "*distintamente,* beralan" and "*diversamente,* bestelan." Nothing else could be expected from a dictionary begun in Spanish with words (and we are again taking a page at random) as "cultural" as *calças* 'breeches', *calçada* 'roadway', *camino* 'path', *calcetero* 'hosier', *caldera de cobre* 'copper kettle', *caldera pequeña* 'small kettle', *calderero* 'kettle maker', *calderería* 'kettle maker's workshop', *calendario* 'calendar', and so on. The Basque words corresponding to these entries were filled in later by asking informants, as is clear from the fact that Basque translations start to be missing with the letter *n,* and after the letter *s* there are only six Euskara correspondences supplied.

The Basque vocabulary Landuchio offers seemed to confirm the devastating impact on the language that Mayans had supposed on the basis of the invasions and conquests of Cantabria, which he carefully enumerates up to the period of the barbarian kingdoms (1873, 334–36). He concludes:

> if their roots are observed, some will be Latin, others Spanish, others French, others from other languages, and very few purely Basque. (1873, 331)

In mitigation of this exaggeration by Mayans, we can say that his documentation, which he was unable to expand, gave him a certain basis for his views. At the same time, the linguistic ideas of his day were unable to help him understand that a language can accept foreign vocabulary to a large extent and nonetheless maintain its own characteristics. It also has to be said that none of the printed Basque literature was accessible to him. He accuses Euskara

> of not being an erudite language, the first and almost only book printed in it, if I am not mistaken, having been the translation of the New Testament that appeared in 1572 [for 1571] and that Nicolás Antonio testifies was in the library of Cardinal Francesco Barberini. (1873, 336)

All the same, Mayans is not mistaken on the fundamental level:

> I will always grant great antiquity to this language, and I will say that this antiquity remains today in the general characteristics of Basque, but not in such a language's particular constituents. I mean that the

multitude of conjugations, the postposition of the articles, and other peculiarities of Basque come from very ancient times, but I am not persuaded that even those words that are considered purely Basque today are the same that they were in ancient times, because if we see that today in order to say 'a little' the Basques say *guchi,* the Navarrese *guti,* and the Bizkaians *gichi,* and there are very many words that differ in this way, forming several very different dialects, how should we believe what they suppose, that this nation alone in the world has the special privilege of preserving its words without corruption, without variation in their pronunciation over the course of many thousands of years? (1873, 332)

The importance of this passage is great, since in it we find proof that Mayans knew Larramendi's first two works. His critique is undoubtedly directed at the argumentation of the brief treatise *De la antigüedad y universalidad del bascuenze en España,* and as far as the *Impossible vencido* is concerned, it is evident that it served him as a source. The "multitude of conjugations" to which Mayans refers is a reflection of Larramendi's treatment of the conjugation, and the "postposition of the articles" is simply the presentation of the postpositions that correspond to our prepositions or cases in the *Impossible vencido.* The dialectological example that Mayans gives as evidence of the differentiation of an *Ursprache* (original source language) comes literally from Larramendi (1729, 371).

Mayans thus acknowledges Basque as "one of the minor mother languages," following Joseph Scaliger's famous classification, which he discusses extensively in his work (1873, 391). Moreover, it is clear that the postscript that he adds to this characterization as a "minor mother language" elsewhere, that "knowledge of it is of very little importance, since it is not an erudite language" (1873, 336), would have to sting Larramendi and other Basques.

The reason for this affirmation is perhaps that Mayans was thinking about the topic of his study; he was writing in order to illuminate the origins of Spanish, and he was primarily concerned with the Iberian Peninsula's Romance languages. It is when discussing etymologies that, responding to Larramendi's protests against the Academy's new dictionary, Mayans reduces Basque's importance in this regard. After a methodological introduction, Mayans affirms:

Where languages are concerned, greater study has to be devoted to those from which more words have been taken than to those from which fewer have been taken. In this way, Spanish etymologists should devote more study to Latin than to Arabic, more to Arabic than to Greek, more to Hebrew than to Celtic, more to Celtic than to Gothic, more to Gothic than to Punic, more to Punic than to Bizkaian, and generally speaking, more to the languages that have been dominant fewer centuries back or belong to nations with whom the Spaniards have traded a great deal than to others that are more ancient or belong to nations with which we have had less communication. (1873, 351f)

In the survey that Mayans once again makes of Celtic etymologies, we find the list of words that has been repeated since Morales, and he says once again that

the fact that these words do not remain in Basque is one of the strongest pieces of evidence that it was not a general language in Spain. (1873, 367)

Mayans observes that these words are preserved in greater number, to the extent that they have survived, in Spanish than in Euskara, and he adds:

it still remains in doubt whether these very few words that Basque preserves are proper to it or were taken from the ancient language of Spain, in which, although I am of the view that it had many dialects, I judge that these dialects, as children of the same language, would have been in general very close to one another and would have had many words in common. (1873, 367)

Here we have to acknowledge that, in the heat of polemic, Mayans has gotten carried away. What could this "ancient language of Spain" be, about which he has been saying so much? The supposed examples that he goes on to cite, taking them from place names (the famous *Uri, Ili,* entangled in his discussion with *Urci* and also with the places ending in *–briga,* as in his predecessors) and drawing for their explanation on Chaldean, Hebrew, and Syriac (1873, 368f), could not offer very clear solutions.

Finally, as rare examples that justify placing Basque in the modest final rank of Spanish etymologies, Mayans comments (1873, 374) on the proverb from the marquis of Santillana's collection, *Sardina que gato lleva, galduda va* 'A sardine taken by a cat is *galduda*' (cf. Michelena 1964, 168), and the Basque derivation of *zatico*, which is indeed attested in Berceo, as Corominas notes.

Summarizing the considerations that Mayans dedicates to Basque in his study of the formation of Spanish, his polemical tone against Larramendi is undeniable. The latter had once again presented the ancient arguments: the perfect language of Adam, or at least a language from the confusion of tongues at Babel, exempt from all change and corruption. Mayans argues against all this, as well as against the attempt to make Basque Spain's only primordial language.

In the area of etymology, Mayans, like Aldrete, lacked this discipline's modern foundation, which it would find in the nineteenth century in the regular correspondence of phonemes. Thus, in a manner that appears rudimentary to us now, he presents a series of

> canons or general rules of the letters that are customarily added, subtracted, or changed. (1873, 398)

Finally, his defense of the Academy's dictionary is also directed against Larramendi's objections. The dictionary appears "diminished" to him (1873, 455), because a vocabulary of the crafts is lacking, and he is still waiting for

> a very complete Spanish dictionary, as we should expect from the leadership of the president of the Royal Academy, the most excellent gentleman Mercurio López Pacheco, marquis of Villena, for whom I profess particular veneration. (1873, 456)

Larramendi Confronts Mayans

Mayans's moderation and discretion in his criticism prevented him from opposing Larramendi directly, although it can be affirmed that he knew Larramendi's first writings. Perhaps he feared the Jesuit's polemical aggressiveness, but he ended up becoming its target.

We will continue our method of extracting from these older works, sometimes difficult to read, what serves to present their authors' thinking, even if the arguments sometimes repeat themselves.

In 1745, the Jesuit's *Diccionario trilingüe* was published in Donostia [San Sebastián]. It was primarily the publication of the Valencian scholar's *Orígenes* that was perceived as a challenge demanding a full response. At the same time, the Royal Academy had continued with the publication of its *Diccionario de Autoridades* while paying scant attention to Larramendi's apologia of the Basque origin of many Spanish words. This explains the peculiarities of the *Diccionario trilingüe*. The first surprising thing about it is that it is not Basque-Spanish or Basque-Latin, but the reverse. Larramendi took the Madrid Academy's dictionary and translated it into his own language. Admirably knowledgeable in the latter, he translated with real words where they existed.

> When the Basques see in this dictionary such a prodigious quantity of their vernacular language, some will ask whether they are all Basque words, and others will resolutely say that they are not, but of my manufacture and invention. To those who ask with modesty and without passion, I say that they are all Basque and that I have not included any that I have not read in printed books or heard in one of the Basque dialects, noting them all down beforehand with all prolixity so that I would not forget them. (1853, XLI)

After accurate observations on the inhabitants' use of foreign words or constructions in Basque, often due to simple ignorance of the correct ones, he acknowledges that he has had to invent neologisms:

> There are others that have been introduced [in the *Diccionario*] out of necessity, as in other languages, and they are of objects that have been newly discovered, and there has not been a Basque who has manufactured appropriate words accommodated to the character of the language, and these necessarily had to be included in the dictionary. (1853, XLII)

He dedicates a special section (§ XXVII) to the defense of the introduction into the dictionary, that is to say, into the language, of what he calls "facultative words," those that "pertain to the faculties, arts, and sciences" (1853, XLII). The language does not have these words because it has not needed them, but

> Basque is now disposed and ready to be spoken in any science and faculty, and this is the occasion to search out the opportune words that it has not had before now, either taking them from other languages, or

inventing them, or forming them from its fertile roots, in accordance with what Cicero says.

Since the work tries to defend the language's capacity to express everything, we can understand that Larramendi, undoubtedly the first to do so, goes on to present a theory of the formation of neologisms, a topic still of current interest today.

Moreover, since he is concerned that the Madrid Academy does not recognize the Basque roots of Spanish, he continually takes advantage of the opportunity to defend this theory in his etymologies.

Like Larramendi's grammar (1729), this new work is dedicated to the province of Gipuzkoa, to which he feels himself ever more united. The material for the work, the author says in his dedication, came from oral inquiries (in which, we should note, he was ahead of his time).

> In the absence of books, I had no choice but to consult the verbal use of our patricians, to listen to the cultured and uncultured, to note how people speak in towns and in villages, to make pilgrimages to various districts, and more so with the determination to include in my dictionary all the dialects of Basque, to take notes, to observe, to combine, to separate use from abuse, to puzzle out the orthography, to research etymologies and roots, and finally, to bring together and organize a body of language that, divided into small bits, was scattered over various places and regions.

In his enthusiasm, Larramendi draws the comparison on the next page that if

> Paradise with all its original pleasantness has been preserved intact amid the waters of the Flood [somewhere on the planet] . . . it will not be a more improper metaphor to say about the pleasantness of our language that in its preservation it has enjoyed the privileges of Paradise . . . [For] Basque, inaccessible to novelty and alteration, and free of bastard imprints, has preserved its ancient purity and beauty so intact that if the first inhabitant of Spain, whether that was Tubal or Tarshish, were to hear the Gipuzkoans speak today, he would understand them without a dictionary and without an interpreter, unless he had forgotten his own language.

The *Diccionario trilingüe* is preceded by an extensive prologue of two hundred double-column pages in which Larramendi includes sections of his brief treatise of 1728, but with more formidable argumentation and an organization into three parts: the first (twenty-nine sections) "reveals the perfections of Basque," the second (twenty-seven sections) defends the theory "that Basque is a primordial and universal language of Spain," and the third, devoted to polemic, opposes Mayans (fifteen sections) and Armesto y Ossorio (eight sections) in turn.

In the first part, Larramendi begins by transcribing sections nine to eleven and thirteen to fifteen of his work of 1728. Beginning with section seven—titled "Basque is a mother language" (and one of the "major mother languages," as the title of the following section announces)—however, Larramendi opposes Mayans, the first to introduce Scaliger's ideas into the debate, and his thesis that, having now forgotten Babel, acknowledges Basque as a mother language but includes it among Europe's minor mother languages.

Often, Larramendi's arguments proceed from personal conversations that resulted more or less by chance. This is the case on matters involving Eastern languages, in which he was undoubtedly not well versed. He spoke with a prelate in Seville who was learned in Hebrew, he had the opportunity to hear some Maronites speak and read in Syriac, as well as an Armenian member of a religious order in that language, and he verified that Basque has no relationship with those languages, thereby confirming its status as a "mother language" (1853, XI). Even without denying Saint Jerome's thesis that Hebrew was the mother of all languages, he reduces its extension and proposes that it has "exceptions," and without denying that Greek, Latin, and other languages with which the learned saint was familiar could be traced back to Hebrew, he denies that such a thing could be said of Basque.

With his dialectical skills, Larramendi tries to attribute to a commentator (1853, XII) the full extension of Jerome's text, forcing the interpretation of the sainted Biblical expert (*In Sophon.* [On Zephaniah], 3, 14ff; *PL*, XXV, 1384), who affirmed *linguam Hebraicam omnium linguarum esse matricem* (that the Hebrew language is the mother of all languages).

Larramendi has his own ideas about how the confusion of tongues took place: a Hebrew extraordinarily rich in synonyms ("it had seventy-two to explain the same object") was divided at Babel into the same number of languages. "The confusion that God caused consisted in restricting those synonyms, leaving each family only one of those that it previously knew," and Basque and other languages, it may be said, according to Larramendi's argument,

> were not born of Hebrew as it remained in the family of Eber after the confusion of tongues at Babel. (1853, XII)

Against Scaliger and Mayans, he proves that Basque is a major mother language on the basis of its importance in the formation of Spanish and of many other languages, starting with Latin and Greek. Larramendi is undaunted by the most daring etymologies, and thus he explains Greek *iesis* 'action of going' (a word invented by Plato in the *Cratylus*) by way of the Gipuzkoan *ies*, *iges* 'to flee', and *kinesis* 'motion' by way of Basque *zin* or *ziñez* 'truly' (in reality, 'oath') plus *iesi* 'to flee'. *Erótico* 'erotic' and Greek *eros* are nothing other than derivations of Basque *ero* 'crazy', and so on (1853, XIII f). With the same facility, he says that Latin *musica* 'music'

> has its origin in the word *musua,* which means 'face, lips, kiss, snout, nostrils' . . . Because the harmony of voices is born from the face, lips, mouth, it was given the name of *musica*, and there is no need to resort to the Muses, who were given that name *berea musu ederragatic,* for their beautiful faces. (1853, XVI)

He goes on likewise to find Basque words in the formation of French and Italian.

Yet despite his sometimes nonsensical theories, Larramendi is knowledgeable and has a sense of what needs to be studied in a language, and so in his section thirteen, which is titled, "Basque is delightful due to the beautiful variety of its dialects," he develops a classification of the latter and accurately indicates their characteristics.

He then continues refuting the criticisms made of Basque, few of which Mayans had left in reserve. For Larramendi, Euskara is a living language, unlike Hebrew, Greek, or Latin, and in addition it is an "erudite language" (1853, XXIX), in the sense that "its words and construction" contain

much teaching and doctrine, which make those who speak and understand them erudite and well-instructed.

In order to counter Mayans's affirmation that Basque had scarcely
more books than Leiçarraga's New Testament, Larramendi offers a
history of printed literature in Basque, with reference to manuscripts
as well (1853, XXX–XXXIII).

After praising the language as facile and eloquent and defending his grammar against critics in Bilbao and Madrid, he devotes the
entire conclusion of this first part to explaining his dictionary, an
explanation from which we have already quoted extracts at the beginning of this section. Permit us now to also note that as a practical purpose of this work, he wanted to establish an instrument for mutual
understanding between dialects, so that "they can all understand one
another easily" (1853, XLI).

The second part of the prologue is a much-expanded development of the first three sections of his treatise of 1728. Larramendi
exhibits all the splendors of his rhetoric, which must have sounded
somewhat provincial and antiquated in the middle of the eighteenth
century, and makes this the longest part of his apologia. Other than
syllogistic argumentation, there is little new to be found in the pages
in which he insists, making use of some classical texts, on the undeniable antiquity of Basque in Spain.

A new argument in support of Larramendi's opposition in his
book on Cantabria to the existence of any paganism among the
Basques appears here in the form of a formidable metal tablet found
in Puerto de Santa María, near Cádiz, on which, in a text in com-
prehensible Basque, quite legible and only with a few abbreviations,
the *escal(dunac)* dedicate it to *gur(e) eguill(e) and(iari)*, "our great
Maker" (1853, LXXIII), displaying Christian monotheism and modern orthography.

Larramendi goes on to mention the coins we call Iberian, inscribed
with "characters of the primordial language of the Spaniards," which
Erro and Cejador will later decipher by way of Basque.

He then draws support from the affirmation of a Madrid academician, Dr. Huerta, according to which "it appears beyond dispute that
the language assigned to Spain was Basque" (1853, LXXV), and this
language, according to the said authority, was brought by Tarshish.

Larramendi values the authoritative texts of Garma, Henao, and Peralta Barneuvo, naturally without forgetting Garibay, who maintained that Basque was the "mother" language of Spain (1853, LXXVIII). Larramendi also returns to the ancient texts to defend the theory that "the Spaniards went out to populate the eastern Iberia" in the Caucasus (1853, XCIV), repeating what he said in his brief treatise of 1728.

Starting from the Basque etymologies he had previously proposed for the Caucasian names he found in Ptolemy, he now proposes, following Garma's indications, other, more nonsensical ones: "*Suecia* ['Sweden'] comes from *su* 'fire', *eciá, ecioá* [*izeki* 'to burn'?] 'lit (on fire)', which is very necessary there in order to resist the rigorous cold," and he maintains on the basis of this argument that the ancient Iberians reached Northern Europe, citing in passing Tacitus's mention (*Agr.* [Agricola], 11, 2) of the relationship between the Silures of Wales and the dark-haired Hispani. He takes up once again the Basque interpretation of names from the Iberian Peninsula, from Setubalia to the Ebro River, now explained, and this is what is problematic, in another way: *ur bero* 'hot water', and so, recalling Moret,

the Ibero spring in Navarre, which is a hot spring,

and the same would apply to the larger river,

if Fontibre, where the Ebro is born, has or once had that circumstance. (1853, XCVIII)

The familiar toponyms in *–briga*, in *–ili*, and so forth likewise parade before the reader yet again (1853, CII ff).

Of great novelty, on the other hand, are chapters eighteen to twenty-four of this part, in which Larramendi attempts, we believe for the first time, to extract statistical results from a dictionary. He analyzes the Royal Spanish Academy's *Diccionario de Autoridades* and counts the etymologies it provides. For example, under the letter A he inventories 319 from Arabic, 168 from Greek, 491 from Latin, 19 from French, 15 from Italian, and so on, and for his part he finds that these figures need to be corrected, since Basque has given Spanish 324 words under this letter. Under B, Latin has given 715, Greek 134, Arabic 30, French 31, and so on, but Basque would again come in second with 139 words. Under G, for example, he attributes a Basque origin to 178 Spanish words, putting it ahead of Latin, which has only 109. In total, Larramendi says (1853, CX), "of 13,365 root words in Spanish,"

> the Arabic words are 555. The Greek are 973. The Hebrew are 90. The Latin are 5,385. The Basque, as will be seen, are 1,951, and there are even more than this number.

There remain at the end 2,786 words of unknown origin, which Larramendi blithely considers to be "those that remain from the primordial language of Spain" and adds as such to those for which he recognizes an origin in Euskara, thereby deducing that "Spanish will have over a quarter, or a bit less, from Basque."

We have to acknowledge Larramendi's merit in having foreshadowed with his calculations the ambitions and possibilities of today's mathematical linguistics, but in reality, only a very small percentage of his Basque etymologies can be saved. Even being more generous in this regard than Corominas, I find in his entire list under A (1853, CXI f), for example, only *abarca, achaparrar, achicar, amodorrarse, amorrar, aroza* (a pure Basque survival), *asco, aurragado, azorrarse*: eight or ten words compared to the 324 that Larramendi gives as Spanish derivates from Basque.

We need not spend time repeating and criticizing etymologies that were nonsensical even then and that the progress of scholarship has reduced to the picturesque. It was of no benefit to Larramendi to apply his ingenuity to comparisons that prove nothing.

In chapter twenty-five, he faces once again the famous list of words from ancient Hispania that we have already seen originate with Morales, who noted that they have not survived in Basque, and in chapter twenty-six, Strabo's affirmation of the plurality of languages in ancient Hispania. The argumentation is based more on syllogisms than on the contribution of new texts or evidence, of which there was none.

Finally, the third part of Larramendi's long preliminary study is dedicated to refuting those who had impugned his earlier writings, Mayans and Armesto Ossorio.

Larramendi needs to demonstrate that Euskara is a language that has not varied, and he first opposes Mayans's affirmation that languages are like rivers. Larramendi compares languages "to the man who has a body and a soul" (1853, CXLVIII); they are individual beings that last, for which reason, he supposes, without taking into account the fact that Latin had turned into the Romance languages, that

> since the Basque of today is the same language as three thousand years ago, it follows that since that Basque was the primordial and universal language of Spain, the same is also the case for this Basque that we speak today. (1853, CLIII)

He objects to the cautious words with which Mayans formulated our ignorance about Spain's first language and debates the Valencian humanist's nuanced interpretations; the arguments that most bother Larramendi are those in which Mayans explains the preservation of Basque by its isolation and lack of cultural development, together with his historical evidence of the subjection of Cantabria by the Romans. Larramendi, obstinate in the traditional identification of Cantabri and Basques, refuses to recognize other possibilities. Even in the face of the accurate stratification of Latin and Romance elements in Basque that Mayans proposes, he claims as Basque words that designate parts of nature, among which he includes, as if they were indigenous, borrowings as obvious as *catua*[3] 'cat' (Spanish *gato*), *martea* 'marten' (*marta*), *gaztaña* 'chestnut' (*castaña*), *guerecia*[4] 'cherry' (*cereza*), *pico*[5] 'fig' (*higo*), *pagoa* 'beech' (Latin *fagus*), and *menta* 'mint' (Spanish *menta*) (1853, CLVIII). Larramendi does not fail to criticize Mayans for the use that he made of a "certain dictionary," which we have already seen was that of Landuchio, and we can be sure that this was the reason that Larramendi condemns this work so categorically. He learned from Mayans of the "short vocabulary that there is in the royal library of Madrid, a copy of which I have in my power," and about which he goes on to say:

---

3. In Unified Basque *katua*. —Ed. note

4. In Unified Basque *gerezia*. —Ed. note

5. In Unified Basque *piku*. —Ed. note

It does not appear to have an author's name, and he did well in keeping
silent about it, because it is a work that accredits him very poorly as
a speaker of Basque and not very well as a speaker of Spanish. (1853,
XXXI)

Larramendi ends his debate with Mayans by defending the inal-
terability of Basque. Even the sensible dialectological argument about
the three forms *guti, guchi,* and *gichi* 'a little' that Mayans had put
forward to prove variability over time and the gradual differentiation
of a shared primordial language fails to convince Larramendi:

let Mayans tell us whether the subtraction, change, or addition of a letter makes a word corrupt. (1853, CLXXVII)

The scale of etymology established by Mayans is inverted by
Larramendi, who had conducted his statistical analysis of the academy's dictionary for this purpose. Not only are the ancient words that
Mayans had considered Celtic Basque for Larramendi, but the same
is also true of words found in many languages of the highest prestige
and antiquity.

Larramendi devotes a few pages to refuting Armesto y Ossorio,
who had intervened in the polemic around those whom Larramendi
calls "theaterists [*teatristas*]" (1853, CXCIV): Feijoo and Sarmiento.

Armesto wanted to defend the Spanish Academy from Larramendi's attacks in his treatise of 1728. Armesto had pointed out that
by the same procedure by which Larramendi explained names from
different countries using modern Basque, it could easily be demonstrated, as a consequence of the similarities in place names, that
Spanish had been the language of Italy or France. Shared Roman
domination explains many of these similarities better than any other
hypothesis. Armesto was not a great linguist, but it was not necessary to be one in order to defend the Academy in almost every case in
which Larramendi risked his Basque etymologies.

In his *Corografía de Guipúzcoa* (Chorography of Gipuzkoa),
an enchanting and very original work, which he left unpublished,
Larramendi summarizes in two chapters his doctrine on the Basque
language and its dialects (1950, 294ff). Of course, he insists on the
identity of Cantabri and Basques, from Galicia to Baiona [Bayonne]
and the mountains of Navarre. He defends the language's personality

and also justifies it on the grounds of its vitality, since according to his calculations, only a quarter of Gipuzkoans understood Spanish in his day. His collection of samples in the Zuberoan, Lapurdian, Bizkaian, Navarrese, and Gipuzkoan dialects is precious for its time.

Garma y Salcedo

This Aragonese expert in heraldry wrote a *Theatro universal de España: Descripción eclesiástica y secular de todos sus reynos y provincias* (Universal theater of Spain: Ecclesiastical and secular description of all its kingdoms and provinces). We comment on it here because although it is a pure example of administrative description, very rich in information and data, and a mirror of the reality of what was still Philip V's Spain, it includes in its first pages a very well-organized survey of the accepted ideas current at the time about Spain's origin.

> The first name with which the moderns give Spain its beginning is that of Tubalia or Jubalia, Tobelia or Jobelia, taking its etymology from Tubal, the son of Japheth and grandson of Noah. The Achilles of this foundation is the authority of Flavius Josephus . . . They add to Josephus's authority that of Saint Jerome . . . (1738, I, 3f)
>
> This opinion . . . was not affirmed until the time of Rodrigo, archbishop of Toledo, and even he did not state it as a certainty about Tubal, although he wrote about the arrival of his sons. He was followed by Lucas of Tuy, the General Chronicle, and others of the older Spaniards. (ibid., 4)
>
> The most celebrated Abulense . . . was the first to affirm Tubal's arrival in person . . . This view remained in peaceful possession of the field from the time that El Tostado promulgated it until the last century, in which, a critical spirit having now progressed further . . . some Spanish and foreign scholars excluded Tubal . . . naming as [Spain's] founder Tarshish, the son of Javan, grandson of Japheth . . . (ibid., 4f)

Garma then promptly mentions Julius Africanus and other late writers who prefer Tarshish as the ancestor of the Hispani, and this leads him into a discussion of the legendary or historical Tartessos.

As a whole, however, Garma does not depart from the Bible and its commentators.

Francisco Xavier Manuel de la Huerta y Vega

Francisco Xavier Manuel de la Huerta y Vega (born in Alcalá, died in Madrid in 1752), first a parish priest in Alcalá, then a visitor and ecclesiastical judge in the diocese of Santiago de Compostela, and finally a member of the Academy of History in Madrid, really belongs to the prior century and is evidence of the difficulties that normal reason found in its path. His curious work (1738–40), dedicated to Philip V, aims to demonstrate the existence of monarchy in ancient Spain, for which purpose it mentions the old histories, including the false chronicles (praised in the prologue).

Basing himself on the Christian author Julius Africanus, known only in fragments, who was the first to attempt to coordinate the chronology of pagan history with that of the Bible, Huerta y Vega is a declared partisan of Tarshish and considers him, not Tubal, Spain's first inhabitant. Like the Tubalians, he accepts the theory that Tarshish's language "remained in Spain" and was one of the seventy-two of Babel (1738, 15ff). This language, however, was then replaced by Latin at the time of Augustus:

> From everything that has been said, it follows that up to the time of Octavian, the primordial language, universally most ancient in all the provinces, was spoken universally in Spain. Afterward, Latin gradually spread further, but without their own language being forgotten, because it is recorded that this language remained in the year 395 after Christ, when Saint Pacianus, bishop of Barcelona, writing to Symphorianus, said: Latium, Egypt, Athens, etc. (1738, 23)

Spain's primordial language, now not Tubalian, but Tarshishian, is Basque (1738, 24):

> because Basque is a mother language, as is evidenced by its lack of commerce or affinity with some of the late-arriving languages, as well as by the common belief . . . because since Basque is a mother language, it cannot be derived from another, and since there is no record of another mother language in Spain, it is necessary for us to confess that this was the primordial language of the entire nation.

He subsequently launches into the traditional arguments: he mentions the eastern Iberia, which he supports with a new and more absurd series of etymologies from Basque (a language of which he clearly knew nothing whatever); he takes up once again Morales's list of words and sees in Suetonius's *dureta* 'bathtub', mentioned in the context of Augustus's Cantabrian campaign, a Basque word; and he accepts Larramendi's arguments about the Basque letters in Spanish, *ñ, ll, ch,* and so on. He even goes into great detail about the conquests of the Spaniards in early Italy, as well as in Ireland, England, and so forth. Even Atlas and his brothers left from Spain to populate the Americas (1738, 144ff).

Preceding Erro in this, he maintains that the Spanish, that is, Iberian alphabet is not only older than the Phoenician (1738, 138ff) but also predates Moses and even Abraham (1738, 140).

We can understand that the good academician continues with all these ancient dynasties and has to debate on equal terms with the Berossus invented by Annius of Viterbo (1740, 90ff).

Juan de Perochegui

This brief book by a colonel, a commander of the artillery of the kingdom of Navarre, is a good representative of the ideas dominant at the time among Euskara speakers of limited education. The friars whose approvals of the text are printed in the original edition were pleased to emphasize that Basque was

> the patriarch Noah's own native language, and consequently the first language in the world.

In this way, its patent of nobility of direct descent from the mother languages of Babel was secure.

Such are the theses that inspired this brief book, and we will content ourselves with an etymology that shows its level: *escuarà* (i.e., Euskara), or (?) *ascogara,* is nothing other than *bayascogarà* 'we are enough' (1760, 5).

Henrique Flórez

The great historian Enrique Flórez (1702–1773) is one of the great figures of our eighteenth century, and as learned as he was judicious.

Among his vast output, we are interested here only in one work, dedicated to an issue repeatedly mentioned in our study: the old iden-

tification of Cantabri and Basques, which had played so important a
role going back to the sixteenth century. He was the one who brought
the illumination of his enlightened age to bear and resolved forever a
confusion that had done harm.

Flórez studied the borders that can be deduced from ancient geography for the territory of the Cantabri, with special attention to the
border between the Cantabri and the Autrigones, thereby excluding
modern Bizkaia from the Cantabria of the ancients (1786, 48f). After
examining the arguments put forward by the partisans of the identification of Cantabri and Basques (1786, 81ff), he goes on to debate the
claims of the Basque authors who locate the setting of Augustus's war
in Gipuzkoa (1786, 102).

He also analyzes the data on ancient Cantabria (1786, 142ff) and
criticizes the interpretation of the labarum as equivalent to the 'cantabricum' or standard of the Cantabri, of which less than impartial
use had been made in support of the alleged primordial monotheism
of the Cantabri-Basques (1786, 152ff).

He recounts the late extension of the name Cantabria to parts of
La Rioja (1786, 159ff) and in Idacius to other regions (1786, 202ff),
and he then discusses with good critical sense topics related to the
ancient geography of Cantabria and the surrounding areas, including
the Basque provinces. With his critical spirit, he also eliminates the
phantasm of the name of Rucones, which made its appearance in the
literature due to a misreading of manuscripts (1786, 204–6).

Flórez's antagonist in this book is naturally Larramendi, the great
defender of the identification with all its consequences. Flórez grants
him "more acumen and familiarity with the scholastic method than
ingenuousness, candor, and clear-headedness in reading the ancients"
(1786, 49).

He also opposes him, along with older chroniclers in the style of
Beuter and Garibay, on the question of locating the Cantabrian War
in Gipuzkoa, with its Arakil [Araquil] and its Mount Hernio.

Against Larramendi, Flórez defends the thesis, like Mayans before
him, that the Cantabri were conquered (1786, 112ff), and that some
inscriptions in Bizkaia prove the reality of the Roman presence. The
Augustinian historian says (1786, 131):

The Basque of today does not exclude the subjection of the territory to the Romans, but only proves the scant spread and permanence that Latin had there, because those of that language were not eager to venture into a place classified as the most rugged and terrible in Spain, and without any utility . . . The legitimate Cantabria, since it was civilized by Tiberius (as Strabo says), adopted the Roman language and lost the ancient Cantabrian due to extensive commerce with the Romans, and afterward with the Gothic kings and the kings of León, such that not even in the most inaccessible parts of Asturias and Montaña[6] is Basque known . . . The same happened in the southern territory of the Vascones, but although the northern part was likewise conquered, it lost its language less, because it kept itself at a greater distance from and with fewer dealings with other peoples. The same applies to the Autrigones and Varduli. (1786, 131f)

Flórez provides a good analysis of the causes of the incomplete Romanization of the Basque mountains. The ambiguity with which he says that Basque was not preserved in the most rugged parts of La Montaña and Asturias could serve us to explain that Basque resisted Latin better, even in areas of comparable ruggedness and isolation, because it was a non-Indo-European language, more different from Latin than the languages of the Cantabri and Astures would have been. Flórez likewise understands very well that the Romanization of southern Navarre and Araba was parallel, and he treats as linguistically equivalent, correctly in my view, the Vascones of the east and the Autrigones and Varduli (and Caristii) of the west.

On the topic of the plurality of languages in the Peninsula, Flórez (1786, 136) follows the more authoritative tradition represented by Morales, Aldrete, and Mayans.

For the rest, Flórez's continuator in his *España sagrada* (Sacred Spain), Risco, would have to return once again to the question of the Cantabri and the Basques (cf. Llorente 1806–8, V, 14).

---

6. Montaña is a historical term for Cantabria. —Ed. note

5

The Age of Astarloa: Flight to Paradise

Nik naiago nuke . . .
gure euskal berbo erromanizatu honetatik
erdal modu guztiak
sustraitik kendu,
nahiago nuke
iberiar eskrituran
eskribitu . . .

— G. Aresti, *Harri eta herri*, III Q (1964)

Joaquín Traggia

This member of the Royal Academy of History in Madrid was born in Zaragoza in 1748 and died after 1813. He was a Piarist and traveled to the Philippines, where he wrote a Spanish grammar in Tagalog, for the use of the natives. Later, he left the order and resided in Madrid.

In reality, Traggia deserves better treatment than Astarloa gave him in his book, since he not only had good sense and was a sensible critic who kept his distance from mythologies, but he had also studied several exotic languages and was able to make a good assessment of Euskara's qualities.

Traggia composed the article on Basque in the *Diccionario geográfico-histórico* (Geographical-historical dictionary) undertaken by the Royal Academy of History. At the start of the article, he says:

> One of the most admirable phenomena of Vasconia is the particular language spoken in many towns in Navarre and in the Basque provinces and the region of Lapurdi [Labourd] in France.

He then recounts the success of Larramendi's doctrine, which has been adopted by well-known scholars, once the first insistence and heat of the dispute eased, even if it faced at the beginning the opposition consequent on new opinions. Nevertheless, it does not seem to me that the point has been as thoroughly demonstrated as is believed. (1802, 151f)

Traggia's mindset is much more modern, and he expresses himself clearly:

> it seems to me a vain effort to want to maintain the view that Basque was born in Senaar . . . With no record of whether Tubal came to Spain in person or his descendants did, the foundations are very weak for attributing to Basque an antiquity coeval to the population of the world after the Flood. (1802, 151)

Like Humboldt later, Traggia knows that this idea that one's own language appears the most authentic and primordial has appeared in many places, and he mentions the Fleming Goropius Becanus. He critiques the traditional etymological arguments for Basque's antiquity throughout the Iberian Peninsula, and he very effectively separates *–briga* from *uri* (1802, 152f), as well as rejecting the popular etymologies of *España* 'Spain' from Basque *ezpain* 'lip', and so on. At the same time, he supposes that Noah and his sons plausibly spoke Hebrew or Chaldean (1802, 154), while Hebrew, which he knows to be a simple, poor, and irregular language, is quite different from the "rich language, full of artifice and very exact rules" that is his characterization of Basque (1802, 155).

Very sensibly, again, he attributes to the ancient Basques' continuous contact with the Romans, starting with Sertorius,

> the abundance of Latin words that Fr. Larramendi believes the Basques gave to Latin, and we believe they took from it. (1802, 155)

It is at this point in his article that Traggia presents an idea that we can characterize as without foundation, and in truth, we do not understand what gave rise to it. The Navarrese, according to Traggia, are not Basques, but a different people who arrived from an unknown location.

Except for this piece of nonsense, all of the rest of Traggia's article is reasonable. On the historical formation of Basque, he says:

The sources of today's Basque were the ancient language of the country; the language of the neighboring Spanish peoples, who spoke in various ways, according to Strabo; the conquering languages of the Romans and Goths; the conquered languages in Aquitaine; and the languages of the Asturians, Galicians, and Aragonese, with whom the Basques had voluntary or forced relations from the eighth century up to the present day. (1802, 156)

He goes on to analyze the language. He denies that the shared presence of certain sounds absent in other languages proves anything for the maternity attributed to Basque with respect to Spanish: neither *ñ* nor *ll* nor *ch* is so characteristic and unique (1802, 159). Nor is the distinction between formal and informal forms of address so peculiar to Basque, since *zu* is the exact correspondent of Romance *vos*. Traggia's knowledge of Malay and Chinese helps him to analyze the morphology of the Basque declination very accurately. On the other hand, he finds the complications of the Basque verb neither so easy nor so interesting:

in this part, they were not so fortunate, and if they thought about simplifying their language, they did not take such appropriate measures as in the nouns. (1802, 161)

Traggia believed that languages are formed consciously and by a choice of elements.

With his intelligence, Traggia saw very well the weak points of the traditional theses. Without naming him, he refers to Hervás and points out the concessions he made to non-Basque-Iberian elements even in the place names of the Iberian Peninsula itself. He says (1802, 164):

One of the modern writers who has discussed languages with the greatest abundance of erudition, and who believes that Basque or Cantabrian is the ancient Iberian, contradicts the claims of those who seek the proof of this language's antiquity in ancient names, when he traces back to Celtic the origin of words ending in *–tania* . . . and those beginning with *il-* . . .

Traggia knew that languages change continuously and cannot maintain themselves without alteration.

To claim that it is the primordial Iberian or the primordial language of Spain, with slight alteration, seems to me a vanity that has nothing more to support it than ignorance of the beginnings and progress of Basque and the etymologies that can be equally claimed for Hebrew, Celtic, Greek, Latin, and any other language. (1802, 166)

Traggia's historical thinking overcomes his rationalist prejudices on the life of languages. He calls attention to the significance for language of the long period of time that has passed since Noah, and he is clear on the influence of important neighboring languages. Consequently, he cannot accept (1802, 165)

that Basque, or any other language, has been preserved without substantial variation, when its people, being small in number, have indisputably lived in contact with and dependent on more numerous nations for almost twenty centuries, and the bordering peoples in the same region have varied their speech to the point of forgetting what their primordial language was.

Francisco Martínez Marina

Born in Oviedo in 1754 and dying in Zaragoza in 1833, this liberal priest, a contributor to the political theory behind the Cádiz Parliament, who began his career as a librarian in Toledo and subsequently became a canon of the Royal Church of St. Isidore in Madrid and an illustrious member of the Royal Academy of History, serving twice as the Academy's director, interests us in this book because he published a study on the origin of Spanish in the Academy's *Memorias* (Memoirs, 1805).

Martínez Marina read Rousseau and Condillac on language and its origins and engages in polemic with them, at the same time that he lays out the theories they had presented. Tubal and Tarshish disappear, like the phantasms that they were, faced with the rational examination of these topics. As far as the primordial language is concerned, the learned canon is, naturally, very prudent:

We are ignorant of the character, nature, and circumstances of that primordial language. We do not know whether it was rich or poor in expressions, whether or not some, many, or all of its roots are preserved in the languages known and existing today around the globe. (1805a, 10)

By the same token, he does not hide his disdain for the theory-builders of his time, whom he does not even deign to cite by name, who had written on the old topic of Spain's primordial language. He writes (1805a, 12):

> Much has been said, written, and done on this topic by our men of letters, whose zeal and good intentions are worthy of praise, but unfortunately, all their researches can only contribute to passing the time pleasantly, as when one reads a fable, and not to multiplying our knowledge.

For Martínez Marina, it is absolutely clear that Spanish has not preserved any ancient words. He supports with all firmness the generalization of Latin in Spain and interprets (1805a, 14) in this sense the debated passage of Saint Pacianus of Barcelona (*Epist.* [Epistolae (Letters)] II, 4, 5) in which he says vaguely that "Latium, Aegyptus, Athenae, Thraces, Arabes, Hispani" (Latium, the Egyptian, Athens, Thracians, Arabs, Spaniards) confess God in their own language, understood by many to mean that the "Spaniards" of Barcelona still had a language of their own in his day.

Afterward, he discusses the decadence of Latin and the corruption of the cultured language, and he sees very well that in general, in the Iberian Peninsula, "there was no other vulgar and common language of the people at that time than Latin" (1805a, 15).

It is a curious fact, and one that reveals the elitist mentality, as we would call it, of a nineteenth-century liberal like Martínez Marina, that for him, the change from Vulgar Latin to a Romance language was not the result of a natural or fated evolution. Language change is decadence, and this decadence is simply barbarism and lack of study. He affirms (1805a, 20):

> The monuments of our history clearly show that the Spanish Romance language owes its origin to the Spaniards' ignorance, negligence, and carelessness in cultivating their ancient Latin language.

Next, like Aldrete two centuries earlier (although Aldrete [see his work, 1606, 176], as we have seen, had a greater historical sense and knew that "languages change with time"), Martínez Marina found himself obliged to defend the position that the Spanish version of the

Fuero Juzgo, the Visigothic law code, was a translation from Latin, against writers as nonsensical as Pellicer (1805a, 25).

Martínez Marina's prejudices can perhaps be explained by the enthusiasms of Spain's eighteenth-century Enlightenment thinkers. The Spanish Academy's motto, "It purifies, fixes in place, and gives splendor," explicitly aimed to fix in place what could only be held fast in that way to a certain extent. For the rest, Martínez Marina's documentary base of medieval texts and the appearance of Spanish in them reveals careful study and a sure critical sense.

His first essay is followed in the same handsomely printed volume by one on Arabic elements, or elements brought by the Arabs, in Spanish. In the introduction to this work, Martínez Marina attacks the misguided national passion that considers its own language to rank first among all, including in time. He writes in opposition to those who give in to this tendency,

> especially if, flattering national passion, we were to insist on raising our language to the summit of honor, showing it to be one of the universe's primordial ones, one of the most wise, rich, sweet, and harmonious, a fertile source and fountain of almost all those known around the globe. (1805b, I)

Since the Tubalic (or Tarshishian) theory applied to Spanish had already disappeared, Martínez Marina is clear that his opponents are the defenders of the Tubalic origin of Basque. Astarloa's book had just appeared in Madrid, and colleagues of his in the Academy of History, such as Traggia, had taken part in bitter polemics. The fastidious academician, without roots among the people and convinced that language is something regulated by literary culture, violently vents his rage (1805b, II f):

> It is indeed true that in some corners of the north of our peninsula, in the valleys as well as in the mountains, some people, especially in the countryside, speak a certain gibberish that has been claimed to be an original language, and even a language of wisdom, and there have even been those who have reputed it to be the mother in large part of our own. However, since during the Middle Ages, during which the dialects known in Spain were born and grew up, the one of which we are speaking either did not exist or did not achieve a reputation among cultured and civilized people, given that nothing has been written and

no public documents have been drawn up in a language of that kind, it should be reputed to have originated in a confused mixture of the common dialect with many other additional words arrived from elsewhere, but so altered, varied, and corrupted, as a consequence of the people's ignorance, the absence of the use of writing among them for several centuries, and the other reasons that, as we have demonstrated in our essay, naturally influenced the corruption of languages, that even if the sources from which the majority of that language's elements come can still be discerned, it is impossible to speak accurately or reach a correct decision with regard to others. The same would have happened to our Romance if it had not been made certain by means of so many books and writings as soon as it reached the point of forming a dialect different from Latin . . .

This violent passage can be understood only in the context of the polemics of the time. The disdainful academician does not even name Basque. Convinced that languages are developed and maintained by the effort of culture, he does not acknowledge anything primordial or original in Basque. Without literature or any kind of cultivation, it derives, like the Romance languages, from the "common dialect," but with a greater degree of barbarism; what cannot be explained in this way is ascribed to "additional words arrived from all over," of unrecognizable origin.

Juan Antonio Moguel

This great Basque writer (Eibar, 1745–Markina [Marquina], 1804) has to be studied in the context of the climate of interest in Basque and Basque antiquities that flourished around 1800 (see Garate 1936). He had close ties to the sailor and academician José Vargas Ponce, to whom Moguel's papers passed before finally ending up at the Royal Academy of History in Madrid.

The editor of the volume in which these documents were published (Moguel 1854, 664) notes in his prologue that

although the author was very well versed in his native language, he was not knowledgeable otherwise . . . So it happens that sometimes he is correct, and the majority of times he errs, especially when he proposes to prove that many common Latin words . . . have their origin in Basque.

The first work included in this volume is a *Disertación histórico-geográfica sobre los iberos y sicanos que entraron en Italia, en el Lacio y territorio de Roma, introduciendo el idioma vascuence* (Historico-geographical dissertation on the Iberians and Sycanians who entered Italy, Latium, and the territory of Rome, introducing the Basque language, 1854, 667–702).

Moguel follows Masdeu and Hervás, whom he calls "great men and heroes of literature" (1854, 669), and with his knowledge of Euskara, he examines the topic of Italian place names, finding Basque names throughout the country. He then continues along the path pioneered by Larramendi and derives Latin *aculeus* from Basque *aculua* and Latin *atrium* from Basque *ataria* (1854, 678f). *Astutus* 'clever, cunning' comes from Basque *astua* 'soothsayer' because "people of this kind are cunning, shrewd" (1854, 680), and so on in succession until arriving at *urbe* 'city', which is none other than Basque "*ur* 'water' and *be* 'below', that is, 'water from below'," since "Rome, built on a hill, has the Tiber River in its lower part" (1854, 697).

This monograph is followed by letters to Vargas Ponce from 1802. In the first (1854, 703), he explains that Campomanes, Masdeu, and Hervás, although they were not native Basques, saw that this language was

very useful for understanding the history and geography of Spain.

Nevertheless, Moguel's good sense led him to see the danger in exaggeration. Consider this observation on Larramendi (1854, 707):

His ingenuity was great, he did a great deal in an entirely uncultivated language, but I have never liked his invectives and mockery impugning learned men. Moderation is half an argument . . .

He provides a very good critique of the false inscription that Larramendi described in the prologue of his *Diccionario*, and he laments the fact that any scholars, such as Luis Carlos y Zúñiga, have followed him (1854, 708).

In his next letter, Moguel offers very interesting information about Astarloa. He notes his trip to Madrid and that he has with him "a new dictionary" (1854, 713). This dictionary, which Hervás seems to have used later, was a triple one: a dictionary of the language, a geographical dictionary, and a dictionary of surnames. Modestly, Moguel does not mention that, if we believe what we read in Hervás's *Catálogo* (Catalog, 1804b, 15), he himself was at least in part an author of this work, compiled under the direction of Josef de Campos. Moguel also says that Astarloa took to Madrid an extensive "art," that is, a grammar. This is the work that Humboldt saw, the *Discursos* (Discourses).

Moguel also expresses his opinion (1854, 714) on Astarloa, who has gone to Madrid to publish his *Apología* (Apology):

> the critics with good instincts will not like his systematic spirit and his heated passion and that he will make Larramendi be forgotten.

The good sense and knowledge of the excellent writer that Moguel was shine in everything that is not an etymology that places Basque at the center of the world. He is able to produce a very good analysis of derivation in Basque (1854, 714ff) and finds the construction of the conjugation "very well organized and very delicate" (1854, 716). If he defends the authenticity of the "Song of Lelo" (which would still deceive Humboldt) against the sharp-eyed Vargas Ponce (1854, 721) and refuses to acknowledge that the Romans ever dominated the Basque-speaking territory, since Flaviobriga "is not Bizkaia" (1854, 720), he has entered the dawning nineteenth century when he says:

> I have not said and will not say that Tubal came in person. Masdeu himself also does not say that he was the one who came, but rather his descendants and those of Tarshish . . .

Pablo Pedro de Astarloa

Pablo Pedro de Astarloa (1752–1806), a priest from Durango, represents a high point in Basque studies, as well as an exaggeration of the consideration of the merits and distinctive characteristics of Euskara. In an erudite book, J. Garate (1936) has informed us about the atmosphere that surrounded this scholar. Astarloa was a friend of Juan Antonio Moguel, who even if he shared his ideas about Euskara, was more accurate in his cultivation of the language, earning indisputable laurels. He formed part of a movement of scholars that still awaits focused research. In our section on Hervás, we will make some mention of them. It is precisely this atmosphere that Humboldt came into contact with during his travels to the Basque Country, which he passed through in October 1799, and in Madrid, where he spent a month in May 1801; he later recalled (1821, 17) his walks with Astarloa through the villages near Durango.

Even without having published anything, Astarloa was already famous, and his ideas about Basque had spread. Samaniego, the Enlightenment author known for his fables, wrote to a friend in Markina [Marquina] in 1786 (Garate 1936, 29):

> Markina, whose inhabitants believe that there is no more to the world than the exiguous territory surrounded by their mountains, a world led by Astarloas and Moguels. Tell the good Pablo Pedro that for a work that I am thinking about writing about antiquities from before the Flood, he should tell me (since he should know) what scribes, tailors, and shoemakers were called in the earthly paradise. Give him a hug from me . . .

Undoubtedly, the material of his *Discursos filosóficos* (Philosophical discourses), which would remain unpublished until the last quarter of the nineteenth century, was circulating among the scholars of the Basque provinces and even farther afield.

The unpublished papers that Astarloa left behind passed into Erro's hands and then into those of his heirs, and finally the Bizkaian provincial government was able to publish the *Discursos* with the assistance of an editor, as we are told in the "Summary Notice" that precedes the book and that was written, according to Garate (1936, 139), by Antonio de Trueba.

We will discuss this work first, since we know that it is earlier than the *Apología* (Apology), and Humboldt was able to use it in manuscript during his trip.

Astarloa begins by posing the theoretical problem, not as absurd then as it seems to us now, of whether there was a primordial language or not, and if so, whether there was one or several (1883, 1). Subsequently, he asks whether this "desired language" remains alive among any nation. In that primordial language,

> infused into the first men by the wise and supreme Maker, after having formed it as a work worthy of His hands,

we would have simply "an open book of all knowledge" (1883, 3f).

Astarloa opposes the idea that the first men lived

> in a brutish state, without arts, without sciences, without society, scattered through the forests in the manner of beasts, unable to articulate a single word . . . (1883, 6)

Along with the "Catholic philosophers" who take their information from Genesis, Astarloa believes that the first men had "the use of a perfect language from the first instant of their creation," and this language was "natural," although not "infused by God" (1883, 6).

Next, Astarloa begins his arguments: men were sociable beings, as Genesis tells us, and their social relationships had to be established not by means of a "language of action," that is, of gestures, but rather by means of one "of articulated words" (1883, 11).

Starting from this basis, Astarloa develops his theory of natural sounds. He supposes (1883, 28f) that a man wants to attract another's attention and pronounces an *o*; he wants to refer to something that is higher than human beings, so he articulates a *g* in the velar region of the palate and pronounces *go*; in order to direct attention to something that is perpendicularly above, he pronounces a *y* and says *goyco*[1] 'from above'; then

> the hearer understands that of the two objects present to his eyes on a perpendicular axis, the higher one was the one that the speaker wanted to communicate to him, that is, the sun. (1883, 29)

In this way, Astarloa reasons, the language of the first men was natural, neither infused by God nor invented by men, but rather just as natural as the neighing or roaring of animals (1883, 39).

Astarloa, who was an erudite man, had read a great deal, and was sufficiently well informed about the ideas of his time, ended up with this idea of natural words, of the natural meaning that he believed he could find in each sound, and which is found in very similar form in the most learned of his contemporaries (see, for example, passages from Humboldt in Arens 1976, 159f). As Unamuno (1902, 561) writes, Astarloa

---

1. In Unified Basque *goiko*. —Ed. note

was the one who inaugurated among the proponents of Basque the highly nonsensical principle of giving an ideological value to syllables and even to letters . . . and he reached such excesses of enthusiasm that he affirmed that he had found something "almost divine" in the abstracted elements of Basque.

Astarloa made much use of some verses he ascribed to Cottunius,[2] and as we will see, Arana-Goiri did the same to an even greater extent. They read as follows:

Clamabunt *a* et *e* quotquot nascuntur ab Eua,
Omnis masculus *a* nascens, *e* femina profert.

[All who are born from Eve will cry out *a* and *e*;
Every male says *a* when he is born, every female *e*.]

Astarloa recounts that he confirmed the truth of these hexameters by experience, since when he was in the portico of the main church in Durango, a group arrived to baptize an infant that

was doing nothing but crying continuously, and across the entire length of the portico, I heard in that crying the letter A, with the greatest clarity. (1883, 44f)

When Astarloa asked how the infant was practicing the alphabet like that, the wet-nurse replied, with no knowledge of Cottunius, in four condensed Basque words that Astarloa glosses as follows:

Well now, isn't this infant male, for you to find the pronunciation of A in his crying strange?

---

2. Astarloa undoubtedly found this text, of which he will make repeated use, in Hervás (1873, 152), who gives a third line,

a genitor dat Adam; *e* dedit Eua prius

[Father Adam gives *a*; Eve gave *e* first]

which Astarloa omits, doubtless because it did not suit his purposes. Hervás found "questi pensieri più da poeta che da filosofo" (these thoughts more fitting for a poet than a philosopher). In my research, I have not been able to identify the Cottunius whom Hervás cites, Cottonius in Astarloa (Catonius by mistake in 1883): perhaps the famous Neapolitan doctor Domenico Cotugno, a contemporary of Astarloa and Hervás and extremely famous for his physiological discoveries, which he presented in books written in Latin.

In confirmation of the same finding, the town's two surgeons, Amezua and Arrugaeta,

> who had often heard that the first letter pronounced by a male was A, and that a female said E,

paid attention to this at Astarloa's request, and "both laid hands on this truth by experience in more than a hundred infants." Moreover, Astarloa confirmed it personally in eight additional cases, five males and three females. Now, Astarloa continues (1883, 45), in Basque *aarra*

> means what in Spanish is 'the one of the A' or 'the one who says A', and that is the noun that means 'male' among us. *Emia*, with which we signify a female, means 'delicate E' or 'delicate crying'. This analogy is most beautiful,

Astarloa concludes, and this provides the anchor for his identification of Basque with the primordial and natural language, the one that he believes to be innate in human beings.

Such ideas about the natural signification of letters (cf. also Astarloa 1883, 161ff) seem gratuitous and even nonsensical to us today, and even Humboldt, who was still near to them in part, criticizes Astarloa and Erro on this point and invites the Basque linguists to give up

> ein solches eitles Bemühen, dessen Vergeblichkeit von andern Nationen längst anerkannt ist. (Humboldt 1821, 13)
>
> [such a vain effort, the futility of which has long been recognized by other nations.]

However, unlike Erro, Astarloa was not an ignorant man, and he was interested in various problems of linguistics and in topics of theoretical and practical interest such as the language and writing of deaf-mutes, with observations of neighbors of his with that disability and ideas of his own in opposition to those of a French teacher of deaf-mutes lauded in Madrid periodicals of the time. The primary meaning of sounds was still invoked in his time and would continue to be so for a somewhat longer period.

We cannot follow Astarloa in his prolix considerations. He replies to many objections, such as the multiplicity of languages, despite their origin on his hypothesis from a single natural primordial language (1883, 70ff). "It is natural to man to multiply languages," and although different languages appear over the course of history for this reason, in

> the mechanism of the languages spoken in the world today we will find . . . a most beautiful analogy. This analogy arises precisely from those traces of the mechanism of the primordial language that have been preserved in them. (1883, 77)

Astarloa views from the perspective of his Basque language the changes in the primordial language, the destruction of the natural language by human caprice:

> In effect, who anteposed the article in the Hebrew language and its daughters, in the majority of European languages, etc., except the caprice of man? Is not the gender of nouns in countless languages a known effect of whimsy and fancy? . . . It was not instinct, it was not nature, it was man who disturbed the ordered mechanism of the primordial language . . . (1883, 77)

Man with his caprice has attempted "to destroy and consign to oblivion the language of his primordial fathers," but

> he has not been able to achieve this . . . There is no language, if we leave one aside, that has not fouled this mechanism. Nevertheless, every language has preserved unequivocal traces of its beauty. (1883, 77)

With reason, Unamuno (1902, 562) found in these ideas of Astarloa a "hymn to the language not lacking in poetry, even if it lacks science." Now, the primordial language that Astarloa believed to be manifest in all its original perfection is none other than Euskara. The characteristics that he demands in the primordial language,

> in its verbs, the five persons, the two hundred and six conjugations, . . . masculine and feminine verbs, . . . ordered . . . syntax . . . (1883, 78),

are found only in Basque.

In the demonstration that Astarloa attempts, the words that have been called "natural" (1883, 88) play a large role, that is, those that are

analogous to their significates, proper, euphonic, and economic,

based

on the child's articulations, on the adult's interjections,

and with that more or less widespread similarity that Schuchardt would later call *Elementarverwandtschaft* (elementary kinship), founded on human nature itself. There are certainly languages, such as Basque, rich in words of this type.

The primordial human language was a single one, since Astarloa is convinced of the monogenesis of the species. Languages as strange as those of the Americas

are of the same mechanism as those that we speak on our continent: we and they know prepositional and postpositional languages ... (1883, 107)

For Astarloa, what are today called linguistic universals exist, and for him, this fact is founded on the primordial unity of the human species, in which he believes.

Having demonstrated by argument the existence of a natural human language, Astarloa (1883, 113) embarks on the "grammar of the primordial language," which fills the rest of the extensive volume.

As everyone does, Astarloa had an incorrigible ethnocentric vision. His knowledge of French and the phonetic description of that language that he was able to study in Destutt-Tracy did not persuade him that there are more than five vowels: the French *u* is simply "imperfect," and the different classes of *e* in the same language are modifications of the fundamental *e*, that is, his own (1883, 124).

"The organ of the mouth cannot produce more than twenty-eight letters," a heading says (1883, 127), and these are none other than the sounds of Bizkaian Euskara laid out for us in columns: five vowels, four labial consonants (*b, p, f, m*), five sibilants that he calls dentals (*c* and *z*, which it seems should be a single consonant; *s* and *ss*, which

I do not know how he separates; and *x*), the two trills *r* and *rr,* two affricates (*ch* and Bizkaian *j*), and finally the three dentals *d, t,* and *n,* the lateral *l,* the two liquids *ll* and *ñ,* and the two affricates *tz* and *ts.* It is incorrect that there are twenty-eight, since that number is only reached by adding the two velars *k* and *g,* which are not included in his analysis.

As far as *v* is concerned, Astarloa (1883, 135) classifies it as "indecent," and

> such that neither the primordial language nor any other perfect one should admit it in its alphabet,

since it does not exist in Basque and is nothing but an invention of the Latin grammarians, who were forced to this expedient in order to differentiate between awkward homonyms in their language, such as *bibo* and *uiuo* and *binus –a –um* and *uinum.*

Astarloa then amuses himself with establishing the possibilities for syllables in a perfect language and with giving rules for how words should be formed. He does not tire of setting in place the ideal qualities of the primordial language, in accordance with their appearance in his native Basque. Basing himself on the identity between actions or gestures and natural words, that is,

> on the analogy between the modulation of both and their significates (1883, 166),

he develops his theory of the natural signification of letters or sounds (1883, 173ff), from which he turns to a study of the formation of words or "modulations of the vocal organ" (1883, 185ff) in the "innocent" or spontaneous articulations of children and the interjections of adults.

With regard to children's words like *aita, tata, papa, ama, mama,* he makes very good use of Hervás's materials to discern their universality (1883, 190ff). The volumes of the *Idea dell'Universo* (Idea of the universe) dedicated to linguistics, which their author, Lorenzo Hervás, sent to him from Italy (cf. Garate 1936, 111), enabled Astarloa to make extensive comparisons between Basque and other languages. The theory of onomatopoeia links up with that of the natural significance of letters and syllables. Further research into the grammatical ideas of the age would be necessary in order to better assess the degree of Astarloa's originality on this point. He constantly relies on his native feeling for Euskara, finding, for example, that the best way to indicate diminutives is with those letters that are most fitted to indicate softness, delicacy, littleness, that is, Basque's *ch*, *ñ*, and *x* (1883, 252f). In the same way, it seems to him that, as in Basque (and in many languages, more or less primordial), the most natural way of counting is by twenties (fingers and toes) (1883, 268).

As Cejador will soon do, he searches languages of the five continents for the *n* of the first-person pronoun, *ni* in Basque (1883, 284). For the second person, the distinction between familiar and polite forms, which Basque shares with modern European languages, seems the most natural to him (1883, 286), and so on in succession.

Astarloa shares in the evolving Rousseauianism of his time and extends it to linguistics in an original and systematic way. In his view, the

> divergence from nature's rules in the invention of words has diversified languages . . . The ants of the Guaraní will understand without difficulty the language of the anthills of our peninsula, and a Spaniard, a Frenchman, an Italian is a tree trunk, a statue, a piece of marble in the congresses of the Moguls. Miserable situation of man! (1883, 297)

For Astarloa, it is certain that the differentiation of languages has resulted from the abandonment of those modes of natural derivation that he discovers in his native tongue. He goes on to devote himself to calculating the number of possible words, according to the numerical combinations of the possible syllables composed of the twenty-eight ideal sounds, and comes up with the theoretical number of five hundred trillion distinct possible words, all this in order to demonstrate that inflection for gender, as it exists in the Romance languages, is unacceptably impoverished, since there are always almost infinite possibilities for making this distinction with entirely distinct words, such as *anai* and *arreba*, instead of *hermano* 'brother' and *hermana* 'sister' (1883, 220). Not without errors, Hervás provides him with data for a discussion of the languages that have to rely on the imperfection of this type of gender marking.

Like Larramendi, Astarloa calls the postpositions that indicate case in languages such as Basque articles (1883, 325ff), and this is the starting point for his theory of declination. It goes without saying that with regard to the famous Basque agent or ergative case, a rarity in Western Europe, it seems to Astarloa (1883, 338) that in the primordial language

> it would indicate that the thing communicated via the noun or pronoun was the agent of the concept the speaker wished to convey.

Specifically, although

> we cannot establish with certainty what this little word would have been, since there are various strong letters and syllables that the vocal organ can produce, we are nevertheless persuaded that it would be the letter *k*,

precisely as in Euskara. He continues in this way, seeking the postpositions of the primitive language in the light of his experience in his native language.

His treatise on the verb (1883, 387–488) remains on the same theoretical plane as this whole part, which is conceived as a set of requirements that the supposed primordial language would have to meet. He draws on Destutt-Tracy, for example, for his doctrine of the formation of adverbs.

There is no doubt that, in his encounter with the doctrines dominant at the time in the field of general grammar, Astarloa had at his disposal his knowledge of and reflections about a language such as Basque, which gave him a very different perspective from those open to scholars who started from the Romance or Germanic languages or from Latin. For example, he has an original doctrine of verbal moods, among which he distinguishes

> infinitive, actual or indicative, habitual, potential, voluntary, necessary, forcible, imperative, intentional or subjunctive, optative, and penitudinary [*penitudinario*]. (1863, 398)

This last expresses "regret for having taken or omitted" the action (1883, 405).

He also attempts a new doctrine of tenses in their combination with moods.

It goes without saying that in the ideal primordial language, the verb will have gender in the familiar second-person conjugation, but not in the polite form *zu*, exactly as in Basque (1883, 429ff). The ideal language would include, as Euskara does in fact, a dative reference to the interlocutor (something that we might indicate with the interjection 'lo and behold!', equivalent to what Latinists call, using a rhetorical term, the ethical dative). This gives us, as basic forms:

> he loves him, o sir = he loves him in relation to you (formal)
>
> he loves him, o woman = he loves him in relation to you (informal feminine) = behold that he loves him
>
> he loves him, o man = he loves him in relation to you (informal masculine) = behold that he loves him

Then, in that ideal primordial language, that is to say, in Euskara and in no other that we know of, it is also possible to intercalate into the verbal forms the dative complement, without omitting the reference to the object (singular or plural) or to the ethical dative of the interlocutor:

> I give it to him, o sir = I give it to him in relation to you (informal masculine or feminine) = behold that I give it to him
>
> he gives it to him, o sir = behold that he gives it to him

and so on. Astarloa does his calculations and finds in that ideal language 206 different conjugations with 1,236 tenses for the active mood, 412 for each of the other moods, and so on. We will limit ourselves to referring the reader to the possibilities reflected in the tables that Prince Bonaparte (1869) left incomplete or the ones that the engineer Echaide (1944) drew up for Gipuzkoan.

Astarloa ends this part with a discussion of syntax (1883, 498–527), in which he establishes a hierarchy of importance or nobility of words, which would determine their order within the phrase in the ideal language. With the support of his native feeling for Euskara and the materials Hervás supplied him in his collection of Our Fathers, he finds the ideal model in postpositional languages:

> this collocation will be dissonant to Spaniards and to all the other nations whose languages are prepositional, but in addition to finding it founded in nature itself, we can affirm that the majority of languages follow this usage. (1883, 518)

As proof, he examines Japanese, Quechua, Araucanian, Mochica, Aymara, Guaraní, Tamanacan, Maipure, Turkish, Georgian or Iberian, Tungus, Burmese, and a couple of Aryan languages from India, the majority of which agree with Basque in a subject-object-verb word order, type III in Greenberg's modern typology.

The last third of this lengthy book, under the title of "Recognition of languages or investigation of whether or not there exists one worthy of having been primordial" (1883, 530), is nothing more than the confirmation that Euskara is the one that precisely fulfills all the conditions demanded in the preceding theoretical discussion. It goes without saying that Astarloa criticizes claims for Hebrew as the first language, as well as those for Chinese, which enjoyed the prestige of an exaggerated reputation for antiquity in eighteenth-century Europe, and repeats his demand that

> if the language of the first men was natural, as we believe, we have to repute it likewise perfect. (1883, 532f)

From the original interjections, it developed into a unique and perfect language in the patriarchal age. Then comes the examination of all the requirements and characteristics that have been noted for the ideal language throughout the length of the work, and we need not say that from its conformity to the ideal and perfect alphabet to its agreement in the collocation of its words, Euskara is the language that meets all the conditions and is manifestly the original language of the human species.

Just as Larramendi found himself forced to debate Mayans in his *Diccionario*, Astarloa had to enter the arena and present his previously unpublished ideas in Madrid. In reality, Astarloa's polemic came in response to the anti-Basque critiques of certain Madrid academicians, specifically the first of them: that of Traggia in the *Diccionario geográfico histórico* that the Academy of History had begun to publish. This polemic, as we will see, arose out of a set of government aims in which the progress of political and administrative uniformity and centralism met an obstacle in the Basques' traditional laws and privileges.

In reality, Traggia, a native of Aragon who had studied exotic languages, seems at first glance to have put forward his critique of

Basque with discretion and without questioning in the least Euskara's originality, its admirable resistance to assimilation by conquerors or neighbors, or its "culture, richness, energy, and smoothness." What the academician permitted himself to doubt was that Basque was in fact one of the original languages that arose from the confusion of tongues at Babel (1802, 152). Perhaps with some irony, he said that time,

> a great discoverer of hidden things, will be able to produce more certain data with which to resolve this issue with full knowledge. (Traggia 1802, 156)

After Traggia's death, Astarloa moved to Madrid. Perhaps we may suppose that this was not because "he was not well thought of in Durango," as Garate says (1936, 116), but rather because someone might have encouraged him to go to Madrid to defend a cause that was threatened by a true government plan. It is enough that we consider that the attacks of Martínez Marina and the very direct legal and administrative ones of Juan Antonio Llorente were to follow for us to suppose that alert residents of the Basque Country may have thought to counter the first of the aggressions that were undoubtedly in preparation at the time.

The *Apología* (Apology, 1803) appeared in Madrid with a prologue dedicated "To the Basques," in which the author recalls his work on the primordial language stretching back twenty years, his comparative studies of Basque and other languages, his examination of Euskara's marvelous properties with regard to its propriety, economy, and euphony, the artifice of its article, its postpositions, its verb, and so on.

The book goes on to crush Traggia's doubts, although, as we have seen, he was not in reality so aggressive about them. The *Apología* is composed of two parts, the first on the

> antiquity of the Basque language, proven with the arguments put forward by the Basques in its favor until now (1803, 8–273),

and the second on the remote times beyond history's reach, proven from Basque's own words (1803, 274–442).

In a work published in 1795, Traggia had been inclined to recognize the Basques as Spain's most ancient inhabitants, admitting as well that they were a cultured nation, in all of which he explicitly followed Larramendi's conclusions. In view of the doubts Traggia expounded in his article in the Royal Academy of History's *Diccionario*, however, Astarloa found himself forced to present his ideas. In persuasive mode, he says (1803, 12):

> No, beloved Spaniards, no; Basque is not the language of the Californians, it is not the language of the barbarians of the North, it was not born on the remote islands of the Pacific Ocean, it did not come to you from the furthest uninhabitable reaches of the globe: it is your language, a language of your own nation, a language of your most remote grandfathers.

Consequently, Basque is not a barbarous and uncultured language;

> it is, finally, worthy of a learned nation such as yours.

Astarloa repeats the familiar arguments on the antiquity of the Basques in their region. In response to Traggia's unfortunate speculation that the Navarrese were not Basques but barbarian invaders, the *Nabaroi* whom Ptolemy mentions in Northern Europe, Astarloa argues, with his etymological method, that *Navarra* 'Navarre' is a Basque word:

> *Na* among us means 'flat, plain' . . . *Be* means 'low', *Ar* is equivalent to 'man', and *A* is an article . . . so that the word *Nabarra* literally means 'plain-low-of-man-the', and in Spanish syntax, 'the man of the low plain'. (1803, 28f)

Mocking Traggia with the conversion of the Basque people, that is, the "mountain people" of the current etymology of *basco* 'Basque' from *baso-ko*, into the *navarros* 'Navarrese' or "those of the plain," he enlarges at length on the mysterious syllables *na, be, ar,* and *a*.

Astarloa sees proof that Basque is Spain's ancient language in the fact that *ñ, ll,* and *z* (?) must have entered Spanish from Basque (1803, 48ff), in opposition to Traggia's not unreasonable view that such "simple sounds" can and do exist in the most diverse languages.

Astarloa marshalled against Traggia evidence taken from Hervás, using it to defend Basque's primacy in certain sounds that it shares with Spanish.

Subsequently, Astarloa lays out the theories he had already formulated in his previous studies, that is, in his great unpublished book, and even goes a step further, developing his theory of the primordial signification of letters. Along these lines, he analyzes (1803, 70ff) each vowel-plus-consonant and consonant-plus-vowel group, discerning the etymology of primordial words in accordance with these interpretations: *atz* 'finger' thus comes from *a* 'extension' and *tz*, characterizing abundance, and a finger is in effect 'of abundant extension'; *ats* 'stench' is from *a* plus *ts*, which is the same as *tz*, so 'of abundant extension, or something that extends a great distance', a description evidently appropriate for a stench; and so on ad infinitum, with words of two, three, and four syllables and the processes of derivation.

It occurred to Traggia to say that Basque was not perfect in that it lacked gender, and once again Astarloa (1803, 120ff) proclaims the excellence of the many languages in the world without gender. Likewise, Astarloa explains the unique perfection with which Basque characterizes what he calls "primary relationships": definite article and causal endings or postpositions (1803, 124ff). Traggia considered Basque nouns indeclinable and dared to assume the six Latin cases in the language. Astarloa had good reason to complain about the fact that every language, from English to Russian, organized its grammar on the Greco-Latin model. If Traggia tried to understand Basque by way of certain comparisons with Tagalog, Chinese, Japanese, and other Eastern languages, however, Astarloa had in his favor an intimate knowledge of the language, as well as the study of others and Hervás's information, more or less sufficient, about many more.

Hence in his analysis of the verb, Astarloa is insightful in his insistence, discerning, for example, a causative formation in *irakatzi*[3] 'to teach' as compared to *ikasi* 'to see', and attempting, as he had already done in his unpublished *Discurso filosófico*, to classify the moods in a new way. In view of the "infuriating multiplication" of verbal forms in Basque, Traggia had dared to think that they were the result of

---

3. In Unified Basque *irakasi*. —Ed. note

mixture: in his view, the Basques had taken them "from contact with many" nations (Astarloa 1803, 161).

Everywhere, Astarloa finds perfections, while Traggia insists on similarities and explanations by way of comparison with the most diverse languages, albeit, it is true, with an abusive overreliance on "perhaps" and "it may be," for which Astarloa reproaches him.

The sections Astarloa dedicates to Basque word order contain interesting observations, amid his apologetic preoccupation with "the learned Aragonese gentleman," and can still be read with profit.

In the *Apología,* sometimes written at top speed, he mixes the examination of the language with the repetition of the Basque scholars' old themes: Basque

> has not been formed since the entrance of the first nation into inhabited Spain. (1803, 189)

It is true that Traggia attributed to the Basques something like the invention of the language, not always using logical or normal criteria. The academician himself had accepted, although not without doubts (see Astarloa 1803, 266), the Basque scholars' thesis that, since Poza, explained the ancient place names of all of Spain by way of Basque, and Astarloa entered victorious into this field to refute Arabic, Hebrew, and Celtic etymologies of the name of Spain and to repeat that only *artz* 'bear' and *tripa* 'intestine' have comparable Celtic words (cf. Hervás 1784, 171). For the rest, Astarloa ignores Hervás's recognition of a Celtic element in *–briga* and maintains its connection with *uri,* against Traggia, who said (1802, 153) that "Basque does not have the noun *briga* in its entire dictionary." On the other hand, Astarloa has the prudence not to join Hervás in extending Basque etymologies to Italy.

A dictionary of geographical names with their etymologies occupies pages 227 to 257, followed by notes on surnames, including (as previously in Larramendi 1729, 10) the explanation of the suffix *–ez* as equivalent to the adverbial postposition in Basque.

Traggia's prudent doubts and reserves on Basque's status as the primordial language of the Iberian Peninsula lead Astarloa to open the second part of his book with a demonstration of the antiquity of the Basque language in the remote times to which history cannot penetrate . . . by Basque words themselves. (1803, 274)

We may suppose that reading Traggia's article encouraged Astarloa to present in the form of a polemical book part of the copious material that he had previously gathered and that remained unpublished. The theory of the primordial language fit like a glove for replying to the doubts and issues the academician had raised.

Basque itself, that is, what the study of its grammar and vocabulary had revealed to Astarloa, could

> present authentic testimony to its existence, not only at the time that Spain was populated, not only in the age of the dispersion of peoples mentioned by Moses, but also in a much earlier age, the assignment of which I happily leave to the decision of men of letters, once they have seen the Basque testimony of which I am going to speak. (1803, 276)

In effect, starting from the fact that

> our language is a true and complete history of itself, in which the descent, customs, sciences, arts, religion of our first grandfathers are found depicted with the greatest care (1803, 276f),

he sets out to explain the etymology of words that appear demonstrative to him: *egun* 'day' means 'ultimate happiness', since *e* 'smooth, sweet, delicious, consoling, happy' and *gun* 'the ultimate' ensure such an equivalence; *ilun* 'dark' is composed of *ill* 'to die' and *une* 'nearness'; and so on for each word.

The correct and, at the time, very new idea that each language is a true archive of its history goes astray in this way with the grant of significance to each letter and each syllable.

Astarloa then continues, after the most general words, with the etymology of those related to time (1803, 309): *goizaldu* or *goxaldu* 'to eat breakfast', for example, comes, according to him, from *goiza, goxa* 'the morning of the day', and upon then discerning the root *al* 'power', he explains etymologically that

> the whole together means to fortify oneself in the morning or make oneself powerful. (1803, 313)

He then takes up the Basque week, a subject that had previously been discussed among scholarly priests in the region, as we will see when we turn to Hervás. In 1802, Astarloa had been named censor of the Basque week in the province of Gipuzkoa, as he tells us (1803, 335), and the province itself published a prospectus that included a study written "at the beginning of the nineteenth century" giving indisputable and authentic testimony of the antiquity of that week, older than all those of the world except the Hebrew. This served as reinforcement for the theory that the pagan gods had never received cult in the region, and Astarloa continued:

> it is also [testimony] to the perpetual immovability and firmness of the Basque people in the true religion throughout the entire prodigious period of their national existence, without declining into the idolatry that dishonored the world, although they saw it be born, tyrannize, and perish; it is also [testimony] to the perfect polity, civility, and morality of the Basques from such a remote and incredible beginning; it is also [testimony] to the elevated science and knowledge of the Basque people in philosophy, astronomy, music, rhetoric, and grammar . . . (1803, 335f)

For Astarloa, the names of the days of the week are incontrovertible evidence of the remote antiquity and culture of the Basques. The goddess Astarte, "a Phrygian divinity," is none other than the *Astearte* 'Tuesday' of the Basque week (1803, 401), just as the Roman god Mars is merely a syncopated form of *marrati* 'lightning-striker, or the one who frequently causes lightning' (1803, 403).

An extremely brief third part (1803, 421–22) completes the *Apología* with the demonstration of the language's antiquity "by its perfection." Traggia had certainly recognized the excellences of Basque and needed merely to recognize its antiquity. Astarloa believes that he has proven Basque's antiquity in having indicated that it shares the perfections of the perfect primordial languages (such as Lule, Tupi, Araucanian, and Chiquito [1803, 425], which he knows by way of Hervás's work) and the qualities of modern languages, such as French, Spanish, and English, which are rich, but not perfect (1803, 422).

Astarloa concludes the lengthy work with a brief discourse he was publishing in Madrid in order to confirm his fellow countrymen in their pride in their language.

He published anonymously a reply to the brief volume that, as we will see, the academician José Antonio Conde published under a pseudonym in opposition to him. These *Reflexiones* (Reflections), addressed to the public and in which Astarloa speaks of himself in the third person, are justified, he says, because

> with Spanish men of letters divided into two bands or factions, the public did not know how to decide.

He reproaches the anonymous critic for his "overgrown forest of Greek, Latin, and Hebrew texts" (1804, 6) and takes shelter behind his great unpublished book:

> Many years ago, Pablo de Astarloa conceived the project of discovering a primordial language by way of the remains that he saw scattered among the languages of the nations. (1804, 7)

Astarloa reproaches Conde for surrendering to the traditional prestige of Hebrew, Greek, and Arabic; he defends himself against the accusation of knowing languages only through Hervás's *Catálogo* (in the process of publication at the time) and refers the reader to the work in Italian (Astarloa 1804, 15); and he maintains unshaken the innate perfection of Basque.

Listening to the two sides in this debate, the erudite academician and the Basque full of enthusiasm for his mysterious language, we cannot help but lament the limitations of both attitudes. Did either one have a future? Undoubtedly not, and this is one of the points at which we are impressed by the obstacles that modern scientific thinking had to overcome in Spain. The study of Hervás confirms us in this opinion.

To conclude, we will select from Astarloa's brief book an argument with which he responds to the Hebrew authorities cited by the Curate of Montuenga (Conde's nom de guerre in his pamphlet):

> Are they more than just some rabbis, some Hebrews just as passionate about a language as Poza, Echave, Larramendi, Sorreguieta, and Astarloa were? (Astarloa 1804, 43)

We end this section with Humboldt's (1817, 334) judgment of Astarloa, of which we accept the first part, but not the second, since the learned Prussian was not sufficiently critical on the point of "the universality of Basque in Spain" and was defending not so much Astarloa as himself:

> Bey Astarloa's Apologie hätte die Gerechtigkeit erfordert, zugleich zu sagen, dass, wenn sie auch viele sonderbare und übertriebene Ideen enthält, sie doch auch reich an trefflichen Bemerkungen über die Vaskische Sprache ist, zuerst wahres Licht über ihren wunderbaren Bau anzündet, und neben her interessante Untersuchungen über die Bedeutung der alten Städte- Völker- und Flussnahmen der Spanischen Halbinsel und über den Vaskischen Kalender liefert.

> [With regard to Astarloa's *Apología*, justice would have demanded that I say at once that, even if it contains many strange and exaggerated ideas, it is nevertheless also rich in apt observations on the Basque language, is the first to shed true light on its wonderful structure, and incidentally offers interesting research on the meaning of the ancient names of towns, peoples, and rivers in the Iberian Peninsula and on the Basque calendar.]

Juan Bautista de Erro y Azpiroz

This heir of Astarloa is a curious figure. He was born in Andoain in 1773 and died in exile in Baiona [Bayonne] in 1854. He studied at the Royal Seminary in Bergara [Vergara] and was an official in the Almadén mines. Subsequently, he held a variety of government positions. In 1818, he was intendant of Madrid, and in 1819, he was named a corresponding member of the Royal Academy of History. In 1820, he took refuge in France from the liberal revolution and returned to Bergara, having retired from his posts. He was an absolutist in his ideas, which caused him difficulties, residence restrictions, and exiles during the latter stages of Ferdinand VII's reign.

Carlos María Isidro named Juan Bautista de Erro general minister (*ministro universal*) in 1836, a position he filled for several months, until the siege of Bilbao was raised.

His three books related to our topic were published in 1806, 1807, and 1815. He was not in the Basque Country when Humboldt passed through, but the anonymous pamphlet we are using (Erro 1954), which was written by Fausto Arocena, states that his relationship with Humboldt "was not a fortunate one," although "it is not easy to determine the motive for resentment."

Erro, whom Hübner (1893, XXIV) benevolently called "uir non mediocriter doctus, sed caeco rerum patriarum amore abreptus" (a man more than moderately learned, but carried away by blind love of country), applies Astarloa's doctrine to writing. In his prologue (1806), he says:

> If I have not been correct in everything, I leave much less to be investigated in an absolutely unknown subject.

On the supposition that Basque is the most ancient language, the primordial one, the alphabet that we call Iberian is also the primordial one, the source from which the Greek and Latin alphabets derive. Larramendi, Erro says (1806, 3), had already called the script of the ancient coins of Hispania "Basque characters." In this way, he is able to apply Astarloa's theory to letters. He interprets the arrow, which is read as *u*, as *i* and attributes to it penetration, which is the sound *i* for Astarloa (1806, 28).

Assuming the remote antiquity of the Spanish coins, he affirms (1806, 114) that "the Spaniards had their own money before the arrival of the first foreigners." His etymologies continue in the line with which we are already familiar: the Roman *as* 'unit; copper coin' is explained by way of Basque *asea,* from *asé* 'to satiate' (1806, 121).

In this way, he is in a position to explain everything, from the Cástulo vase (*MLI*, XLI) to the Trigueros one, which was a German bell (1806, 144ff).

In his next book, *Observaciones* (Observations, 1807), dedicated to Euskara speakers in Euskara, he engages in polemic against Conde, who denied, like Unamuno later, that languages were "philosophical" (1807, 46).

Erro published his *Mundo primitivo* (Primordial world) in 1815, after the disastrous years of the Napoleonic Wars, although he had finished writing it in 1807.[4] In this book, we likewise remain in the world of Astarloa, whom he calls "my dear friend" (1815, 54).

---

4. In the prologue, he refers to "last year, 1806," and he subsequently signs it in Elche de la Sierra, January 30, 1811.

Chapter 2 demonstrates that "The primordial language was infused in man at his creation and not formed by him." Moreover,

> the confusion of Babel, in any of the senses in which it might be understood, neither extinguished the primordial language nor deprived us of the satisfaction of proceeding with the most solid hopes of finding this precious language and of contemplating in it the unknown and important events of the primordial world. (1815, 66)

With this assurance of discovering in Euskara the language that predated Babel, Erro ventures into the fields of etymology. He devotes many pages to the numerals, on which topic we will limit ourselves to giving the etymologies of *bat* 'one' and *milla* 'thousand', since Erro believed that he found in them the "first part of the physical system of the universe" (1815, 97):

> *Bat* is *at, ata*, an articulation of infancy, which means 'father', and the letter *b* added for the fullness of the word in composition. The root *at*, which with the characteristic is *ata*, also means 'generation', as a quality essential or inherent to that of fatherhood, and so we say *b-at-aitz-a* for 'baptism', as if we were saying 'abundance of generation'. (1815, 110)

Note the similarity to Astarloa, reducing the same Latin-Romance form *bataiatu* to Basque etymology. He continues in the same way with the rest of the numerals up to a thousand, where *millá*

> is composed of the initial *m* and the participle *illá* of the verb *ill* 'to die'. (1815, 158)

In a note on this point, he adds, reminding us of Larramendi:

> The Latin *mille* ['thousand'] comes from this noun *millá*, and it was for a reason that the Romans wrote it with double *ll*, despite the fact that the alphabet of their language is unfamiliar with this letter in its true pronunciation, and this is also the source of *miles*, that language's name for a soldier, due to his office and profession of annihilating, destroying, and killing the enemy of the state of which he is the defense and guard.

Erro goes on in the same way, confirming the appropriateness of the Basque names of plants, minerals, and animals, followed by that of place names from around the globe, beginning with Asia, from *asi* 'to begin', because

> no one is ignorant of the fact that the human species, cities, religion, laws, and arts and sciences had their origin in this region. (1815, 208)

The same for Assyria, Senaar, Armenia, Ur of Chaldea . . . Then all of Africa, in a prelude to the explanations of "Africa," that is, the rest of the Iberian Peninsula, by Arana-Goiri. Understandably, the volume concludes with a well-engraved map of the Near East, with the exact location of the Earthly Paradise (1815, facing page 260).

José Antonio Conde and Juan Antonio Llorente

The historian and academician José Antonio Conde (1765–1820) turned his hand to polemic, reinforcing us in our belief that the struggle between theories about the Basque language was really a cover for political and administrative issues. The unitary state of the French Revolution, with which the Spanish monarchy was in conflict, and not as a matter of doctrine, but with the grave consequence of the effective occupation of parts of the Basque Country, aroused in the government—at the time in the hands of the omnipotent Godoy—the desire to put an end to the region's traditional privileges and laws. We cannot go into detail about historical topics, but it is not by chance that the popular revolt known as the Zamacolada, one of the ingredients of which was the desire to impose mandatory military service on the Bizkaians, coincided with the polemic about the Basque language that we are narrating.

Conde (who published this pamphlet and the following one under the pseudonym of "the Curate of Montuenga" [*el Cura de Montuenga*]) begins his text against Astarloa (Conde 1804, 5) in this way:

> So that it not be believed that the portentous discoveries of those who discuss Basque antiquities are applauded by all, and so that such a miserly judgment of the national erudition of the Spaniards not be formed, I thought to write these reflections on the subject.

Conde represents the generally held ideas of his time, and his knowledge of Latin, Greek, Hebrew, and Arabic, on display in their original alphabets in the handsome edition by the Royal Press, allows him to flaunt great superiority over Astarloa. Like Martínez Marina, he does not acknowledge any dignity or importance of Basque, which he repeatedly characterizes as "gibberish" (1804, 6, 21, 33, etc.). He mocks Astarloa's scraps of Hebrew, with his verbs *hifil* and *hofal* and *nifal*, and he accuses him of not knowing any more languages than what he had learned from a superficial reading of Hervás's *Catálogo*. For his part, Conde is unfamiliar with the ex-Jesuit's voluminous Italian publications and pays no attention to the far from scanty information contained in the vocabularies, Our Fathers, and comparative tables of the Italian work. At the same time, Conde researched the Basque tradition on the subject and was familiar with Poza, Larramendi, and even Echave, which must have been a more rare book. However, the tone of these academicians, whom I believe acted on the instigation of Godoy's government, was harsh, and so Conde repeats Mariana's comments about a "rude and barbarous language" (1804, 27).

For someone who, like Conde, was not interested in Basque or in problems of general linguistics, and who therefore could not appreciate the good knowledge of the language that Astarloa sometimes demonstrated in his analyses, criticizing the *Apología* was very easy. Conde analyzes the story of Tubal as an ancestor of Iberians and Basques and easily reaches the conclusion that

> we cannot prove that the Iberians were fellow tribesmen of Tubal, nor whether the tradition is true that this patriarch or his descendants came to Spain . . . (1804, 40)

After this, he makes fun of Astarloa's ingenuous etymologies, sometimes, it must be said, with good reason, as when Astarloa, after explaining that the *po* of *potzua* means 'round', goes on to explain another Spanish word by way of Basque:

> *Bola* ['ball'] is composed of *bo*, which is the same as *po*, and *la*, which means 'maker', meaning 'maker of roundnesses',

in response to which Conde exclaims that such an etymology is stupid (1804, 49).

Conde knew about the tradition of the plurality of languages in ancient Spain and rightly insists on the Celtism of the ending –*briga* (1804, 60).

Next, Conde responded to Erro's epigraphy. In this work (Conde 1806), the academician exhibits his knowledge of the bibliography about Spanish coins, beginning with Lastanosa and continuing with Velázquez and the occasional foreign author. He is aroused to act because

> there have appeared in public new and prodigious Oedipuses who claim to have solved the riddle of those recondite enigmas. (1806, 4)

He attacks a certain Zúñiga, curate of Escalonilla:

> He has been preceded in this erudite mania by Mr. Hervás in his catalog of all the languages, a work that discusses dialects of nations whose existence is not well established and distinguishes their affinities, origins, and kinship by way of the comparison of a few barbarous and poorly transcribed words of each . . . (1806, 6)

What the curate of Escalonilla did, like Erro, was read and interpret Iberian coins. The characters found on those of Obulco correspond, according to him, to the Basque (?) words *iri gali*, *belza gala*, which he interprets with the help of the plow and heads of grain engraved on the coin as "pleasant wheat field, the black wheat" (1806, 9).

Conde goes on to analyze Erro's *Alfabeto*, exclaiming in academic Latin:

> nec uidi umquam maiorem confidentiam cum maiore imperitia coniunctam. (1806, 11)

> [nor have I ever seen greater confidence joined with greater lack of expertise.]

Later on, he makes the same comment he had already made about Astarloa:

> The Basque writers have the rash presumption to prefer their gibberish to Hebrew. (1806, 45)

For the rest, he has no difficulty casting ridicule on the fantastical explanations of Iberian coins and monuments known at the time that Erro offers in his book. He reviews his explanations of inscriptions from Sagunto, Iglesuela, Numancia, and so on, and makes fun of the one he offers of the Cástulo vase:

> he infers that it was an offering or purse or measure for an expiatory fine by the magistrates, and he wanted the vase's Celtiberian inscription to allude to this. (1806, 57)

He ends his philippic with the words "sed satis iam nugarum" (but enough now of trifles, 1806, 70).

If we had any doubts about the hidden undercurrent of the debate we are narrating, Juan Antonio Llorente's *Noticias históricas de las tres provincias vascongadas* (Historical notices of the three Basque provinces, 1806–8) would remove all our hesitations. It is a formidable brief, with very abundant documentation, to combat the idea that

> Araba, Gipuzkoa, and Bizkaia were free, sovereign, and independent republics until of their own will (each one in its respective time) they surrendered their sovereignty, independence, and freedom to the kings of Castile, upon terms and conditions . . . (I, XVII)

This work by the famous canon scholaster of Toledo (1756–1823) does not interest us directly, since it is not concerned with language, but rather with historical, constitutional, and fiscal problems. The relevant point is that when a Basque, Francisco Aranguren, a judge in the criminal chamber (*alcalde del crimen*) of the Royal Chancellery of Valladolid, wrote in opposition to Llorente, the themes we know well were revived. The good Don Francisco thus attacked Llorente, and the canon defended himself against the accusation that

> being a member of the clergy, it is unworthy of my state to take sides in these matters, as if historical truth was incompatible with the clerical state. Fray Henrique Flórez and Fray Manuel Risco, who denied that the Bizkaians were Cantabri, were priests and members of religious orders. (III, XXIV)

In volume five, responding to Aranguren, Llorente recounts the history of the polemic, which he remembers as beginning with the Royal Academy of History's *Diccionario*. The root of the problem was that Aranguren maintained that Charles IV was not the king of Bizkaia, but only its lord, and the historian of the Inquisition devoted the entire volume to reviewing events since the Romans and Goths dominated in Bizkaia.

6

Tubal Vanishes: From Hervás to Humboldt

Lorenzo Hervás (y Panduro)

Lorenzo Hervás is highly representative of the Enlightenment in Spain, even if he acquired and developed his encyclopedic knowledge in Italy. At all events, the six volumes of his *Catálogo* (Catalog) appeared in Spain between 1800 and 1805. It was the eve of Trafalgar, and the disasters of the Napoleonic invasion would subsequently put an end to public education in Spain, where it is still not restored today.

An examination of Hervás's copious works demonstrates that he learned about a subject by writing about it. In his great Italian work *Idea dell'Universo* (Idea of the universe), he dedicated the last five volumes to linguistics, gathering astounding documentation. He discussed Basque to some extent in those volumes, and then in the six volumes of the *Catálogo* in Spanish he went into much greater detail, with ever greater knowledge. What was perhaps his last work, as we will see, was dedicated to Basque.

Hervás (who in his works published in Spain added his second surname, "y Panduro," in gratitude to his maternal uncle) was born in Horcajo de Santiago (Cuenca) in 1735 and died in Rome in 1809. He entered the Society of Jesus and studied in Madrid and Alcalá, after which he taught in the Society's schools in Cáceres, Murcia, and Madrid. He left Spain when the Jesuits were expelled in 1767 and settled in Italy, where he remained except for a few years during which he went back to Spain. From his definitive return to Rome in 1802 until his death, he was a librarian at the Quirinal. He was a man of incredible industry and productivity.

Hervás was not a linguist. When he arrived in exile in Italy with the rest of the expelled Spanish Jesuits, he sought his bearings in the new surroundings, and in the freedom of Italy, having taken up residence in Cesena (1774), he became a scholar of universal interests. His *Idea dell'Universo* (1778–87) is an unfinished encyclopedia in twenty-one volumes that covers the life of man, with a physical-philosophical anatomy of the human being; then describes the universe, in a "static voyage to the planetary world"; subsequently addresses the history of planet Earth; and finally takes up the subject of languages.

Hervás did not aspire to be an original thinker. We might say that he was struck with wonder at the progress of scholarship in his age and wanted to bring together its results as quickly as possible in an encyclopedic work. We know that he wanted to publish his gigantic compilation in Spanish, which was impossible for a series of reasons, first of all political ones, given the situation of the exiled Jesuits. Only later, between 1789 and 1805, was he able to publish a Spanish redaction of almost the entire work (except volumes eleven to sixteen of the Italian version, the *Storia della Terra* [History of the Earth]), and it was then that the Italian volume seventeen, the *Catalogo delle lingue conosciute* (Catalog of the known languages), was expanded into the six volumes of the Spanish *Catálogo*.

Hervás's interest in languages was only one aspect of his universal curiosity. In addition, the circumstance that he was able to work on this topic while taking advantage of the presence in the Papal States of so many Jesuits from various parts of the world developed his great capacity for conducting surveys. The result was really the largest and most reliable collection of data and information achieved up to that time. Hervás's biographer, F. Caballero (1868, 87), had good reason to state that the linguistic part of Hervás's work is "the most interesting part, the part that has spread the author's fame the most, the part that will survive . . . Here is found concentrated Hervás's genius, showing him to have been a man of large ideas, with the will and force to put them into practice, of an industrious character. . ."

Hervás was forgotten because he could have no successors. The disaster of the Napoleonic Wars in Spain prevented others from benefiting from his work. At the same time, Hervás disappeared from the scene at the moment that modern linguistics arose in Germany with Humboldt and Bopp, and Adelung and Vater's (1806–1817) encyclopedic work made use of all of Hervás's immense study, completing it with the fruits of the excellent libraries that already existed in Germany.

We will limit ourselves to the part of Hervás's work that refers to Basque and, in connection with this language, to the primordial languages of Hispania. Hervás's enormous merits in the ordering and classification of languages, especially those from exotic continents, where he applied his method of questionnaires addressed to his fellow Jesuits, do not shine in his study of Basque. He followed his conservative and traditional tendencies, surely accentuated during the years he spent in Spain (1798–1802), and maintained many ideas that were already outdated even then. The authority of his fellow Jesuit Larramendi remained unshakeable for him, and his relationship with Astarloa and other Basque scholars contributed to reinforcing this excessive weight of the past.

We find the echo of his earliest research on Basque in his Italian volumes. Larramendi's influence is visible from the first. After noting (1784, 155f) Basque's relationship with Georgian and the agreement between certain Caucasian names and certain Basque ones, as evidence of the travels of Tubal, the father of the two Iberias, he makes reference (1784, 200ff) to Basque as a language "eccellentissima e nobilissima pel suo artificio, civiltà e coltura" (most excellent and most noble for its artifice, civility, and culture), then sets out a curious theory about the ancient days of its Golden Age:

> la perfezione, o dicasi, il secolo di oro della lingua Bascuenze fu prima che nella Spagna entrassero i Romani, allorchè il Latino idioma era ancora nella sua infanzia o nella sua prima formazione. (1784, 205)
>
> [the perfection or, as it were, the Golden Age of Basque was before the Romans entered Spain, when Latin was still in its infancy or first formation.]

Also from Larramendi is the idea that Latin has many elements that originated in Basque (1784, 206ff). Basque's frequent Latinisms are for Hervás, as for Larramendi, ancient Basque elements that have been preserved in Latin. An example that he gives as certain (1784, 173 and 210) and that serves us as a good example of his method is the relationship of derivation he asserts between Basque *urre* and Latin *aurum* 'gold', as well as the Welsh Insular Celtic *aur* 'gold', and so forth.

Even more indebted to Larramendi is Hervás's (1785, 99) unfavorable opinion of the Spanish Academy's *Diccionario,* due to its failure to make use of Basque as the root of many etymologies. He believes that Oscan is Basque, a theory he had already supported in the preceding volume (1784, 212ff) with nonsensical interpretations of place names: Osco from *ots* 'noise'. He explains the name of the Sabellians by way of Basque *sabel* 'womb' and claims that the Hernici of Latium bear the name of Mount Hernio in Gipuzkoa.

With this Larramendian idea, Latin for Hervás does not deserve classification as a mother language and is simply (1784, 182f) a mixture of Etruscan, Greek, Celtic, and Cantabrian. Like Larramendi, he finds Basque elements in Etruscan as well (1785, 234).

In his first *Catalogo* (1784, 171), Hervás had to occupy himself with separating Basque from the Celtic languages, with which the Celtic enthusiasts of the day grouped it. Faithful to his survey methodology, he charged his fellow exile José de Beovide with composing a brief Basque grammar for him, and with that work and an Irish grammar that he had requested from his friend Charles O'Connor, he found that Basque had nothing to do with the Celtic languages. Beovide himself examined, at Hervás's request, Leibniz's great vocabulary and found only two words that might indicate a relationship between Basque and Celtic (1784, 170ff).

We will select among the observations found in Hervas's Italian work on Basque the one he makes (1784a, 14f) on the place-name element *–briga*, which he conflates with the Basque *uri* 'city', a confusion in which he follows Garibay, citing him. He goes on (1787a, 16) to use and abuse *ur* 'water', finding it in Spain and in Italy.

In the same volume, coming a little nearer to Astarloa (whose studies he could not have known at the time), he attributes the Latin *b* to Oscan, which, he says, acquired it in its turn from Cantabrian or Basque (1787a, 116). *D* also came to the Latins from the Cantabri of Campania (1787a, 117).

Hervás's mixture of original ideas and fortunate observations with unsustainable theories based on a tradition that had to be interpreted in forced ways is evident on this point of the influence of Cantabrian or Basque in Italy and Spain. Undoubtedly worthy of recognition as a precursor to Ascoli in the substratum theory, as Coseriu has pointed out, and prejudiced by the need to always start from the mother languages of the Tower of Babel, Hervás attributes the greater similarity between Spanish and Italian and the differentiation of French (1784, 188f and 206) simply to the fact that the two peninsulas both had a Cantabrian, that is, Basque substratum, while the substratum in France was Gaulish (cf. Coseriu 1978, 527).

When he discusses Basque in his collection of Our Fathers (1787b, 207ff), he distinguishes four dialects and offers the Lord's Prayer in three different forms, since he was able to go to the Barberini library, see the famous copy of which Nicolás Antonio spoke, and transcribe it in its oldest form, that of the Huguenot Leiçarraga (1787b, 41; cf. Olarra 1947, 310). He presents this documentation about Basque with an assertion of its interest for history, since

> gioverà ad illustrare quella della Georgia, dell'Italia e della Spagna.
>
> [it will help to shed light on that of Georgia, Italy, and Spain.]

In the very much expanded redaction of the *Catálogo* in Spanish, Basque became, starting with volume four, a central axis of the work, and not to the latter's advantage. In this volume, Hervás begins with the "Primordial European nations: Their mother languages and dialects of these."

The unfortunate idea of continuing to take the sons of Japheth into consideration burdens this part of Hervás's work, and Tubal makes an immediate appearance (1804a, 22). It might be said that in his Spanish edition, Hervás insisted on these old opinions even more than in the Italian redaction, perhaps due to the atmosphere in Spain, where the Enlightenment had stopped short in horror when faced with the French Revolution, and perhaps also due to Hervás's correspondence and relationships with Basque scholars.

Olarra (1947, 311) has rightly noted how Hervás's interest in Basque was reciprocated in the region. He cites this passage from a 1799 letter by José de Iturriaga to Juan de Leyza:

> Fr. Hervás is owed the eternal recognition of every Basque.

Moreover, the author himself informs us that in the same year, Antonio María de Letona wrote to Hervás recommending that he contact Basque scholars and giving him the names of Astarloa and Moguel.

José Antonio de Campos, another member of that flourishing
group, invited Hervás, who had returned to Spain, to move to the
Basque provinces, where the climate was so benign, but Hervás, who
was unable to work in the Spanish libraries, had written to him something that the good Campos transcribed with regret:

> You tell me that if Abadiño [Abadiano] was a country of useful books,
> you would come in search of them, but that country is not found in
> Spain. (Olarra 1947, 311)

In 1801, Manuel María de Acedo, in Bergara [Vergara], invited
him to take up a teaching position in the seminary and even to serve as
its rector, but the attitude of the Spanish government, which expelled
the Jesuits again, made these projects impossible. Only in 1805 did
the Royal Basque Society of Friends of the Country name Hervás a
member, with a patent issued in Bilbao (Olarra 1947, 312).

In the *Catálogo* in Spanish, Hervás develops a classification of
European languages as primordial and latecomers. In this classification, the primordial mother languages—those that did not arrive
subsequently, but rather with the population that dispersed after
the confusion of tongues at Babel—are Basque (that is, Iberian or
Cantabrian), Celtic, and Greek; on the other side, the Germans and
the Slavs, like the Turks, the Hungarians, the Albanians or ancient
Illyrians, and the Roma are the late-arriving nations (1802, 23). Curiously, here and in many other analogous passages, Hervás makes no
mention of Latin. He writes (1802, 6):

> In the most remote antiquity, the Cantabri, leaving Spain, conquered
> many regions in Italy and established themselves in them, as the tradi-
> tion of the Spaniards has constantly taught, denigrated by illustrious
> critics because they did not find evidence to authorize it.

Undoubtedly, his years of residence in Spain confirmed Hervás
in his ideas and made him much more decisive, we would almost say
imprudent, in presenting them. His difficulties in obtaining information were great, and this explains, for example, the fact that he was
unaware of a work such as Flórez's *Cantabria*. On the other hand,
he established contact, as we have already seen, with Basque scholars
who were working very actively at precisely this time, and not only as
a consequence of Humboldt's travels. The dedication of volume four

of Hervás's *Catálogo* (1804) is "To the three most noble provinces of Spanish Basques," dated April 30, 1803, when he was already back in Rome. In the introduction, he thanks Juan de Leyza for a gift of Basque books and affirms that, without doubt, the primordial language of all of Spain was Basque:

> its use was universal throughout Spain before any foreign nation entered.

The whole Tubalic mythology, the passages from Flavius Josephus and Jerome, and the Basque etymologies of geographical names (Axpe [Aspe] from Basque *aitz* 'peak', Ibero from *ur-bero*, Berones from the same root, and *España* 'Spain' from Basque *ezpain* 'lip' [1804a, 79ff]) parade through the extensive volume unsupported by new arguments.

In the following volume (1804b, 15), Hervás recounts that already from Barcelona he had written to Leyza to draw up a "triple Basque vocabulary," which

> began to be written by Juan [Antonio] Moguel under the direction of Josef de Campos.

This triple dictionary is described as a list of Basque root words, one of geographical terms, and finally one of Spanish surnames that are neither Latin, Arabic, nor foreign. For his part, Hervás contributed in this same fifth volume a collection of various common surnames in the Spanish dominions and an examination of topographical names in the Spanish Basque Country (1804b, 264ff).

With such materials, he aimed to demonstrate that many Italian and Spanish place names were Cantabrian: from Cecinna, Asta, Alba, and Urbino to the Roman Valentia and Pollentia . . . (1804b, 34ff); Arretium from *arichá* (*aritz* 'oak', *aritx* 'holm oak') (1804b, 57); and so on to the Betis River, which is the Basque *beti* 'full' (1806b, 150).

After a review of all the scholarship on the subject (1804b, 184ff), in which he corrects Archbishop Ximénez de Rada on the Cetubales, not the *coetus Tubalis* 'company of Tubal' accepted by many, but the *kedhah* of Tubal, with a Hebrew first component of similar meaning, and continuing on from El Tostado and Marineo Sículo to Moret and Larramendi, Hervás (1804b, 220) comes to cite Humboldt and his materials, still unpublished at the time, which he says he has used in Rome for the appendixes of this volume.

He expresses his thanks for the information he has received from his Basque friends and confesses that in his linguistic works in Italian, he still knew little of Basque and had to rely on his colleague Beovide. He admires (1804b, 221) the

> praiseworthy tenacity of the Basques in preserving the language they received from their progenitors.

The sixth and last volume (although not the final volume of the work, which remained incomplete) discusses the Celts. There is no doubt that in it, Hervás improved the general approach to the languages of this branch, then in the hands of Celtic enthusiasts in France and the British Isles. He makes a very good survey of what ancient historiography transmits about the settlement of the Gauls in France and about the conquests they made from there in Central Europe, Italy, and the southeast as far as Galicia, as well as in Great Britain. More fantastical is what he says (1805, 103ff) about the presence of the Celts on the Black Sea and their arrival from there in the western part of the Iberian Peninsula, in order to reach Ireland via the Atlantic; he knows that the Scots Gaels came from Ireland, and he attributes the same origin to the Picts themselves. Nevertheless, it must be recognized that he was able to a certain extent to distinguish between the P-Celts or Gauls and the Q-Celts or Gaels and Celtiberians.

In this volume, he corrects many of the ideas that he had followed in earlier works, precisely under the influence of Basque scholars. He now correctly classifies the place names with *–briga*, of which he gives an extensive list (1805, 303ff), alongside the other Celtic ones in *–durum, -dunum, -magus*, and so on. (1805, 311ff), and he closes the volume with "Indexes of words from three Celtic dialects with the corresponding ones in Greek, Latin, and Hindustani" (1805, 344-71), in which, leaving aside loans and errors, a noteworthy number of instances of Indo-European agreement are recognized for Breton, Irish, and on a smaller scale, Welsh.

If we consider the date of this volume, and that it was only in the fourth decade of the century (Thurneysen 1916, 282f) that the Indo-

European character of the Insular Celtic languages was indicated by J. C. Prichard (1831), A. Pictet (1837), and finally F. Bopp (1838), we must acknowledge Hervás's good information and sharp perception when he compares (1805, 59) Celtic to Sanskrit.

It seems that Hervás's last work, sent, according to an autograph note in the manuscript, to Tomás de Sorreguieta, a priest in Tolosa (Gipuzkoa), in 1808 (Olarra 1947, 308), was the *División primitiva del tiempo entre los vascongados, usada aún por ellos* (Primitive division of time among the Basques, still used by them). It remained unpublished among the papers left by the ex-Jesuit and now in the Archivi di Stato in Rome, where José de Olarra (1947) discovered and studied it.

In this brief work, Hervás took a position on a topic that, as we have already seen, also occupied Astarloa (1803, 309–402); it was precisely Sorreguieta who had initiated an extensive debate on the subject. Sorreguieta had sent Hervás two monographs of his on the Basque week, published in 1804 and 1805, and Astarloa, in his interaction with Hervás, had also arranged for him to receive his *Apología*.

Hervás, who on the one hand acknowledges that the week "was the first period of time, which began with the creation of the world" (in Olarra 1947, 315), thought on the other hand that, given Basque's origin at Babel, this language might preserve an authentic form. He recognizes (ibid., 314) that, unlike his Basque interlocutors, he is "without the particular helps that they have in Basque, their native language." Instead, he is in a position to discuss with great erudition the names of the days of the week in the most diverse languages: Hungarian, Turkish, the Slavic languages, Tagalog, and so on. We must not forget that in volume nineteen (1786) he had discussed the *Divisione del tempo fra le nazioni orientali* (Division of time among the eastern nations).

In the etymological realm, he debates the Basque words with Astarloa, and he generally corrects this author's overly personal ideas. Hervás's experience with many languages leads him to interpret, generally with accuracy, not only the names of the days of the week, but also those of the months and seasons of the year. Curiously, he believed that the use in Basque of numerical forms that appear very

early, suggesting a week of three days, not of seven, *astelen*[1] 'Mon-
day', *asteazken* 'Wednesday', was comparable to the use of numerals
in Slavic (in Olarra 1947, 333), where it is the Church's influence that
has substituted them for the ancient pagan names.

In the history of our topic, as in that of linguistics in general,
Hervás stands at the moment at which modern scholarship was born.
As Lázaro Carreter (1949, 71) justly notes, "his religious faith did not
offer him secular solutions." With regard to language, consequently,
he accepts, according to a quotation Lázaro gives us (1949, 157), that

> the first one spoken by men was infused, and that the diversity of lan-
> guages in words and syntax cannot be the effect of any other cause than
> the admirable confusion of languages mentioned by Moses.

Alongside this traditionalism, which still weighs more or less
explicitly on his acceptance of the Tubalic tradition of the arrival
of Basque, Hervás, who collected and compared many vocabularies
from the most diverse languages, discovered that the key to their community of origin was not in their words but in their structure, in what
he called "grammatical artifice." The comparison of vocabulary and
especially of structure is very well formulated in the introductory part
of the Spanish edition of the catalog:

> The method and the means that I have had in view in order to for-
> mulate the distinction, gradation, and classification of the nations . . .
> consist chiefly in the observation of the words of their respective lan-
> guages, and chiefly their grammatical artifice. This artifice has been, in
> my observation, the chief means on which I have relied in discerning
> the affinity or difference of the known languages and reducing them to
> determinate classes. The particular artifice with which the words are
> ordered in each language does not depend on human invention, and still
> less on caprice: it is characteristic of each language, of which it forms
> the foundation . . .

Exaggerating, Hervás affirms that nations become civilized, that
is, accept cultural influences, and change,

---

1. In Unified Basque *astelehen*. —Ed. note

but they never change the foundation of the grammatical artifice of their respective languages. (1800, 23)

In this permanence of language, the mystic idea of the confusion of tongues at Babel continued to weigh heavily.

Juan Francisco de Masdeu

In this erudite and industrious Jesuit (1744–1817), a somewhat younger colleague of Hervás in exile, we observe very similar qualities. Both were extremely prolific writers, whose knowledge was greater than their critical sense; both received a magnificent stimulus from Italy's climate of freedom and culture; and both were patriots who wanted to communicate with Spaniards, publishing their books in Spain, the results of their studies. The advantage was certainly on Hervás's side, due to his having dedicated himself to linguistics, which was at the time perhaps a more promising field than the ancient and medieval history that Juan Francisco de Masdeu preferred. Hervás was able to teach something to a linguist as important and well-situated as Wilhelm von Humboldt, while Masdeu's extensive historical research could not be continued in nineteenth-century Spain, and the progress of studies in ancient history, epigraphy, and so on during that century left the learned Catalan far behind.

We will limit ourselves to the part of his lengthy historical work that interests us, that is, the part that deals with Basque and its relationship to the Iberian Peninsula's primordial languages.

The reader of this book will understand by now that Masdeu had to begin his study of origins by vanquishing the fabrications of the Dominican Giovanni Nanni, famous under the name of Annius of Viterbo (1784, 38ff). This forger dedicated his commented Berossus to the Catholic Monarchs, which did not cease to win him credit among us. Annius was the one who brought Tubal to Tarragona, where he installed him as king and the head of a line of succession that culminated in the Gargoris mentioned by Justin. Masdeu still shielded himself (1784, 47) behind Luis Vives's conclusive critique of this fabricator.

Unfortunately, Masdeu was not such a good critic of the other tradition, the one based on Genesis and its commentators, and he spoke of Tubal as a descendant of Japheth (1784, 62ff). He falls for the traditional Setubalia, for which he derives from Larramendi the suggestion to understand in the first syllable the Basque *sein* 'child': the children of Tubal (1784, 68). He also acknowledges, because it was defended by a Christian writer, Julius Africanus, the legend of Tarshish (1784, 68). It is thus still the case for him that

> the Spaniards originate from the trunks of Tubal and Tarshish; but I do not therefore assert, as various modern authors think, that these patriarchs or some of them penetrated into Spain. (1784, 71)

Once it is granted that the Spanish population had a double origin,

> the languages of the ancient Spaniards necessarily had to be two; let us call them Tarshishian and Tubalite. The language of the Tarshishians was probably Iberian, and that of the Tubalites Celtic.

Masdeu's ideas are not very clear. For him, Iberian mixed with Phoenician and perhaps "was entirely lost" (1784, 82). Celtic, on the other hand, had a long life ahead of it, in more or less mixed form, since it is

> the same that subsists today with the name of Basque . . . I would not have the boldness to give Spain this glory (if such it may be called) of having preserved one of the mother languages, if I did not see the situation of Cantabrian Vasconia . . . (1784, 82)

that is, its geographical isolation and the robustness of the Cantabri, "these formidable northern Spaniards" (1784, 83). In this section, he follows Moret and Larramendi with their linguistic arguments, including with regard to place names.

Masdeu studied widely in epigraphy and numismatics and was familiar with the scripts of Hispania. He distinguishes, accurately enough, between the "Celtiberian," that is, what we would call today the northeastern, and the "Turdetan," or southern, and he says that they derive from the Greek and Phoenician scripts respectively (1784, 100ff; cf. 1785, 159–63). Terreros y Pando, a fellow Jesuit, had already called the Iberian script Basque (Masdeu 1784, 132). Velázquez and Pérez Bayer are Masdeu's sources in this part.

Masdeu was guided by a somewhat immoderate patriotism, which led him to carefully separate the offspring of Tubal and Tarshish from those of Gomer, the ancestor of the French and English (1784, 62f), and to suppose that the Iberians were great conquerors who dominated Italy and were "perhaps founders of Rome" (1784, 127), spread to Sicily under the name of Sycanians (1784, 132ff), and reached the eastern Iberia, on the shores of the Black Sea (1784, 139).

Masdeu (1784, 277–93) discusses Basque under the title of "Nature, construction, and origin of the most ancient Celtiberian language," after having affirmed (1784, 151ff) that Celtic is not French but Spanish and is preserved precisely in Basque. He even affirms that French Basque is much more mixed than the Spanish variety (1784, 278).

For the rest, Moret and Larramendi are Masdeu's chief sources in this section. With Larramendi, he accepts the idea that the Greeks themselves took words from Cantabrian (1784, 279). Contradicting himself as Hervás did, he now vigorously opposes those who included Basque among the Celtic languages and even made it an inheritor of Gaulish (1784, 279f). Of course, we must suppose that Masdeu was in direct communication with Hervás, since in precisely the same year that this volume came out in Madrid in translation, Hervás's first volume on languages appeared in Cesena.

After this, Masdeu debated the thesis of Italian scholars that the Basques were Etruscans who spoke Latin (1784, 281) and reviewed the list of words from ancient Hispania compiled by Morales, finding, with a great deal of exaggeration, that

> they are pure Vascon, and all are used with very little variation. (1784, 283)

Finally, he drew on Moret and on information given him by Hervás to demonstrate the language's ancient establishment in Spain.

The historian Masdeu could not fail to be aware of Flórez's book on ancient Cantabria, and so, when he discussed Augustus's war later on, he affirmed, incidentally in agreement with Moret, that

> neither Bizkaians nor Navarrese had any part in the Cantabrian War. (1807, 16)

Wilhelm von Humboldt

Wilhelm von Humboldt (1767–1835), a founder of the University of
Berlin, together with his brother Alexander, and undoubtedly one of
the creators of modern linguistics, received Spanish influence via two
routes. One was his Basque friends, Moguel and Astarloa, whom he
got to know and was in contact with during his trip to Spain (1799–
1801). The second, about which much still remains to be said, was by
way of Lorenzo Hervás (see Batllori 1951).

Humboldt's Basque studies were primarily crystallized in two
published works, his *Berichtigungen* (Corrections) in Adelung-Vater's
work on world languages (1817) and his famous monograph on
Basque and place names, the *Prüfung* (Examination, 1821).

Berichtigungen begins with the confession that he has been interested in Basque for over ten years (allowing us to suppose that the
manuscript was in the editor's hands for several years before publication), and that this interest led him (during his travels) to seek
oral information, since the published works were not sufficient for
the knowledge of this language and its problems. Vater's invitation
to contribute an appendix to this great work found him at a moment
in which he did not know what to do with his gathered materials and
in which his occupations did not allow him to put them in order and
make use of them. Finally, there came a pause that enabled him to
work, and at that point he was faced with the problem of Basque
in relation to the primordial population of Spain and even of other
countries, such as Italy.

On this point, it is curious to find that Humboldt in this work is
completely under the influence of Larramendi's tradition (which had
a similar excessive sway over Hervás). We still find him at this stage
making the mistake of believing that the Italian place name Astura
is an example of "ganz Vaskischen Namen" (entirely Basque names,
1817, 278), just as in another passage he derives the Italian Urbino
from the name of a Cantabrian called Uchin or Urtino in the fantastical "Song of Lelo" (1817, 352f).

As we will see, the method of and the information available to the
great Prussian scholar improved greatly between the composition of
Berichtigungen and *Prüfung*. In this first study, however, we find Humboldt not only accepting the traditional etymology of *vasco* 'Basque'

from *baso-ko* but also analyzing the Spanish *vascuence* 'Basque' (a clear derivative of Latin *Vasconice*) into *vasco* plus *antza* 'resemblance' (1817, 279). After other such etymologies, nonsensical but in conformity with the Basque tradition, Humboldt reduces the Basque dialects to three (1817, 280–82), forgetting those that Larramendi had previously presented in a more complete form.

Subsequently, he reviews Adelung's Basque vocabulary with greater knowledge. In truth, every study of Basque lexicography before Azkue was faced with uncertain words and phantasms on all sides. For this reason, Humboldt believes himself justifiably required to offer a more reliable vocabulary over eighteen pages of his *Berichtigungen*. His conversations with Moguel and Astarloa were no doubt the basis for the confidence with which he was able to present it.

His etymologies, taking into consideration the state of that discipline, are not always acceptable. For example, he is correct to reject Hervás's explanation of *amaika* 'eleven' by way of a supposed *ca* 'one', but his own proposal, to relate *–ika* to the verb *igan* 'to go up', supposing that it means "am Abhange liegend, steil" (lying on a slope, steep), is impossible (1817, 288; cf. for the etymology Tovar 1958, 832).

In presenting his dictionary, Humboldt is very critical of the previous attempts in the great collections of Hervás, Pallas, and Mirievo. In order to compare words, he rightly demands an analysis of their derivation and the elements of which they are composed (1817, 306). His small dictionary can thus be put forward as a model in contrast to the rash and unreliable comparisons made by lexicographers working with vast quantities of poorly analyzed material, whether in Hervás's case or in that of Catherine II's lexicographers (1817, 305f).

Less convincing is Humboldt's attempted analysis of certain vowels with affricates and other consonants, although the importance of the expressive element and "natural words" in Basque leads him at times, alongside misguided and dangerous efforts, to successes like that of relating *etsi* 'to close', *estu* 'tight, compact', and *ertsi* 'to close' (1817, 310). At the same time, the importance of palatalization and liquids in the formation of diminutives escapes him, as he says that these are phonetic details that the linguist can leave out of consideration (1817, 311).

He goes on to begin an analysis of the elements of Basque words, with good observations on derivation, and he naturally criticizes Astarloa's theory on the special meaning of each letter, giving an example: "so soll *atza*: der Finger, von *a*, dem Zeichen der Stärke, und *tz* dem des Überflusses, eigentlich *Ueberfluss von Stärke* heissen" (so *atza* 'finger', from *a*, the letter indicating 'strength', and *tz*, the one indicating 'excess', is supposed to actually mean 'excess of strength', 1817, 313).

In his examination of declination, he completes Adelung and points out, as someone more familiar with the language, the importance of the ergative case, so characteristic of Euskara.

Analyzing the Basque conjugation, he finds both Larramendi and Harriet insufficient, and he says that Astarloa is "der erste und einzige, der die systematische Anordnung der Vaskischen Conjugation entdeckt und aus einander gesetzt hat" (the first and only one who has discovered and expounded the systematic arrangement of the Basque conjugation, 1817, 319). We see that Humboldt was able to study Astarloa's manuscripts, unfinished and never to be finished, since in Astarloa's printed works (especially in what we read in his posthumous publication) we find that, as Humboldt says,

> Indess gehn diese Mängel meisten Theils nur die Flexions-Formen selbst, nicht das Gesetz ihrer Bildung an. (1817, 320)

> [For all that, these defects most often affect only the inflected forms themselves, not the law of their formation.]

Astarloa's manuscripts (chiefly the *Discursos filosóficos*) are the source for the contrast between the active voice and a passive one, as well as for the table of inflectional morphemes (1817, 328). In what Astarloa called "active recipient conjugations," Humboldt recognizes a dative. In his indications about Basque literature, he praises Moguel and Astarloa and expresses reservations about studies like those of Erro, who applied Basque to Iberian coins. He informs us that Astarloa has a work composed in two manuscript volumes, from which he extracted the *Apología*. This work was titled *Plan de lenguas o Gramática Bascongada en el dialecto Vizcaino* (Plan of languages, or Basque grammar in the Bizkaian dialect). It is not included, at least under this title, among the manuscripts that Mateo de Erro, the heir of the author of the *Alfabeto de la lengua primitiva,* placed in the hands of the Bizkaian provincial government in 1856–58 (prologue to Astarloa 1883, VI).

Humboldt concludes his labor of "correction" with an interesting Basque anthology, including two texts by Moguel and the apocryphal "Song of Lelo," which was given to Humboldt during his travels in Bizkaia (1817, 351ff; cf. for the "Song of Lelo" the youthful work of Caro Baroja 1941, 161–86).

Humboldt's other work in the field of Basque studies, the famous *Prüfung* (1821), can be considered to "close a long period of search," in the words of A. Steiger, the author of the prologue of the most recent Spanish edition (1959, 6f). More debatable is what Steiger adds, that

> it brings together the conclusions and results of its predecessors and debates them with scientific rigor, including them within a framework of concrete and organic concepts.

As we will see, Humboldt still depends too much on his predecessors, and although he is naturally part of the cultural Golden Age of the Germany of his time, he does not manage to free himself from such a quantity of ingenuous theories as we find in those who transmitted to him his curiosity about the problem, as well as all the materials he had available for studying it: Larramendi, Astarloa, and Hervás. We place the three names together here, because even if Humboldt never denied what he owed to his guides in Basque studies, he had very little generosity toward Lorenzo Hervás.

From the supreme cultural observation point that was the Germany of his time, apart from his travels and those of his brother Alexander, Wilhelm von Humboldt realized the importance of the remnant languages of the extreme West, Basque on the one hand and the Insular Celtic languages on the other, for discovering Europe's primordial inhabitants.

After exaggerating to a certain extent the importance of what he had succeeded in learning about Welsh and Irish, and in ignorance of the long tradition we are examining, Humboldt defends the importance and originality of his efforts with this affirmation:

Von der Vaskischen Sprache dagegen war, bis auf die neuesten Schriften
Spanischer Gelehrten über dieselbe, noch wenig Gebrauch für diese
Zwecke gemacht, und auch jene Schriften haben nicht eigentlich die
gegenwärtige Untersuchung zum Gegenstande, sondern gehen nur
gelegentlich auf dieselbe ein. (1821, iii)

[Prior to the most recent writings of Spanish scholars on the Basque language, on the other hand, very little use had been made of this language
for these purposes, and even these writings are not really concerned
with the current topic of research, but only touch on it occasionally.]

From the exalted vantage point of the full nineteenth century, he
forgets poor Hervás, who, like Astarloa, disappeared from the scene
on the eve of the Napoleonic catastrophe that overwhelmed Spain,
with no pretense at politics or civilized war, and he reduces Basque
studies to the work of local scholars, whose capacity for systematic
scholarship he denies. However, even the dangerous temptation of
using Basque for Italy as well (with nonsense like the etymologies of
Astura and Urbino mentioned above) seduced Humboldt in his prologue, as it had Larramendi and especially Hervás. Permit us to quote
the following passage:

erst, wenn über diese ältesten Völkerstämme mehr Licht verbreitet ist,
wird auch eine sichere Grundlage für die Untersuchungen über die
Urbewohner Italiens gewonnen. Dass diese bisher so wenig gelangen,
lag wohl vorzüglich daran, dass man sie auf dem umgekehrten Wege
anfing. Anstatt zu ergründen, welche Urvölker in den Ländern gesessen
hatten, mit welchen Italien vormals gleiche Bewohner gehabt haben
kann, und welche Spuren ihres Daseyns in Ortnamen und Sprachen
übriggeblieben sind, um auf diese Weise zur Kenntniss des Grundstoffs
zu gelangen, auf den man bei Zergliederung der Italischen Denkmale
stossen konnte, wandte man bloss das Griechische und Lateinische
zur Erklärung derselben an, ohne zu bedenken, dass die Hellenischen
Einwanderungen gewiss nicht die frühesten waren, und dass die
Römische Sprache *erst selbst einer Zerlegung in ihre Elemente bedarf.*
(1821, iii–iv)

[only when more light has been shed on these most ancient tribes will
a sure foundation have been obtained for research on Italy's earliest
inhabitants. That so little has been achieved in this regard up to now is
likely due above all to the fact that the problem has been taken up from
the opposite direction. Instead of establishing which early peoples settled in the lands that might once have had the same inhabitants as Italy,

and what traces of their existence have survived in place names and languages, in order to acquire by this route a knowledge of the original base that one might uncover in analyzing Italic monuments, Greek and Latin have simply been used to explain them, without considering that the Hellenic migrations were certainly not the first and that the Roman language itself first needed to be broken down into its elements.]

The reader familiar with Hervás thinks immediately of that non-sensical idea that Latin is not properly a mother language, but rather a mixture of Greek, Celtic, Etruscan, and . . . Cantabrian components. It is for this reason that we have taken the liberty of emphasizing the final words of the passage quoted.

In this work, Humboldt is going to use the studies of Larramendi, Astarloa, Hervás, and Erro, as he confesses (1821, 1), and is going to undertake "[e]ine neue unparteiische Beleuchtung" (a new impartial examination, 1821, 2), that is, one made from his advantageous perspective in Berlin, with more abundant documentation and new critical ideas. Curiously, Humboldt does not have all the necessary materials, a fact explicable by the unfortunate situation in Spain: he is unfamiliar with the six-volume Spanish edition of Hervás's *Catálogo*, in which Hervás devotes so much attention to this problem, and uses only the *Catalogo* volume of the Italian work, according to what we see in this reference.

The chief novelty of Humboldt's work is without doubt methodological, the attempt to fix the limits of this dangerous field of place names. As Humboldt justly observes, Hispania is the region with the greatest surviving quantity of ancient documentation, outside of Greece and Italy (1821, 3), and in order to establish the reliability of the method, he once again rejects Astarloa's theory that Basque

> hat ... jedem Buchstaben und jeder Silbe eine eigne Bedeutung beigelegt, welche ihnen auch in der Zusammensetzung bleibt. (1821, 7)
>
> [has ascribed a meaning of its own to each letter and each syllable, which it also retains in composition.]

Humboldt compares this method of Astarloa's to the very similar one of the founders of Welsh grammar and lexicography, John Davies and William Owen, in order to correctly point out

wie schwankend, willkührlich und selbst abentheuerlich ein solches
Verfahren ist, wenn es sich nicht auf Wahrnehmung wirklicher Tonver-
wandschaft nach einem festen Ableitungssystem gründet. (1821, 9)

[how variable, arbitrary, and even quixotic such a procedure is when it
is not based on the recognition of real kinship of sounds in accordance
with a fixed system of derivation.]

We already have here modern historical linguistics, which Humboldt's precursors in these studies had not yet attained.

In his opening chapters, Humboldt establishes on well-thought-
out principles how to analyze words by distinguishing roots and
derivational elements. The progress of Sanskrit and Indo-European
linguistics helps Humboldt to establish his method, as we see in his
citations of Wilkins and Bopp. Consequently (1821, 14–15), he is able
to reject proposals by Astarloa and Erro as picturesque on occasion as
Cosetania 'land of hunger' (Basque *gose* 'hunger') and Sagunto 'place
of mice' (Basque *sagu* 'mouse').

Having dismissed these fantastical methods, with the help of
phonetic correspondences (still called "real kinship of sounds") and
the analysis of words in accordance with their derivation or composition, Humboldt begins his review of the interpretation of Iberian
names by way of Basque.

To begin with, he is free of the prejudice of the supposed Basque
unity of the Iberian Peninsula. The name Rhetogenes, for example,
with its initial *r*, cannot be Basque but rather must be Celtiberian
(1821, 21), given that

die Bildung der alt-iberischen Ortnamen im Ganzen dem Lautsystem
des Vaskischen folgt. (1821, 22)

[the formation of ancient Iberian place names generally follows the
Basque phonetic system.]

In effect, on this point of phonetic similarity, without entering
into the question of whether it proceeds from a common origin or a
"phonetic alliance" between neighbors, a principle of this kind is still
maintained today.

It is in these methodological principles that the novelty of Humboldt's book resides. His materials recall, even in their arrangement,

the first index of place names that Andrés de Poza had compiled two-and-a-half centuries earlier: we find, for example, Asta with the traditional explanation (1821, 23–24), *iria* in relation with Ulia, and so on (1821, 24–30), and the comparisons involving *ura* 'water' (1821, 30–33) and *iturri* 'fountain', albeit mixing in forms such as Turiaso that we would consider Indo-European (1821, 34–36). However, the demand for rigorous phonetic correspondence leads him to see clearly the Celtic element –*briga*, finally leaving behind the Basque scholars' conflation of this element with *uri, ili*. Naturally, he finds Celtic names in Gaul and Iberia (1821, 94–106).

It is curious how Larramendi's old idea of a Basque presence in Italy persists in Humboldt. Even Campania reminds him of the Basque adverb *campoan* 'outside', which he had read in Larramendi's grammar (1821, 116), and which he does not seem to recognize as pure Latin or Romance. A great deal of rigor in speculations about Iberians, Pelasgians, and other peoples of more or less shadowy existence cannot be demanded in his day. Very discreetly, he opposes any relationship between Basque and New World languages (1821, 173–77).

The chief conclusions of Humboldt's monograph (1821, 177-79) were accepted almost without debate, especially in Germany. Both Hübner and Schuchardt based their studies on this foundation, and in our time, this theory, which Caro Baroja called "Basque-Iberianism," persisted without becoming outdated until after 1940: the identification of Basque with Iberian, the presence of Basque throughout the Iberian Peninsula, as seen in place names, and the presence of Iberians, mixed with Celts, in Lusitania and the northern regions were very generally accepted theses. The importance of the Celts in the Peninsula, on the other hand, was less generally recognized. On other points, Humboldt was not so accepted: although it was generally believed that the Basque (or Iberian) influence in France was limited to the south, the presence of Ibero-Basques on the large islands of the Mediterranean and even the possible Eastern origin of all the Iberians were not proposals taken up by others. The possibility of Basque names in Italy, which Humboldt was not ready to give up, was also not accepted, and neither was the thesis of a possible relationship of origin between Iberians and Celts.

With regard to Erro, Humboldt was highly skeptical, and rightly so, of his readings of the coins that we call Iberian (1821, 179–82).

As a whole, however, Humboldt was dependent on the tradition of Basque scholars on these issues, as Bahner has previously indicated (1956, 64).

7

A Still Pre-scientific Age

The only thing that is known here is that nothing is known.

— A. Cánovas del Castillo, prologue to Rodríguez-Ferrer, 1873

Antonio Cánovas del Castillo, Miguel Rodríguez-Ferrer, and Aureliano Fernández-Guerra

In 1873, the magistrate Miguel Rodríguez-Ferrer published an informative book on the Basque Country, a topic of current interest at the time due to the renewed outbreak of the Carlist Wars. This explains why the prologue to the book was written by Antonio Cánovas del Castillo, who curiously, for political reasons, defends the region's autonomous institutions and traditions against the laicizing republic, even though a few years later, as prime minister, he would attack those same institutions and traditions by suppressing the region's traditional laws and privileges (the *fueros*).

Cánovas's introduction (Rodríguez-Ferrer 1873, XI-LIX) is very interesting because it reflects the ideas about the Basque regions that were current elsewhere in Spain. As in the past, Cánovas begins by equating Bizkaian with Basque. He then declares himself in favor of the traditional institutions:

> Far from desiring that similar institutions disappear from there, I would want to spread them, if it were possible, to the rest of Spain. (in Rodríguez-Ferrer 1873, XII)

In the Basque language he sees, with a lens justified at the time, the reason for the traditional and religious spirit that had led a very considerable number of Basques into the Carlist camp:

> Shut up in his solitary language, unknown to any other nation, even more and better than in inexpugnable mountains, the Basque (_vasco_ or _vascongado_ or _vascuence_, whatever name is preferred) has defied until now the impetuous current of new ideas. (ibid., XIV)

Moreover, Cánovas goes on to display knowledge that was uncommon among non-Basques: not only does he know that Garibay makes Basque one of the seventy-two languages of the dispersion from Babel, but he also provides a very good analysis of the circumspection with which Ximénez de Rada had discussed this point.

Rodríguez-Ferrer, in love with the Basque Country, reveals himself to be well informed not about the language but about the debates surrounding it. He can serve as an introduction to a French or Basque-French literature that is generally of little value and that we cannot address here. He still mentions the two Iberias, identifying the eastern one not with the Georgians but with the Circassians (1873, 89), and he could be considered a precursor of the Soviet linguist N. Marr in characterizing the Basque-Caucasian relationship as Japhetic.

His information is better on Basque written literature and on the studies of Prince Bonaparte.

Greater pretensions and greater confusion are to be observed in two works by the academician A. Fernández-Guerra (1816–94), who once again took an interest in the topic of the Cantabri and the Basques.

We also find in his works the idea that the "Japhetic tribes" were found throughout the northern part of the Iberian Peninsula, from Finisterre to Bidasoa (1872, 13).

> They called themselves Iberians, that is, 'shore people', in opposition to the Celts, or in other words, 'mountain people'. (ibid.)

It is hard to believe that after Flórez, a passage such as the following could be written:

> The Cantabri, meaning the most daring of the Dragani Celts, possessed the coast that runs from Villaviciosa to Laredo and the inland area bordered by the mountain fastnesses of Covadonga and Liébana, the sources of the Carrión, Buenavista on the banks of the Valdavia, the confluence of the Fresno or Amaya River with the Pisuerga, and from the ancient Moreca (today Castro-Morca, east of and on the border

with Villadiego) to the Agüera River, west of Castro-Urdiales. (1872, 17)

Basque provides Fernández-Guerra with etymologies such as the following of Santoña:

> from *Sand'onia*, the equivalent in Euskara of 'Sanda's foot', quite properly, since Santonia Peak (as it was still called in 1639) serves as a stepping-stone and base for the Ason River, which the Iberians called Sanda or Sanga, according to Pliny's testimony. (1872, 21)

He goes on to indicate that the Basques and the Cantabri were always enemies, since while the former spoke Euskara, a language that "is similar to none of those of Europe, since it is still living today after thirty-seven centuries," the latter spoke Cantabrian, from which Spanish derives (1872, 24).

In his other monograph of 1878, Fernández-Guerra returned to these topics. In this work, he is not so convinced of the distinction between Basques and Cantabri, and he says that

> Asian Iberians, Japhetic tribes, abandoning in the primordial age the banks of the Ibero, the Arrago, and the Araxes (rivers that are today named Kur, Iora, and Araks, between Mount Ararat and the Caucasus), passed along the southern shores of the Black Sea, crossed the Bosporus in Thrace, followed the right bank of the Danube and the Drava, entered the Eastern Alps, Liguria, the district of the Rhône, and the Pyrenees, and occupied Spain. (1878, 10)

Fernández-Guerra is still working with the idea of comparing Mount Ararat to Mount Aralar, as we have seen repeatedly in this history. Subsequently, he takes up the Cantabri, with references to the classical sources.

In this period, Fernández-Guerra was influenced by Fita, to whose speech upon entering the Royal Academy of History he would reply the following year, and he quotes paragraphs from the Jesuit's letters with interpretations of the Academy's own tessera (*MLI*, XXXIX), which becomes a dedication *Nibak quer Zakkara* 'to the genius of the city (?) of Záncara' and with new references to the history of the cantabricum, the Constantinian labarum, and the famous Basque *lau buru* (in Fernández-Guerra 1878, 35 and 37f).

Francisco M. Tubino

This Cádiz autodidact (1833–88) attempted a prehistory of the Iberian Peninsula, with attention to archeological remains, in accordance with his general interest in art history, and also including anthropological results on human races and cranial measurements. His 1876 synthesis, which we have been able to study, has some interest for our central topic.

He begins by gathering information on the megaliths found in Andalusia, Extremadura (very little was known about these at the time), and Portugal. He recounts, for example, the first work done on the Menga Cave in Antequera, by an architect, R. Mitjana, between 1842 and 1847, and allows us to measure the pan-Celtism dominant among those interested in this field at the time when he interprets the name of Menga as Mengal, said to be none other than Breton *Men lac'h*, translatable as 'sacred stones', according to him. Tubino is familiar with the studies of Vilanova, Góngora, and other pioneers of Spanish prehistory. He then recounts the immature theories of the day on the megalithic monuments and lays out some possible ethnic filiations for the group or groups that spread them.

He is aware of what we call the "Sea Peoples," but he attributes the spread of megaliths from North Africa to Spain fundamentally to Egyptian influences, which, combined to a greater or lesser extent with Phoenician trade, provide the explanation. Recognizing that the Aryan or Indo-European expansion in Southern Europe (and Central Europe, he says [143]), should be dated between 1200 and 1300 BC, he asks about the races that existed in ancient Western Europe, including the British Isles.

As far as the Iberian Peninsula is concerned, Francisco Tubino denies Iberian unity (1876, 150). He opposes the thesis of Humboldt and others who insisted on translating Iberian inscriptions using Basque; against them, he draws on the numismatist A. Delgado in order to deny the "dreamed-of unity of Iberianism" (1876, 152f).

In an examination of the place-name arguments already familiar to the reader of this book, he opposes Humboldt's explanations and points out, entirely correctly, that the element *–ippo*, frequent in the southwestern Iberian Peninsula, is not Basque at all (1876, 154). He accepts W. J. van Eys's denial that names of the Asta type can be explained using the Basque *aitz* 'rock' (1876, 156), and after acknowledging that the widespread place-name form *Ili-*, *Iri-* may have a connection to Basque *iri*, he very justly ridicules the explanation by way of Basque of the name of Urbino (1876, 157). He concludes, reasonably enough:

> since what has been said is sufficient to trim the most considerable part of the lists of our Basques scattered throughout the Peninsula, we do not believe ourselves obligated to exhaust the subject. (1876, 157)

He accepts from Delgado and Zobel de Zangroniz the variety of alphabets used in Spain and notes, with a prudence not excessive for the time, that in general the Iberian inscriptions on coins and elsewhere "do not go back further than the third century at most" (1876, 159).

He denies the existence of any certain witness to the Basque language before the tenth century, and in his view, once Humboldt's Basque-Iberianism (the Basque antecedents of which the reader is already familiar with) has been eliminated, the determination of Iberian ethnicity depends on archaeological and craniological arguments. He is aware of the presence in Egyptian sources of the *lebu* or *rebu*, that is, the Libyans, and connects them to the Berbers of western Africa (1876, 171ff) and even, with the *Shardana* of the Egyptian inscriptions in mind, with the Sardones (that is, Sordones) of Roussillon (1876, 178), thereby arriving at the conclusion that

> the Berbers form the nucleus of the great population that inhabited the caverns of Baetica and Portugal during what we have called the meso-lithic period, the same group that built the megalithic monuments. (1876, 181)

With regard to the Berber linguistic problem, he bases himself on the proposals of a broad Hamitic-Semitic unity advanced by F. Müller, and among numerous hypothetical constructions, he proposes a hypothesis about Basque as an offshoot of a common Hamitic-Semitic root.

> Bring together all these results, and our conjecture will not appear forced: the primordial Euskara, which we do not know, could have very well represented one of the first Hamitic derivations, one of those first

shadowy languages to split off from the lost common dialect. (1876, 183)

Fidel Fita y Colomer

The Jesuit Fidel Fita (1835–1917), who at the end of his life served as director of the Royal Academy of History in Madrid, marked his entrance into that academy with a discourse of formidable erudition. The young Unamuno, who prepared his doctoral dissertation on the topic shortly afterward, called Fita in his dissertation, perhaps with some irony, "learned and reverend Father" (1884, 109).

Fita, who was Catalan, chose as the topic of his entrance speech a work by Juan Margarit, bishop of Girona [Gerona] and a supporter of the Catholic Monarchs. This work, a commentary on Chronicles dedicated to Ferdinand and Isabella and preserved in manuscript in the National Library in Madrid, discussed the origin of the inhabitants of Hispania, as El Tostado and many other Biblical commentators did. The bishop of Girona follows in the footsteps of his medieval predecessors, mentioning the Caucasian Iberia (Fita 1879, 46) and commenting on the topic of the Iobeli or Tobeli of Flavius Josephus (1879, 49).

For his part, Fita knew something of the Celtic languages and was familiar with the Celtiberians and the Gauls (1879, 48f); in addition, he was undoubtedly informed of the recent studies of A. Luchaire and knew about the Basque words he had found and interpreted in the Roman inscriptions of Aquitaine (1879, 51).

Fita (1879, 52) was also aware of the criticism by French authors of the Basque-Iberian thesis, which the Germans had followed since Humboldt, and of their tendency to stress instead the importance of the Indo-Europeans in Spain, as E. Philipon would ultimately set down in his book.

Fita, who was the discoverer of the famous Roman inscription with the word *paramus* (to which he refers in his speech [1879, 55]), attempted with some rashness to apply Celtic to the etymologies of the Iberian Peninsula. He thus turns for Lauro and Iluro to the Irish *lár* and Welsh *llawr* 'soil', which he also identifies with Basque *lur* 'earth' (this comparison, accepted by a number of scholars of Celtic, is still repeated today; Tovar 1949, 73). Similarly, he explains (1879,

63f) the Extremaduran inscription BANDIEAPOLOSEGOLV (*CIL*, II, 740, with variant readings) by way of Celtic elements such as Irish *ban* 'woman', Irish *die* 'day', and a *segolu* that he finds similar to Welsh *llosgaw* 'thermal' (which I am unable to confirm; perhaps it derives from *llorg* 'burning, inflammation').

Nothing stops Fita in his etymologies of place names. The names of rivers such as the Arga, the Aragón, and even the famous Araxes, already familiar to us from Garibay, are for him derived from Basque *erreka* 'stream, gully'. Occasionally, he is accurate, as when he links Basque *zi(h)ar* 'silver' to the Germanic *silver.*

Guided by the bishop of Girona [Gerona], that is, by the Biblical tradition going back to Jerome, Fita ventures into the eastern Iberia, where, invoking Hervás's authority, he discovers in Georgian similarities with Basque, beginning with the declination (1879, 79) and with etymologies like that of Iturissa = Viscarret (?), with a Georgian counterpart that he transcribes as *htsqarro-sa* 'place of fountains'.

We cannot follow Fita in his final cavalcade. After comparing the Basque conjugation to the Georgian one (1879, 88f), he resolves the problem of the etymology of *Euskara* by way of the Georgian *uhtsq* 'to speak' and supposes that the Aryan Georgians in their lengthy voyage to the Iberian Peninsula paused in Hebros in Thrace and—as Hervás and Larramendi believed—left their trace in Italy in the form of the Opici and the Sycanians, both Iberian peoples.

Sabino de Arana-Goiri

This founder of the Basque nationalist party was born in Abadiano,[1] near Bilbao, in 1865. His father was a marine outfitter. Of a Carlist family, and the youngest of eight children, Sabino de Arana-Goiri had to go into exile in France with his family in 1873, in a dramatic voyage, due to his father's activities in the civil war. Back in Bilbao, he completed his secondary education at the Jesuit school in Urduña [Orduña], where the principles of "religion" and "*fueros*" (Basque traditional laws and privileges) were inculcated into him. He studied

---

1. Abadiano (Abadiño today) is a town near Durango; Arana was in fact born in Abando, a separate town at the time he was born, but which later became part of the expanding city of Bilbao. —Ed. note

Euskara beginning in 1882, under the influence of his brother Luis, two years older, who had left Bizkaia for his studies and thereby gained an awareness of its difference from other provinces of Spain. After a life of great political activity and having written a very great deal in newspapers that served the nationalist cause, resulting in persecutions and several periods of imprisonment, he died in 1903.

He began his Basque studies following the Dutch scholar of Basque E. J. van Eys, but it is beyond doubt that Astarloa had greater influence than anyone else on the formation of his ideas about the language. We can say that the autodidact Arana-Goiri did not have a scientific spirit, nor did he ever aim to pass as a scholar, but as a man of action, an organizer of a controversial party that took root among people of very solid convictions, he formulated a certain number of historical and linguistic principles, without concerning himself with supporting or debating them. In the years in which he lived with his family in Barcelona in order to study law, he was not influenced by Catalan regionalism or nationalism, which was already being formulated at the time by Valentín Almirall and others (Corcuera 1979, 193ff).

What in Astarloa were speculations based on a profound knowledge of Basque and on traditional ideas that made the Basques, the preservers of the primordial language, into the most authentic Spaniards, uncontaminated by Phoenicians, Romans, Goths, or Moors, becomes in Arana-Goiri the mark of a nationality, Bizkaian first of all and then Euskaran, that should separate from Spain and so achieve full racial identity, based not only on language but also on Basque blood (*euzkoodola*). In an instructional text for children written in the form of a catechism, Arana-Goiri asks and answers:

> How does one know the race of a family?
>> By their surnames.
>> How?
>> If the surnames are Basque [*euzkerico*], whoever posseses them is Basque; but if they are not Basque, whoever posseses them is not Basque. (1897, 1059)

In the journal *Bizkaitarra* (1893–95, 545ff), it is clear that this idea of Arana-Goiri's is the updated translation of "purity of blood" and "nobility of descent [*hidalguía*]" in the old "terminology of Spain."

The rapidity is surprising with which Arana-Goiri settled on his principles and ideas, including in the linguistic realm, and began to act and fight to put them into practice.

At the same time, his "dogmas," as he formulated them in his programmatic work *Bizkaya por su independencia* (Bizkaia for its independence, 1892, 107ff), had a very long tradition behind them, and authors such as J. Caro Baroja and A. E. Mañaricúa (cf. Corcuera 1879, 15ff) have noted their weight as far back as the sixteenth century. The supposed battle of Arrigorriaga, the myth of the Cantabrianism of the Basques, the hypothesis of an early monotheism that excluded all contamination by pagan idols in Euskalerria, and so on, are topics that, as we have already seen in part, are repeated in Basque writers and serve as a stimulus for studies of and theories about the language.

In his first work (1887, 33), we find Arana-Goiri preoccupied with the famous etymology of *vasco* 'Basque' from *baso-ko* 'mountaineer', citing Astarloa's *Apología*, and a little further on (1887, 36ff) debating against Astarloa the controversial topic of the Basque etymology of *España* 'Spain' (from *ezpain* 'lip'). This is the same world of traditional Basque erudition in which Unamuno was taking up a more critical position in the same years. Already the holder of a doctoral degree from the University of Madrid, Unamuno was living in Bilbao, waiting for an opportunity to obtain an academic position and supporting himself as a private instructor.

Already at this time, Arana-Goiri came into conflict with Unamuno, who had published in a local newspaper an article on orthography (OC, VI, 187–91) in which, in passing, he declared his opposition to *k* in writing Basque, citing Moguel as an authority. Arana-Goiri (1888, 43–47) quickly responded with a defense of the use of this letter against the "doctor of philosophy and letters."

The lecture Unamuno gave in 1887 at the premises of the "El Sitio" society of Bilbao (*Espíritu de la raza vasca* [Spirit of the Basque race], OC, VI, 192–227) and the polemic that followed were an opportunity that Arana-Goiri did not fail to take advantage of in order to maintain his doctrine (1888–89, 70ff): the Euskaran race had no ties of brotherhood at all with Iberians, Celts, or any other primordial inhabitants of Spain; what Unamuno called fictions, the histories of Aitor invented by Chaho and those of Navarro Villoslada's novel,

are for Arana-Goiri that "ancient, real, and practical" way of life
in the region that its patriots love; Bizkaia should be independent;
and the "Bizkaian philologist" Astarloa should not be criticized, as
Unamuno does, since "so long as the arguments of the learned native
of Durango have not been destroyed, his theory remains standing,
and reason remains on his side" (1888–89, 77).

Faced with Unamuno's famous speech at the 1901 poetry competition (*juegos florales*), Arana's reaction naturally had to be a violent
one (1901, 1989–92 and 1993–2001; see also 1901–3, 2155–60). He
found that the "most illustrious rector of Salamanca" had performed
his role as presider in a lamentable fashion, and he considered his
speech "worthy of Diogenes." He attributed Unamuno's attitude—
a point repeated over and over—to his resentment arising from the
"three different reversals" he suffered in Bilbao, his native town: in
the competition for the provincial government's famous professorship
of Euskara, won by Azkue, and in other competitions for the professorship of philosophy at the Institute and for the post of provincial
archivist.

He did not pardon Unamuno for wanting to be at the same time
Basque and Spanish. The final phrase of the text in which Arana-
Goiri protested with his signature against the presider's speech was
one that undoubtedly would not have displeased Unamuno: "let us be
practical and not poets."

Given his racialist identification of Basqueness, it is understand-
able that as soon as he had settled on his political doctrine, he dedicated
himself to writing a *Tratado etimológico de los apellidos euskéricos*
(Etymological treatise on Euskaran surnames, 1895, 702–807).

In his desire that whatever was Basque should quickly acquire
differentiating characteristics, he thought up a revolutionary naming
system. Already in his first writings, he signed his name as Arana eta
Goiritar Sabin (cf. 1887, 31), and he established on the basis of the
ethnonym *tar* a system that, according to his perennial critic Azkue,
as I myself have heard him say, turned the Basque provinces into Western Tartary.

On the first page of his calendar (*Egutegi bizkaittarra*, 1896, 983–
1015), we already find all at once all the invented forms of Euskaran
baptismal names: Luis becomes Koldobika (from Hlodovvich, he
explains), and Peru becomes Kepa (from Cephas, the Aramaic, albeit

not Basque, translation of 'rock', as the Evangelist says in John 1:42). In the same way, Josu comes from Jheossuany, and Miren from Miriam. Without further explanation, he thus creates a naming system different from any other. Subsequently, he also corrects the signs of the zodiac and forges neologisms with greater or less success, such as *aberri* 'fatherland' and Jaungua instead of Jaungoikua (1896, 1013–15). In the same year (*Ortografía* [Orthography], 1896, 826), we have the invention of the *agaka*, an alphabet based on curious phonetic ideas that makes the dictionaries that have followed it very difficult to use.

Starting on January 1 of his *Egutegi*, he puts into practice the Astarloan doctrine that, on the basis of the lines from Cottunius that we have already seen in Astarloa, prefers –*e* for feminine names, such as Euportsiñe for Euphrosyne (Spanish Eufrosina), and –*a* for masculine ones, such as Arka for Argeus and Titta for Titus (1896, 987).

Nothing stops him in his critique. He corrects the great writer Antonio Moguel on his spelling and vocabulary (1893–95, 211ff).

It is evidently unjust to treat Arana-Goiri's writings as those of a scholar. He was the founder of a party, convinced of his ideas and trying to convince others, and for this reason he did not need to justify his innovations, nor did he explain them, but rather tried to impose them.

In the feverish activity he conducted as a publicist over an incredibly small number of years, he went on to publish (1897, 1016–66) a "Children's First Friend" (*Umiaren lenengo aizkidea*), dedicated to parents and in which he presented a first reading book for children, progressing from the alphabet to a nationalist catechism in question-and-answer form inculcating the racialist doctrine we have previously mentioned. At the end, we find an interesting list of neologisms.

Proud of his Bizkaian heritage, he feels no need for a unified Euskara but rather, at most, for more organized dialects: a single Gipuzkoan, a single Navarrese, but with the Euskaran group as a whole maintaining "variety in unity" (*Ortografía*, 1896, 822). However, love for his native territory leads him to go on to affirm (1896, 823n), "It seems that the *euskeldun* [Basque speaker] who best understands those who do not speak his dialect is the Bizkaian. It might be said that Bizkaian Euskara in a certain way includes the other dialects within itself . . ."

In his reasoning, Arana-Goiri upholds whatever favors his effort
to separate the Basques from any historical relationship to others.
Since the Latin etymology is clearly recognizable in *lege* 'law', he prefers as his term the dialectical variant *lagi*, and debating the word
with Astarloa, he allows himself etymological speculations in which
he compares it to *lagatu* (better, *lagetu*) 'to permit' (with alongside it
laketu 'to permit' and also 'to be grateful for', which, alas, like *laket*
'to please' is none other than Latin *placet* 'it pleases' once again).
Instead of accepting the evidence, however, he turns to Astarloa's
theory of the meaning of each letter, according to which "the consonant *l* indicates the idea of 'attachment'," as he confirms with a long
series of words: *lagun* 'company', *lar* 'bramble', and so on. In *agi* he
discovers the root *agin* 'to command', and so *l-agi* will mean 'imposed
subjection or command of subjection, promulgated or published subjection' (*Ortografía*, 1896, 957–59).

For Arana-Goiri, the tradition of the region's scholars of Basque
was valid in all its parts: the development of linguistics and history in
the nineteenth century did not exist for him, and Astarloa was alive in
all his affirmations. What was important for him was to demonstrate
that the Basques could not be traced back to any other people:

> The origin of the Euskaran race is completely unknown until today; its
> language is without known sisters or a known mother. (1882, 72)

Moreover, this affirmation from the beginning of his published
output was one to which he would always return:

> Neither a mother nor sisters for our race have yet been found among
> all the races of the world, nor is it even known whether it came from
> the north, the south, the east, or the west to this corner of the earth.
> One finds an affinity with the "redskins" (west); one, with the Geor-
> gians (east); this one, with the Finns (north); that one, with the Berbers
> (south); but no one has obtained sufficient marks of affinity to dare to
> establish our race's brotherhood with any of those compared with it.
> All the other races have been classified into primordial groups, original
> branches, and later derivations; ours remains a virgin forest for scien-
> tific research, a true island in the midst of humanity. (1893–95, 182)
>
> This most original race is neither Celtic nor Phoenician nor Greek
> nor Latin nor German nor Arab . . . It is isolated in the universe in such
> a way that data cannot be found to classify it among the other races of

the Earth . . . We foresee an objection, and it is the following: "If the Euskaran race," we will be told, "were the original inhabitants of the Spanish peninsula, it follows that the true Spaniards are the Euskarans, among whom are the Bizkaians." Granted that the Euskaran was the aborigine of the peninsula; however, he was also the aborigine of North Africa, Italy, a large part of France, and the British Isles. Therefore, if we are called Spaniards for having been the aborigines of Spain, we should be called Moroccans, Italians, French, and English for the same reason . . .

Finally, in the weekly *Baserritarria,* he repeated:

We are accustomed to represent to ourselves the races that live in Europe today as arriving now by way of the Urals, now by way of the Caucasus, now by way of the Mediterranean, now by way of the Straits of Gibraltar, but the *euskeldun* race is older and greater, as its language reveals, and it is very probable that it spanned Africa and Europe at once, without having separated itself notably from its cradle. (1897, 1342)

This belief had been set from the beginning and was not subject to debate. The old tradition of Poza, Larramendi, and Astarloa continued without variation. We seem to still be hearing Hervás, their follower: the Oscii of Italy are Basques (Arana-Goiri 1901, 1818), and so are the Etruscans, from *Atria-euzko* (1901, 1820), and the Casci (the *casci Latini* 'old Latins' of the archaic poet Ennius) are likewise none other than *euzkos* (1901, 1821) . . .

In an article in which he replies to another by Antonio Valbuena titled "El vascuence en toda España" (Basque throughout Spain), Arana-Goiri engages in a critique of Valbuena's etymologies and his own. Approving this famous method and starting (1901–3, 2219) from Tubal's arrival in Spain, he titles his reply "El baskuence en toda Africa" (Basque throughout Africa), with derogatory etymologies:

the man destined to be the patriarch of the West had scarcely made out from a distance the lands known today under the names of Africa and Spain when his face fell as he slowly moved his head up and down. Those who accompanied him most closely, concerned at the unaccustomed expression of the jovial vine-grower, asked him the cause, to which he answered, "*Alperrik a*!," a Basque expression that means as much as "*Uselessly* have we left *that* land from which we come!"

With etymologies as burlesque as this one of Africa and those that follow of prominent regions and cities, such as Barcelona from *bart ze lo ona* 'what a beautiful dream last night' and *Castilla* 'Castile' from *ke asto illa* 'ass dead (from) smoke' (1901–3, 2222 and 2231), the fantastical cycle to which Humboldt had vainly attempted to bring a little order comes to a close.

Francisco Fernández y González

Francisco Fernández y González, a professor at the Central University of Madrid, a distinguished scholar of Eastern languages, and a man of great curiosity, took up the enigma of Basque on repeated occasions. In two 1893 lectures, he compared it to numerous languages of North, Central, and South America on the basis of superficial similarities in words and forms, especially pronouns, numerals, and verbs: Aleutian, Nahuatl, Aymara, Arawak, and Cumanagota, among others, show some resemblance. To give one example, we cite the one he proposes for Aymara *killa* 'moon', Basque *il-* (1893b, 31).

He attempted a more systematic theory in his speech upon entrance into the Royal Spanish Academy (1894), the first part of which is dedicated to proving that Basque belongs to an earlier age than the Aryan and, according to Menéndez Pelayo's extracts (1941, 198), Semitic languages. The Basque people, in his view, are

> something like the union of a people with affinities to the Berbers and another northern people analogous to the Finns or the Lapps, and external similarities can even be found with the type of the Mordvins and the "redskins."

The language, as an agglutinative one, appears to him to be similar to Turkish and Hungarian, along with the languages of the New World and what some at the time called "Turanian."

The mixture of anthropological and linguistic arguments and the daring of the comparisons do not create any clarity.

In his speech, he dedicates the first pages to insisting on the "copious and evident analogies between Basque, Berber, Galla, Ancient Egyptian, Assyrian, Sumerian-Akkadian, Turkish, Samoyed, and Nahuatl" (1894, 3). The comparisons are all over the place and unreliable, although Fernández y González sometimes discovers very tempting relationships, for example, that of Basque *izen* 'name' with Hebrew *sem* and Arabic *ism* 'name' (cf. Tovar 1970, 43).

The same is true of the study he sent to the Hamburg Orientalist Congress (1902), in which nothing is clarified by the comparisons with Chaldean and Aramaic, sometimes ones that had been previously noted by others or have been advanced since, and sometimes as nonsensical as *zigorra* 'stick' and *ezkurra* 'acorn' compared to the *zikkurat* or Babylonian pyramids. It is true that *bait(h)a* 'house' resembles the Semitic *bait,* which is an interesting problem. As a whole, however, the author's efforts in this monograph were unable to convince. Here, too, we find again the old story of Tertullian's and Prudentius's labarum as an inheritance from the Cantabri, that is, the Basques.

With Menéndez Pelayo (1941, 196f), we must lament that "our dean had abandoned, although no doubt temporarily, the paths of Semitic erudition, in which he can teach us so much and so well, to become entangled in arid disquisitions on the indigenous languages of the Americas and the kinship of Basque with Turkish."

Juan Fernández Amador de los Ríos

The son of the former and a professor at the Instituto de Pamplona (Iruñea [Pamplona] Institute), this scholar, remaining piously in his father's orbit, published the beginning of an impossible Basque-Chaldean dictionary. In thirteen fascicles that I have been able to see in the library of the Royal Academy of History, he did not get beyond the letter A. The extensive introduction repeats Fernández y González's ideas, reducing them chiefly to the comparison with Chaldean.

Julio Cejador y Frauca

Julio Cejador y Frauca (Zaragoza, 1864–Madrid, 1927) was as tireless as he was disorganized. His ambitions as a linguist were unlimited by any sense of discipline.

He belonged to the Society of Jesus and traveled to the Near East. He taught in Jesuit schools and later outside them. He was a professor of Latin at the University of Madrid.

He wrote as many as twelve volumes of a work with the general title *El lenguaje* (Language, 1908–14). The work began publication with volume four, which was continued by all the following ones under the general title of *Tesoro de la lengua castellana: Origen y vida del lenguaje: Lo que dicen las palabras* (Treasury of the Spanish language: Origin and life of the language: What the words say). It is a kind of etymological dictionary, in which references to Basque are exaggeratedly frequent. It remained unfinished, and the occasional original observations it contains are smothered by arbitrary doctrine. According to a contemporary critic, J. Alemany y Bolufer, in a laudatory review included in volume five (18), Cejador wanted to demonstrate the unity of all languages, a topic that had also occupied Astarloa and that had a great defender at the time in the Italian linguist Alfredo Trombetti (1861–1929).

Cejador's ambitious work began in volume one with an *Introducción a la ciencia del lenguaje* (Introduction to the science of language, 2nd ed., 1911), including a list of the world's languages and a plan for examining them using the comparative method. In volume three, under the title *Embriogenia del lenguaje* (Embryogenesis of language), with a dedication to Euskara speakers, he adheres to Astarloa's thesis, joining him in discovering in Basque elements scattered around the world. He once again pursues the pronoun *ni* 'I' in Chinese and Quechua (cf. Cejador 1922, 94ff), and since he has little time for phonetics, he has little difficulty in demonstrating that Basque *zu* 'you (formal)' is the same as the *tu* 'you (informal)' of European languages (cf. 1922, 108). The repetition of a genius's attempt with an autodidact's disorientation has very poor results.

Later, as an appendix to his extensive history of literature, Cejador (1922) published an updated exposition of his doctrine. It is a dialogue in which one of the interlocutors, Aurelio, represents the author, and Astarloa, the inspiration for all this doctrine, appears as Don Pablo. Reading Cejador, we seem to have gone back a century in time, to Astarloa and Erro.

Naturally, Cejador sometimes presents Astarloa's ideas in a more modern form. For example, he points out the resemblance between the Basque genitive and adjectival suffix *–ko* and the same Indo-European suffix (a thesis that would find later defenders; Tovar 1959, 68ff), as well as the combining forms *–zko* in Basque and *–sko–* in Indo-European. However, this possibility leads him to affirm (1922, 84) that all Indo-European suffixes originate in Basque, so that the *n* of the Basque relative is nothing more nor less than the Indo-European adjectival suffix *–no–*.

He goes on to affirm that Spanish originates in Basque (1922, 113ff), and to demonstrate this, he develops and surprisingly expands the place-name arguments that we have already found in Larramendi. Cejador maintains that certain equivalences in the meaning of place names are based on the possibility of "translating" such names not into Latin but into Arabic, since "Iberian" place names were still understood by the inhabitants of Hispania in the eighth century (1922, 150).

These are some of Cejador's examples: Arriaca corresponds more or less to Guadalajara. This Arabic name, which means 'river of stones' (*wad al-hizara*), is said to be the translation of a name derived from Basque *(h)arri* 'stone'. The Turia River (if it is granted that this name is a form of Basque *zuria* 'white') will have been translated into Arabic as Guadalaviar (*wad 'al-abyad*). If Calatañazor, 'castle of the crows' in Arabic (*qal'at' annasur*, which Asín translates 'of the eagles') is the ancient Veluca (better, Voluce), it can be supposed that in that ancient form it is derived from Basque *vele* 'crow'. Occasionally, the explanation is more complicated, as in the case of Zorita de los Canes (Zorita 'of the Dogs'), which has to be corrected to Zorita de los Canos (Zorita 'of the White-Haired Men') so that the name and specification can once again be explained by way of the Basque *zuri* 'white' (1922, 120).

Amid this delirium, Cejador finds some Basque elements in Spanish, as in *bruces* (1922, 121), and others that are less certain, such as the suffix *–orro, –urro* (1922, 133), but he has to turn to the good Larramendi in order to maintain that Latin "was not a general language in Spain" (1922, 122), while Euskara was (Cejador 1915, 25ff). Permit us to note a few successes: that of the relationship between *mina* and *mena* (1922, 168), that of a possible Basque explanation for the word *balsa* (1922, 168), and above all, that of the identity between the Basque vowels and those of Spanish, which Unamuno had previously noted (OC, V, 559) and Navarro Tomás would subsequently demonstrate.

In a monograph that appeared posthumously (Cejador 1926, publication delayed), Astarloa's theses are combined with Erro's. For Cejador as well, the Iberian alphabet was "Spanish or Euskaran," precisely when Gómez-Moreno had just made public his admirable decipherment. It is with good reason that Cejador accuses himself at the beginning of this work of his "Basque hobby-horse [*chifladura de vascuence*]," which leads him to use it as a universal key.

We will limit ourselves to presenting a few examples of Cejador's "decipherments," as a lesson to "translators."

There are some coins from Iliturgi (*MLI* no. 119b) with the inscription ILDITVR ESNEG, that is, the Latin adjective *Ilditurgense* with the final letters reversed. Cejador dauntlessly translates 'dead source of milk', combining without any syntax the Basque words *iturri* 'source, fountain', *il* 'to kill, to die', and *esne* 'milk'. On another coin, likewise in the Latin alphabet, we read DETVMO on one side and SISIPO on the other (*MLI* no. 127), read by Cejador, no doubt by reference to a defective example, as SISIRS. These two words, the names of two cities, become, with scant Basque syntax, *det* 'I have' *umo* 'ripe' *ziziri* 'lentil(s)'.

The Alcoy lead tablet, in the Greek alphabet, presents quite legibly the word *ilduniraenai*, in a context that somewhat recalls Basque, but that no one has explained. Cejador translates 'to those of mine who died', on the basis of the Basque elements *nire* or *nere* 'my, mine', *ildu* 'to die', and apparently, the genitive postposition *en* and the dative postposition *i*.

Our final example is the interpretation of the Iberian stele from Cretas (*MLI* XVIII), on which everyone agrees with Gómez Moreno in reading *ca-l-u-n s-e-l-ta-r*. It is a funerary stele on which five lance heads have been carved, admirably confirming the information Aristotle gives us (*Politics* H 2, 1324b16) that the Iberians placed over the tomb of a warrior as many lances as enemies who had died at his hands. The two words, which may be supposed to be the warrior's name and 'stone, tomb', are turned by Cejador, reading the letters we know not how, perhaps in Erro's fashion, into *algamatseltcho*, which means nothing less than 'imbiber (*eltzu*) of a tasteless or powerless (*al* 'power', *ga(be)* 'without') grape (*mats*)'.

8

Demythologization

Unamuno and Basque

Miguel de Unamuno y Jugo (1864–1936), as a native of Bilbao and the descendant of families with deep roots in Bizkaia and Gipuzkoa, had direct experience of the problematical situation of Basque throughout his life and applied his powerful intelligence to it, at the same time that, having heard the Carlist canons as a child and seen the parade of the liberating army on May 2, 1874 (OC, I, 285, and X, 55f), his sentiments in its regard were not unconditional.

We will begin with a passage in which the great writer expresses very well what he and many others of his contemporaries thought in Bilbao. In the words of the rector of Salamanca (1902, 1578),

> I will never forget the words of a curate who told his congregation, preaching in Basque, "Don't send your children to school, because they will teach them Spanish there, and Spanish is the vehicle of liberalism." Modern culture is called liberalism.

I cannot help continuing to quote. Unamuno goes on:

> Nor do I forget what a fellow countryman, a fervent admirer of the so-called traditions, said to me once: "Culture! . . . Culture! . . . You're always on about that! It's better to be happy than to be cultured." The bad thing is that the one who resists culture is not left to enjoy his happiness, if there is such a thing in willing and remediable ignorance.

From this perspective, against this political and religious background, which is also highlighted if we recall the Carlist origins of Arana-Goiri, as well as of Azkue and Urquijo, we can understand Unamuno's attitude toward Basque, something that is now not easy

for more recent generations to explain. Unamuno denied that Basque
had a future as a modern language of culture. I jump ahead of my
story to present that fact, which he affirmed before his fellow countrymen in his famous speech at the 1901 poetry competition (*OC*,
VI, 334f) and which we will examine in the second part of this chapter, and turn now to consider his scholarly studies on Euskara, which
are his doctoral dissertation and his classification of the Latin and
Romance elements in the Basque lexicon, the first serious efforts in
Spain for a long time.

I

The student of philosophy and letters who attended classes at the
University of Madrid between 1880 and 1884 chose as the topic for
his doctoral dissertation a *Crítica del problema sobre el origen y prehistoria de la raza vasca* (Critique of the problem on the origin and
prehistory of the Basque race). He defended this dissertation on June
20, 1884, before a tribunal chaired by Francisco Fernández y González,
a man of great and miscellaneous erudition who would later devote
some attention to Basque, and in which his supervisor or sponsor was
Antonio Sánchez Moguel.

Manuel García Blanco, in his edition of Unamuno's works (*OC*,
VI, 20f), has opportunely pointed out that according to Unamuno's
own testimony, Sánchez Moguel, a professor of the history of Spanish
literature, dedicated a large part of his course to also discussing the
history of the language, a subject that was not yet part of the official curriculum. Granted the limitations of his doctoral supervisor, to
which his own student testifies in passages cited by García Blanco's
erudition, it is evident that he contributed to awakening Unamuno's
sense of history, a current that held absolute sway in the linguistic
scholarship of the day and that Unamuno absorbed through the study
of authors with whom he was already familiar, such as A. Schleicher
and W. D. Whitney, cited in his dissertation, or would soon come to
know, such as the patriarch of Leipzig, K. Brugmann, with whom
Ortega y Gasset would study Sanskrit two decades later.

Unamuno's doctoral dissertation, which remained unpublished
until the posthumous edition of his complete works and which was
produced by a boy less than twenty years old, who could boast upon
presenting it (1884, 88) that its "weak sketch" was for him the "fruit of

long labors,"[1] was in reality a notable achievement. Unamuno begins by realizing that the way the problem is posed is itself defective "due to the exaggerated local spirit that vitiates our research" (1884, 90). For this reason, no doubt, he titled his dissertation a critique, which he situates, already firm in his ideas, at the moment of crisis for the Basque language, which will lead the people, according to him, "not to be annihilated, but to be assimilated, to lose themselves as a stream is lost in the great currents of a wide river" (1884, 91).

After a review, natural if we remember that the title speaks of a "race," of the results reached by anthropologists and specialists in crania, and reference to the little that was known up to that time of the region's prehistory, he insists on the value of the language as

> a living and manifest monument that has reached us across centuries and centuries, the sole inheritance of a people in perpetual succession. (1884, 94)

He goes on to acknowledge the disadvantage for research of the lack of a long written tradition in Basque, added to the historical uncertainty represented by the possibility that race and language do not correspond, since it so often happens that a people changes its language and receives a foreign one. All this has given rise to "phantasmagorias, more than doctrines, that have divided scholars of Euskara" (1884, 95).

Unamuno next proposes to review and critique the different opinions. The newly minted scholar recounts the most important, from Rodrigo Jiménez de Rada in the thirteenth century to Aureliano Fernández-Guerra. In the copy that García Blanco used for his edition, bibliographical references were left blank that Unamuno must be assumed to have completed with library research in the definitive copy submitted to the university. These lacunae and some omissions or negligences are evidence that it must not have been easy to work in

---

1. In effect, he tells us (OC, I, 343) that in his last year of high school, he began a Basque-Spanish etymological dictionary, the manuscript of which, written in school notebooks, I remember having seen at the University of Salamanca's Unamuno House. He goes on to say that a friend of his at the time, Práxedes Diego Altuna, planned, upon going to Madrid to study, to write a history of the Basque people "in sixteen or twenty folio volumes."

the Madrid public libraries of the time: for example, it appears that he did not study Mayans (he accuses him in another work [1902, 559] of "extremely scant knowledge" of Basque), and he lacked reliable information on Moguel's *Peru Abarca*, which he believed had some resemblance to Juan de Valdés's *Diálogo de la lengua*. However, he studied Marineo Sículo, Esteban de Garibay in debate with the Valencian Beuter, Poza, whom he justly presents as a precursor to Humboldt, Larramendi, Astarloa, and others, and he would go over the history again later, returning to the topic (1902, 558ff).

Out of all this material, the problems that struck Unamuno (1884, 101), precisely after citing Astarloa and Wilhelm von Humboldt, were those of the relationship between Basque and Iberian and of the origins of the Basques.

Unamuno draws on the old Basque tradition of Garibay, Poza, Echave, Larramendi, and Erro, who supposed that Basque was Spain's primordial language, but he resists the Basque-Iberian thesis. Despite the fact that Humboldt, with a certain amount of critique and a more modern presentation, had maintained the same theory (supported in its most exaggerated form by Lorenzo Hervás), Unamuno cites the subsequent criticism that permits him to affirm, with reason, that "such a hypothesis is down at heel [*de capa caída*] today" (1884, 103). A. Hovelacque, basing himself on work by J. Vinson and W. J. van Eys, had no doubt gone too far in his criticism, but Unamuno finds that it can only lead to nonsensical results to interpret by way of Basque place names not only from the Iberian Peninsula but also from France, Italy, North Africa, the Caucasus, and even the Urals.

Unamuno does not enter on a critique of the examples, which are counted in the hundreds in Humboldt, as in Larramendi and in Hervás. What is more, he is not closed to the possibility of those explanations that have a certain logic, and so he defends the possibility that Humboldt might be right to explain the place-name element *asta* by way of the Basque *aitz* or *acha* 'rock' in some cases (1884, 103). The identification of Vascon and Euskara, accepted by Hervás and others, appears doubtful to him (although he will approve it in his last years, *OC*, I, 902), and he believes that the traditional explanation of *vasco* 'Basque' by way of *baso-ko* 'of the mountain, mountaineer' is absolutely unacceptable (1884, 106). Unamuno is inclined to follow the opinion of the learned Hispano-Philippine numismatist

Jacobo Zobel de Zangroniz, according to whom "the Iberianism of the Basques . . . does not rest on solid foundations and . . . is as risky to affirm as to deny, because the problem has still not been posed" (1884, 107).

With reason, the problem of the Basques' ethnic origins appears to him even more complex and inaccessible, and he considers the linguistic method the most applicable one (1884, 107).

Unamuno intelligently liquidates, with a critique somewhat *more hegeliano* (in the Hegelian style), a methodological problem, that of the comparison and rapprochement between Basque and the Indo-European languages. This comparison was made between Basque, an "agglutinative" language, and a "supposed agglutinative form of the Aryan languages," with the result that one empirically given, "real term" was compared to another "transcendental" one (1884, 108).

Such a Basque-Aryan theory had been formulated in its most wide-ranging form by the Basque Frenchman Agustín Chaho, in an entirely unscientific manner, and Fidel Fita had supported it once again in his speech upon being received as a member of the Academy of History in Madrid (1879), like Fernández-Guerra as well. Fita's speech was a display of knowledge as extensive as it was confused, and in this aspect of the comparison with Indo-European languages, the young Unamuno dares to criticize him, saying with reason that

> as many words as Fr. Fita . . . has found in common between Basque and Sanskrit, a Sinologist would find in common between Basque and Chinese. (1884, 109)

Unamuno subsequently debates the relationships that Fita, with a long tradition behind him, discerned between Basque and the eastern Iberia, that is, Georgia, in the Caucasus. Fita entangled this topic with what he calls Euskara's "fundamental Turanian artifice." Unamuno correctly resolves the difficulty, pointing out that a resemblance of this kind, like the one that Prince Bonaparte, H. de Charency, and in Spain Fernández-Guerra had proposed with regard to the Finno-Ugric or Uralic languages, could be reduced to "forming a *natural* [today we would say 'typological'] group of all the agglutinative languages."

With great clear-headedness, the young Unamuno resolves problems that were not yet mature. He rightly rejects the term "Turanian,"

> since while for some it designates the languages that are neither Aryan nor Semitic, for others it is a synonym of Altaic in geography, and for the majority, a synonym of agglutinative in linguistics. (1884, 112)

Like Humboldt, he is inclined to explain as typological (in our terminology) and not genetic all resemblances between Basque and New World languages (1884, 111f). He denies that Basque is Semitic in character, a theory that has also had its defenders (1884, 112f), and he suspends all judgment about the relationship between Basque and African languages, due to a lack of documentation (1884, 113).

In the same way, he reviews and dismisses a series of absurd theories: that of a Basque language without personality of its own, a conglomerate of Latin and Provençal remnants, or that of a language brought by barbarian tribes who invaded the Roman Empire or defended it against the Germans in the time of Honorius; that of Basque as a Celtic language, as maintained by British and French enthusiasts for Celtic (1884, 114f), a theory against which Hervás had already fought; and that of Basque as a relative of Etruscan, as defended by W. Betarn (1884, 115) and still in our own day by the Basque Argentine bishop Nicolás Esandi (1946).

On this point, he cites Whitney's opinion, which appears the most solid today, that Euskara is "*perhaps* the last vestige of a Western European civilization destroyed by invaders of Indo-European race" (1884, 116, and 1886, 165). Although Unamuno would subscribe not long afterward (1886, 164) to the thesis he heard from Menéndez Pelayo, that "the Basque people are the remains of an aboriginal people who preceded the first Iberian and Celtic invasions," he disliked this reasonable proposal by the great American scholar. It spoke of "civilization," and for him it was evident that the only civilization that had reached the Basques was the Latin one. The cultures of megalithic Europe and the spread of metals from Spain did not seem to be civilization to Unamuno, when the enchantment was yet to be discovered of those distant cultures that Ortega y Gasset would praise among us, calling them Atlantises. This entire first part of the dissertation, covering ground that rightly appeared to Unamuno "scant and poorly gleaned" (1884, 89), is summarized in his first two conclusions: that all the comparisons previously made between Basque and other languages "lack scientific foundation" and that there are not "*sufficient reasons either to affirm or to deny*" Basque-Iberian kinship (1884, 139f).

In the second part, which he summarizes afterward in his third and fourth conclusions (1884, 140), on the "lack of method" applied to the problems and ignorance of the Basque people's prehistory, Unamuno raises issues of a more methodological slant.

Starting from the biological ideas dominant among the linguists of the time, Unamuno accepted that languages are organisms that pass "through three moments or phases in their development, which linguists call monosyllabism, agglutination, and inflection" (1884, 117). Since Unamuno believed, with reason, that the study of these "groups" (today we would say "types") had only begun, comparison of Basque with other languages was not possible. The work of the most famous Basque scholars, such as Larramendi and Astarloa, was deficient due to the lack of scientific method (1884, 119). A phonetic history of Basque, made difficult by the absence of ancient literature, was lacking, although Campión had already begun work in this field, and this lack undermined Fita's comparisons, for example. After that, it was necessary to separate the Latin and Romance elements in the Basque lexicon, a field in which Unamuno would go on to make definite advances, as we will see. Unamuno's program included the correct idea that "before comparing Basque to other languages, it is necessary to compare it to itself" (1884, 123). The evolutionary biological idea led him to believe that, by means of the establishment of phonetic laws, the language could be traced back "to its primordial roots, if possible to its monosyllabic state."

Following a critique of the "spirited Astarloa," with his theory of the primordial meaning of each sound of the language, a "fantastical and arbitrary" proposal that had the attraction of "absurdities that please and enchant, as everything that has a poetic flavor and appeals to the imagination enchants and pleases" (1884, 124), Unamuno acknowledges that all comparative research is premature so long as the language itself in its living form has not been better studied.

He dismisses the fantastical legends invented by Chaho, whom Unamuno would later call to mind more than once as a substitute for what he called the nonexistent Basque history, and who had enchanted him a few years before: "The *koplari* sang to the sublime Aitor, who came from the land of the sun, from the eastern Iberia, where the Ark came to rest; he sang to Lelo, the killer of Zara; he sang to Lekobide, lord of Bizkaia, who made peace with Octavian, lord of the world" (OC, I, 174). In other passages he recalls Juan Zuría, who came from Ireland, the imaginary battle of Arrigorriaga (OC, I, 344), Don Lope and Don Pedro (OC, I, 157f), and other heroes of a mythology that had its measure of success.

Subsequently (1884, 127f), he reviews the topic of the traditional confusion between the Basques, the people who have preserved their pre-Roman language, and the Cantabri, the last people to resist. With this motive, he collects (1884, 129f) the scant information about ancient Basque paganism and that of the other regions of northern Spain, dismissing along the way the legends and fantasies of Basque authors who, for example, have interpreted the word *lábaro* 'labarum' as *lauburu* 'four heads', with reference to the swastika found on ancient monuments in the region. He also criticizes Joaquín Costa, who had accepted the idea of traditional historical poetry among the Basques (1884, 136).

Finally, Unamuno (1884, 137f) recounts that something that he later read in Charencey had also occurred to him, that *aitz* 'rock' could have given rise to words such as *aitzur* 'spade', *aizkora* 'ax', *aizto* 'knife', and *aiztur* 'scissors', which would date the language to the Stone Age. Azkue has told me that when he heard one of these words in Erronkari [Roncal] and exclaimed that the etymology must be from *aitz*, his informant said that Bonaparte had said the same.

The newly minted doctor, less than two years after defending his dissertation, published in the *Revista de Vizcaya* (Bizkaia Review) two articles titled "Del elemento alienígena en el idioma vasco" (On the element of foreign origin in the Basque language). In this work, he said that although it was not his desire "to strike a sour note in the midst of almost universal harmony," he wanted to be heard: "I sing my part and nothing more" (1886, 143).

His thesis was the demonstration that there are many elements in Basque taken from Latin or Romance. This seems obvious now, but at the time it was in opposition to a doctrine that had in its favor the immense authority of Larramendi and had been accepted by Astarloa and by Hervás himself. This doctrine supposed that, once the primordial character of Basque had been demonstrated, and on the assumption that this language had been spoken in Italy as well, the Latin words in Basque were not loans taken in Hispania from the Roman conquerors but the reverse, a Latin inheritance from Basque.

In a later critique of P. Novia de Salcedo's *Diccionario* (Dictionary), Unamuno selects from the latter work a few ridiculous examples that are a caricature of this kind of idea: *arima*, the Basque form of Latin *anima* 'soul, life force', has the original meaning in Euskara, according to this kind of delirium, of 'what is smooth, what is delicate in its movements'. *Arrazoyá*, which is the Basque form of Spanish *razón* 'reason', turns out to be 'what is usual, what is customary among the lineage, among the race'. *Baba*, which is nothing more nor less than Latin *faba* 'bean', means, as Unamuno comments ironically, 'much low extension'. And so on to infinity.

Unamuno reviewed Basque vocabulary and isolated into determinate semantic groups the Romance and Latin loans that had accumulated over the course of history: in religion, in general ideas, in utensils and tools, and so on. An impartial observer cannot fail to recognize that in his eagerness to deny any primordial culture to the language, Unamuno denies Basque's capacity to express general ideas. We have an example in his insistence that Basque had no word for 'tree' in general, or that *gogo* never meant more than 'appetite' (OC, III, 573); even in his famous speech at the Constitutional Assembly of the Spanish Republic, he aroused the indignation of the Basque-Navarrese deputies with his insistence on denying that the old word had the meaning of 'spirit' (OC, V, 691). In defense of the young scholar that Unamuno was at the time, it must be said that in his extensive and well-founded list of Latin and Romance loans, the most complete compiled up to that time, he could rely on nothing more than his practical knowledge of Bizkaian, with limited reading, since Basque books must have been rare at the time, and without the help of good dictionaries, since the best, and almost the only, one was still that of Larramendi.

II

Doubts have been raised about whether Unamuno knew Basque. We will bring together some data about his relationship with this millennial language.

You are my land and my terrain,

he says to Bilbao in his late *Cancionero* (Songbook, OC, XV, 714). He wrote of the poet Iturribarría that "Iturribarría, a native of Bilbao, was unfamiliar with Basque. He thought and felt in Spanish" (OC, V, 576). It has been said with exaggeration that Unamuno's Spanish writings have the roughness of the native Basque (and he himself exaggerated at times, comparing himself, for example, to his friend Arzadun, who was from Bermeo and would be expected to know Basque as a native; cf. OC, VII, 146), but Bilbao was not a Basque-speaking city, except, naturally, in its relations with villagers from the surrounding area. At most, as he himself explained in a footnote written in 1903, "in the time of my childhood there still persisted a special speech, with the accent of a Basque who has learned Spanish, with special turns of phrase and with a vocabulary in which there was a great deal of Hispanized and muddled Basque . . ." (OC, I, 223).

All his childhood memories of Bilbao, with their emotional freight, were linked to this Bizkaian Spanish heard in his family and in the street. His memories of his *bochito*, an affectionate nickname for Bilbao, "which was, as it were, the mold or form of my civic soul" (OC, VII, 398), led him to protest against the Bizcaitarras [Basque nationalists], against "barbarism, whether Boeotian or troglodyte" (OC, VII, 401). In prose and in verse, he idealized that Bilbao of Artecalle and Tendería, with the villagers doing their shopping (OC, I, 113f), and later, when he no longer lived there, he was disturbed by the progress and growth of his native town (already in 1900; OC, I, 216ff). One of his most beautiful poems is the one titled "En la basílica del señor Santiago de Bilbao" (In the basilica of the Lord Saint James in Bilbao, OC, XIII, 254ff). However, it is a sentimental memory, in which, in addition, the town appears, even as industrialization advances, more remote from the countryside and from Basqueness as expressed in Euskara. García Blanco dates to 1911 a poem in which Unamuno says:

my town is strange to me
my Bilbao no longer exists. (OC, XIII, 817)

The first impression of a foreign, non-Spanish language that he remembered is the one he received at the age of six, when he heard, not Basque, but his father speaking French with a visitor (OC, I, 235f).

It was in his youthful romantic years at the end of high school when Unamuno came to know the Basque literature of "Navarro Villoslada, Goizueta, Araquistain, Vicente Arana, Trueba . . ." (OC, I, 342). At that time, "I studied Basque with all earnestness, in books above all, and then seeking every occasion to hear it spoken and even to speak it" (OC, I, 343). This is the same atmosphere, Unamuno recalls (OC, I, 346), in which Sabino Arana was educated.

The high point of Unamuno's Basque enthusiasm is found in his prose poem on the tree of Gernika [Guernica], published in the review *Euskal-Erría* in 1888 (OC, VI, 243f). In his interest in Basque as a living language, Unamuno's courtship of Concha Lizárraga, his beloved wife, undoubtedly played a decisive role. This text reflects Unamuno's enthusiasm for the tree, so often referred to by him using Iparraguirre's words, and for Gernika, where, as he says in his Bizkaian Basque, "the most intimate part of my heart dwells" with his fiancée. In the *Cancionero*, written during his years in Hendaia [Hendaye], he will recall that time of courtship strolling through the streets of Gernika (OC, XV, 352f).

In his Basque text, he laments that the traditional laws and privileges have been taken away (agreeing in this with his rival in the competition for the Basque professorship at the Bilbao Institute, Azkue, who expresses his sorrow with such pathos on the first page of his grammar), but Unamuno, with his doctorate and having already made up his mind about the language's future, ends this lyrical page with a certain ambiguity. It is true that spring and new leaves are awaited after winter, but in the invocation to this tree that springs up from the iron entrails of Bizkaia toward the heavens, there appears to be an echo of Campión's phrase, upon which Unamuno commented (OC, I, 518), "Basque is rising to the heights and taking refuge there in order to die closer to heaven."

So Unamuno knew Basque, and not only read it (it is clear that he read Axular; OC, VI, 330), understood it, and spoke it (he still recalls speaking it in 1909 with the errand-runner of the Navarrese sanctuary of San Miguel de Excelsis; OC, I, 526) but also wrote it. In addition to his page on Gernika [Guernica], I have found included in an anthology of Basque poetry (Onaindia 1954, 675f) a composition of his in a popular style, titled "Gabon abesti" (Christmas Eve song). The friar who compiled the anthology gratuitously attributes to Unamuno's loss of the competition for the Basque professorship to Azkue his subsequent complete abandonment of Basque, as well as what he considers "quite a few vile things" (*zikalkeri naiko*) that he said about the old language. The compiler characterizes the brief poem of Unamuno's youth that he publishes (and about which he does not say where it appeared) somewhat derogatorily as a "little song" (*abestitxo*).

The Unamuno who launched his career as a thinker and writer in the years on either side of 1900, abandoning his linguistic studies, which he might have been able to develop in a more favorable atmosphere, did not return to the topic of Basque as a scholarly problem. As far as his relationship with the language itself is concerned, his absence from Bilbao accentuated his distancing of himself from it. In 1901, he gave a speech in Bilbao as the chair of a poetry competition (*Juegos Florales*). On this occasion, this writer of the Generation of '98 proclaimed as compensation for the loss of Spain's last Western Hemisphere colonies a policy that would be no longer centrifugal, but "centripetal," in which the regions and towns would have to renew and save Castile and all of Spain. For this program, "Basque is now too narrow for us" (OC, VI, 335).

García Blanco rightly points out that this speech had an antecedent in the one that he gave in 1887, still during his period of residence in Bilbao, before the competition for the Basque professorship, at the "El Sitio" society, proclaiming at the same time his love for "the common fatherland" and "the fatherland within the sound of the church bell" (OC, VI, 32).

From the perspective of our century, which has seen the resurrection of languages such as Hebrew and the more or less successful conversion into languages of culture of the languages of so many peoples, we can have another vision, recognizing that Renan's phrase about an "ongoing plebiscite" is applicable to a nationality's will to preserve its own language. However, Unamuno continued to think the same way, and in his beautiful speech to the Parliament of the Republic in 1931 on the designations of Castilian and Spanish for our language, a topic that has come up for debate again in reference to the monarchical constitution, he opposes all language planning (as we would call it now), and says of the Basque language that

> just as I would consider it a true impiety to try to hasten the death of someone who is dying, it seems equally impious to me to inject a moribund mother with drugs in order to artificially extend her life, because drugs are what the work is that is being done today to make a cultured language out of a language that, in the sense ordinarily given to that word, cannot become such. (OC, V, 690)

Undoubtedly, Basque for him had become a sentimental memory. It is in poems where he dreams of himself as a Basque, as in his striking "Salutación a los rifeños" (Greeting to those of the Rif), written on the occasion of the 1909 Melilla War, in which he speaks at the beginning of his lineage,

> that of Legazpi, Saint-Cyran, Loyola,
> of Zumalacarregui,

and recalling the Basque-African theories to which he had alluded in his doctoral dissertation, he asks himself,

> are we Moors amid the mists,
> exiled natives of the Rif?

This is Unamuno's anti-European moment, when Ortega y Gasset called him "possessed (*energúmeno*)" and a "Muslim hermit (*morabito*)," and when the rector of Salamanca wrote in his notebook:

> Alas for my hermetic forest race,
> my shamefaced race,
> not yet born for aesthetics . . . !

The great saints of this race, "Christian hermits (*morabitos cristianos*)"—Loyola, Saint-Cyran—were for him in this period comparable to the fiery saints of Africa,

> Cyprians, Augustines, Tertullians,

whom he contrasts to

> this green, soft, greasy Europe

that pairs Christianity with the "golden calf," greedy for the mines of the Rif, for the sake of the great furnaces that already existed in Bilbao, where the poem began. The hermit of Salamanca wrote in secret about a dreamed-of alliance of Basques and Berbers,

> in close formation,
> the peoples in their infancy,
> against the other old ones, the Gentiles,
> let us fight for the faith, the faith of the living God . . .

This surprising poem remained unpublished until García Blanco's edition many years after Unamuno's death (OC, XIV, 794–800).

Such bolts of inspiration, or the use of a Basque epitaph for the dead of the European war (*orhoit gutaz* 'remember us') in a poem (OC, XIV, 622–24), or the recollection of Michelet's story that in reply to a French aristocrat who boasted of his ancestors dating back to the eighth century, a Basque proclaimed, "Well, we Basques don't date" (OC, X, 820, and V, 692): this is what is left to him. The poet and writer who made his career in Salamanca finds Basques and Castilians extremely similar, and he goes so far as to say, in opposition to Basque racialists, that

> from the fact that the Basque people still preserves, in large part, its aboriginal language, and the Castilian people has lost its aboriginal language, it cannot be deduced . . . that the former is more pure than the latter, since a change of language does not in itself suppose mixture. (OC, V, 559f)

He likes to repeat the phrase of the Catalan writer Jaime Brossa that "Basque is the alkaloid of Spanish" (OC, X, 953).

We have limited ourselves to presenting as completely as possible Unamuno's thoughts and feelings about the Basque language. Contradictory as they are, like the thoughts and feelings of the poet from Bilbao on other topics, they reflect that Hegelian aspiration that he learned as a student in the Swabian genius's *Logik* (Logic), in which synthesis is only possible by means of tension and destruction.

What Is Known about Basque

We should now respond to the many questions posed in the history recounted in this book, but that would lead us to write another one.

Although somewhat belatedly, with the generation of Azkue and Urquijo, contemporaries of Menéndez Pidal, we have solid studies here. See the speech given in Oñate by Julio de Urquijo (1918), in which he draws up a first balance sheet of Basque studies, very cautiously and prudently, as in everything he wrote. He concludes by defending himself against an elderly Gipuzkoan gentleman, a friend of his, who reproached him, "There is no doubt that you are a great demolisher."

Evidently, scientific study put an end to all the Tubalisms and fantasies of Annius of Viterbo that had posed an obstacle to the study of early Spain and of Euskalerría.

Today we are certain, thanks to the gradual pursuit of the "works of information" for which Unamuno asked, that Basque is indigenous to the region in which it still lives. We can affirm (as proven by the presence of personal and divine names of an undoubted Euskaran character in inscriptions in the Pyrenean region, as far as the Aran Valley itself) that the Romans found Euskara already there. We can also say that there is no doubt that the territories of the Vascones, Caristii, and Varduli (and possibly the Autrigones) were already at that time Euskara-speaking territory, at least in the northern part. It cannot be supposed that a more or less belated colonization or invasion, as has sometimes been said, determined the Basquization of Gipuzkoa, Araba, and Bizkaia, as well as the regions south of the Atturi [Adour] and the Errobi [Nive] rivers to the north. The roots of the language, as demonstrated by place names and certainly by dialectology, are equally deep throughout the territory in which Basque is historically found.

It is true that the names of those four mentioned tribes do not appear to be Basque, and the same is true, with rare and not always clear exceptions, of the personal names offered by the Roman inscriptions of Bizkaia, Araba, and Navarre, as well as certain Indo-European place names in the Basque Country (Michelena 1964, 121ff). However, we know that Indo-Europeanizing elements reached central and western Hispania by way of the Basque-Navarrese Pyrenean passes, and it is consequently possible to suppose that the tribal organization of the Vascones, Caristii, and Varduli was more or less Celtic or para-Celtic, like that of their neighbors the Autrigones, Cantabrians, and Berones. On the other hand, we can be certain that the territory where Euskara is spoken today was already such when the Indo-European waves arrived, perhaps around 1000 B.C.

Indo-Europeans undoubtedly established themselves in the Euskaran regions, but they did not impose their language, unlike what happened in other regions, such as Cantabria and Celtiberia. Basque thus survived with its full personality, as the only pre-Indo-European language in all of Western Europe.

Neither in the Alps nor in Great Britain, nor in Ireland, nor anywhere else do we have a linguistic survival of this kind, a language with characteristics alien to the world of Latins, Germans, and Celts who cover, with no other exceptions, the linguistic map of medieval and modern Europe.

The ancient diffusion of Basque was no doubt greater. However, it also seems to be the case that we can affirm that it never appears to have been anything like a language that was spread throughout Western Europe. The typological characteristics of the Insular Celtic languages (Tovar 1980), in which it seems possible that we have traits inherited from vanished pre-Indo-European languages, are completely different from those of Basque (Tovar 1977, 1978, 1979), while they show undeniable coincidences with Hamitic-Semitic. It appears that, with J. Pokorny and other authors, we can affirm that there was an important Hamitic element in pre-Indo-European Western Europe, uniting this part of the world with North Africa. However, we also find that Basque has very different typological traits from those that link Insular Celtic to Berber. It is only in a few of the characteristics considered by Greenberg's word-order typology (noun-adjective order, postnominal demonstrative) that Basque coincides with Insular Celtic and Berber.

In all the rest (verb at the end, postpositions, prenominal genitive, relative clause before the antecedent), Basque agrees with languages that appear to have their center in Eastern Europe or farther afield, such as the Caucasian languages and the most ancient Indo-European languages (Sanskrit, Hittite, in part Latin).

At the same time, Basque lexicostatistical tables confirm the presence in Western Europe of the Hamitic element, since in the basic list established by M. Swadesh, we find that Basque and Berber have 10 percent of their words in common. Of course, these tables also point, to a lesser extent, to a kinship between Basque and two of the three Caucasian languages with which this comparison has been made, with a 7.5 percent match with Georgian and Circassian.

In order to make comparisons with Basque, we have to turn to quantitative methods, less reliable and less productive than the traditional historical comparative method used for language branches like Indo-European and Semitic, or for families like Romance, Germanic, and so on. The reason is that, since it is an isolated language, surrounded by late-coming languages (to use a term pleasing to the Basque scholars of old) for, let us say, three thousand years, it has evolved in this environment, while its possible "relatives," if it had them and they have not all disappeared, have necessarily evolved in different environments. In addition, for the study of Indo-European or Semitic, specialists have available texts that are sometimes three or four thousand years old (Mesopotamian and Hittite tablets, the Hindu Vedas, Homer), but that is not the case in the West, where writing arrived later.

With regard to Basque's ancient borders, we know that it persisted throughout the length of the Pyrenees. J. Corominas (1965, 67–217) has proved that in the Middle Ages, in the Pyrenean regions on the borders of Aragón and Catalonia, Basque survived until very late, and a name such as Tossa de Mar, on the Costa Brava, Turissa in a Roman mosaic found there, is linked to the Iturisssa that Ptolemy mentions among the Vascones and that is evidently explained by Basque *iturri* 'fountain, source'. Corominas (1971) himself has written about Roman lead tablets from a medicinal spring in Roussillon on which the nymphs are invoked with the Basque word *neska* 'girl' (NESKAS, NISKAS).

To the west of the Bilbao estuary, the original diffusion of Basque was covered over very quickly by Indo-European invasions, and it becomes increasingly obscured from Las Encartaciones across Cantabria and Asturias (Tovar 1959, 90ff).

To the north, from what we can tell from place names, Basque must not have ranged far from the Pyrenees. Nevertheless, let it be noted that the closest etymological rapprochement to the name of the Basque language, Euskara, is that of the tribe of the Ausci, whose name survives in that of the city of Auch.

To the south, Basque bordered on Iberian, and the problem of the relationship between these two languages, which have to be distinguished, but which belong to the same world, can be formulated in Corominas's words (1976, 122): the language of the inscriptions of the Algarve, "different from Turdetan and its Tartessian antecedent, although perhaps not very radically so, and very different from Iberian, itself very different from Basque, forms part of a single family with what was surely a common, albeit quite distant, origin, with these two or three pre-Indo-European languages of Hispania." In occasional cases, it is possible to find elements common to Basque and Iberian, in a limited number, but undeniable, and it is even possible to discern the different treatment of the same element in the two different languages, Basque and Iberian (Tovar 1979b, on *irun/ildun*).

The preservation of Basque is explained, in my judgment, by two reasons. First, the isolation and independence of the region at the time of the fall of the Roman Empire: the Vascones who rebelled against the Visigoths and Franks were not subject to the administration of those kingdoms, which continued the Romanizing work of their predecessors, and since Christianity had not entered the region, the influence of the Christian Church, a great Romanizing element, was also absent. Second, as a non-Indo-European language, Basque did not lend itself to progressive assimilation and the development of intermediate forms.

When the Basques emerged into history, around the ninth century, they found themselves included in part in the kingdom of Navarre and among peoples that each had their own peculiar identity: Castilians, Gascons, and so on. The maintenance of their language in a quite isolated territory, like their valleys and mountains, was perfectly possible. A conservative and traditional spirit did the rest.

Surrounded by Romance languages, however, Basque has been in communication with them, and there have been a series of mutual influences. We know that Euskara received Latin words in Roman times, recognizable by their pre-Romance phonetics: *lege* 'law' and *errege* 'king', *bike* 'pitch, tar' and *errota* 'mill' (from Latin *rota* 'wheel'), *gela* 'room' (from *cella* 'cell'), among others, are forms prior to phonetic changes that took place in Hispania and Gaul at the beginning of the Middle Ages. Christian Latin words, like *zeru* 'heaven', are already Romance, but others, such as *dekuma* or *tekuma* 'tithe', may still be ancient. Naturally, the number of Romance loans in Basque is large.

It is a known fact that Spanish developed in the territory of the ancient Autrigones and the surrounding area. That ancient tribe had the Cantabri to the west and the Varduli (Euskaran territory) to the east. It is a consequence of this circumstance that the five vowels of Spanish are exactly the same as the five Basque vowels. If we compare the vowels of Galician-Portuguese, Catalan, and the Gallic Romance dialects, we find distinctions between open and closed vowels that do not exist in Spanish (Tovar 1978, 1979).

Prestigious authors like A. Martinet (1956, 297-325) accept that the loss in modern Spanish of distinct voiced consonants (in the old oppositions *s- -ss-/-s-*, *x/g j*, *ç/z*) is a consequence of contact with Basque, which lacks precisely these sounds. The shift from Latin *f* to *h* on both sides of the Basque territory, in Spanish and Gascon, is reasonably attributed to the same Basque adstratum.

At the same time, if we analyze the Basque conjugation, Romance influence is beyond doubt in the compound perfect and the periphrastic future and conditional. Larramendi (1729, 60) had already noted the coincidence in the opposition 'I have eaten / I ate', although in conformity with his theory, he interpreted it in the reverse direction, as Basque influence on Romance. Basque also shares with the European languages the distinction between the polite form of address *zu* and the familiar *(h)i*, like Spanish *vos* and *tú*.

We might maintain that there is a true linguistic alliance or *Sprachbund*, in Trubetzkoy's sense, between Basque and the languages of the entire Iberian Peninsula (sometimes with extensions in southern France). Traces of this are the *r/rr* opposition (simple and multiple), the diffusion of the word *izquierdo* (for which I have defended a Basque etymology), and the pronunciation of intervocalic voiced occlusives as fricatives (note the difference in words like *baba*, *dedo*, and Basque *gogo*, with the initial occlusive and the medial fricative).

We should conclude these indications on the relationships of Basque by noting its coincidence with some linguistic and cultural elements of European antiquity, who knows whether of pre-Indo-European origin. Just as the witchcraft of the *akelarres* resembles the

Walpurgisnacht of German superstition, the Basques share with the ancient Celts and Germans the practice of counting not by days but by nights (Tovar 1959, 81ff).

What shall we say of Euskara's current situation? I am not Basque, nor do I live there, so as to be well informed about the rapid evolution of recent years, nor do I feel that I have the authority to express an opinion on the dominant tendencies in Basque.

In the Middle Ages, and still in the early modern period, and in Spain until the twentieth century, languages were spoken for the most part by illiterate people and were chiefly inherited by oral tradition, as in the earliest times. In this way, Basque survived until yesterday, and in this way, a living oral literature has been preserved among the Basques until today.

However, the current crisis, an unfortunately bloody crisis that is affecting the Basques, is a political crisis, but also a linguistic one. In today's world, where illiterates cannot exist, because the economy prohibits it, the transmission of the language is no longer predominantly oral, nor does it happen in the tranquil, age-old retreat of the mountain villages. The Basque Country, as industrialized as it is and as attractive to immigrants as it has been, has arrived at an identity crisis.

It would be stupid not to acknowledge it. A language cannot subsist today without schools and modern communications media, and a unified form of language is necessary in order to serve these purposes and those of the autonomous regional administration. Depriving a language of this today is the same as condemning it to death.

The road to peace in the Basque provinces and in Spain passes through politics, and as can be seen in this book, through linguistic politics. "The current situation," King Juan Carlos has said to a foreign journalist (*El País*, March 23, 1980), "is the fruit of enormous historical mistakes."

To those nostalgic for Franco's regime, this book can teach them that the linguistic and political problem of the Basques is not one that has just been posed now, and that the long silence imposed up to the rise of ETA did not resolve anything, but rather embittered everything.

This book has also been written so that many Basques might leave behind what a politician (G. Peces-Barba, *El País*, March 2, 1980) has rightly called "the chimera of their own imaginings," as well as so that non-Basques can see the complexity and importance of the problem.

When Unamuno, in his lack of faith in Euskara's future, believed it impossible to act on languages and direct them to a certain extent, he was unaware, as a man of his historicist age, that languages have always suffered such operations, and as F. Marcos Marín now reminds us, Spanish itself has undergone them at the hands of Alfonso the Wise in the thirteenth century and Philip V's Royal Academy in the eighteenth.

The gravity of the disturbance in the Basque soul can be measured by reading the work of the poet Gabriel Aresti (1933–75), who took on the challenge of creating, in unfavorable circumstances and motivated by those circumstances themselves, a language with its grammar and lexicon, its meter and rhythm, and thereby succeeded in expressing the violence of his feelings, with elements reminiscent of Solana's paintings, with outbursts of *irrintzi gorri*, dreaming of destroying the beech forest that has ended up in the usurer's possession and of pulling out the teeth of those who prohibit everything, agitated by the memory of all the acts of violence that put an end to the old, and in part imaginary, Basque idyll. In this book, we have sought to locate the origins of that disturbance that has erupted in our time.

Madrid, January–March 1980.

Bibliography

J. Chr. Adelung & J. S. Vater, 1806–1817, *Mithridates oder allgemeine Sprachkunde,* 4 vols., the third divided into three volumes. Berlin. Reprint in Hildesheim, 1970.

M. Agud, v. Landuchio.

Antonio Agustín, 1744, *Diálogos de medallas, inscriciones y otras antigüedades,* Madrid.

E. Alarcos (García), 1934, "Una teoría acerca del origen del lenguaje," *Bol. de la R. Acad. Española,* 21, 209–228.

Bernardo de Aldrete, 1606, *Del origen y principio de la lengua castellana o romance que se usa en España.* Rome. Fascimile edition and study by Lidio Nieto Jiménez, 2 vols., Madrid, 1972 and 1975.

José Amador de los Ríos, 1862, *Historia crítica de la literatura española,* II, Madrid.

Sabino de Arana-Goiri, 1965, *Obras completas.* Editorial Sabindiar-Batza, Buenos Aires. From this edition the following writings are cited: 1887, *Etimologías euskérikas;* 1888, *Pliegos euskeráfilos;* 1888–89, *Pliegos histórico-políticos;* 1892, *Pliegos euskeralógicos;* 1893–95, *Bizkaitarra;* 1895, *Tratado etimológico de los apellidos euskéricos;* 1896, *Lecciones de ortografía del euskera bizkaino;* 1896, *Egutegi de bolsillo para 1897;* 1897, *Umiaren lenengo aizkidia;* 1897, *Baserritara,* weekly; 1898, *Lenengo egutegi bizkattarra;* 1901, *Euzkadi,* journal, 4 numbers; 1901–03, *La Patria,* weekly; posthumous, *Etimología de vascuence; Clasificación del verbo vizcaíno; La semana vasca.*

Pablo Pedro de Astarloa, 1803, *Apología de la lengua bascongada o ensayo crítico filosófico de su perfección y antigüedad sobre todas las que se conocen: en respuesta a los reparos propuestos en el Diccionario geográfico histórico de España, tomo segundo, palabra Navarra,* Madrid.

————, (published anonymously), 1804, *Reflexiones filosóficas en defensa de la Apología bascongada o Respuesta a la Censura crítica del Cura de Montuenga*, Madrid.

————, 1883, *Discursos filosóficos sobre la lengua primitiva o gramática y análisis razonada de la euskera o bascuence*, Bilbao.

Werner Bahner, 1956, *Beitrag zum Sprachbewusstsein in der spanischen Literatur des 16. und 17. Jahrhunderts.* Neue Beiträge zur Literaturwissenschaft, Band 15, Berlin. (There is a 1966 Spanish translation titled *La lingüística española del Siglo de Oro*, Madrid.)

Miguel Batllori, S. J., 1951, "El archivo lingüístico de Hervás en Roma y su reflejo en W. von Humboldt." *Archivum Historicum Societatis Iesu*, 20, 59–116.

Pero Antón Beuter, 1604, *Primera parte de la Crónica general de toda España, y especialmente del Reyno de Valencia*, Valencia.

Prince Louis-Lucien Bonaparte, 1869, *Le verbe basque en tableaux*, London.

G. Bonfante, 1954, "Ideas on the Kinship of the European Languages from 1200 to 1800." *Cuadernos de Historia Mundial*, 1, 679–699.

————, 1973, *Studi Romeni*, Roma.

Fermín Caballero, 1868, *Conquenses ilustres*, vol. I, *Abate Hervás: Noticias biográficas y bibliográficas*, Madrid. Cánovas, v. Rodríguez-Ferrer.

J. Caro Baroja, 1941, *Algunos mitos españoles: Ensayo de mitología popular*, Madrid.

————, 1945, *Materiales para una historia de la lengua vasca en su relación con la latina*. Acta Salmanticensia, Salamanca.

Julio Cejador, 1908–1914, *El lenguaje*, 12 vols., Madrid.

————, 1915, *Historia de la lengua y literatura castellana*, vol. I, Madrid.

————, 1922, *idem*, vol. XIV, Appendix: "Diálogos familiares acerca del eúsquera y el castellano," pp. 69–276. Madrid.

————, 1926, "Ibérica, I. Alfabeto e inscripciones ibéricas." *Butlletí de l'Associació Catalana d'Antropología, Etnología i Prehistoria*, 6, 130–225.

D(on) J(osé) A(ntonio) C(onde), Cura de Montuenga, 1804, *Censura crítica de la pretendida excelencia y antigüedad del vascuence*, Madrid.

————, 1806, *Censura crítica del alfabeto primitivo de España y pretendidos monumentos literarios del vascuence*, Madrid.

Javier Corcuera Atienza, 1979, *Orígenes, ideología y organización del nacionalismo vasco*, Madrid.

Joan Corominas, 1965, *Estudis de Toponimia Catalana*, I, Barcelona.

————, 1975, "Les plombs sorothaptiques d'Arles," *Zeitschrift für Romanische Philólogie*, 91, 1–53.

————, 1976, "Elementos prelatinos en las lenguas romances hispánicas," *Actas del I Coloquio sobre lenguas y culturas prerromanas en la Península Ibérica*, Acta Salmanticensia, Salamanca.

E. Coseriu, 1972, "Andrés de Poça y las lenguas de Europa," *Studia Hispanica in honorem R. Lapesa*, III [Madrid), 199–217.

————, 1978, "Hervás und das Substrat," *Studii si cercetari lingvistice*, 29, 523–530.

Crónica de España, v. Docampo.

Cura de Montuenga, v. Conde.

Florián Docampo, 1541, *Las quatro partes enteras de la Corónica de España que mandó componer el Serenísimo Rey don Alonso llamado el Sabio . . . Vista y emendada mucha parte de su impresión por el maestro . . .* , Zamora.

Ignacio Ma. Echaide, 1944, *Desarrollo de las conjugaciones euskaras, perifrásticas y sintéticas, respetuosas y familiares*, San Sebastián.

B. de Echave, 1607, *Discursos de la antigüedad de la lengua cantábrica vascongada: Introdúcese la misma lengua en forma de una matrona venerable y anciana que se queja de que siendo ella la primera que se habló en España, y general de toda ella, la hayan olvidado sus naturales y admitido las otras extranjeras. Habla con las provincias de Guipúzcoa y Vizcaya que le han sido fieles, y algunas veces con la misma España*, Mexico. (There is a facsimile reedition, Bilbao, 1971.)

Juan Bautista de Erro y Azpiroz, 1806, *Alfabeto de la lengua primitiva de España y explicación de sus más antiguos monumentos de inscripciones y medallas*, Madrid.

————, (published only with initials), 1807, *Observaciones filosóficas en favor del Alfabeto primitivo o Respuesta apologética a la Censura crítica del Cura de Montuenga*, Pamplona.

————, 1815, *El mundo primitivo o Examen filosófico de la antigüedad y cultura de la nación bascongada*, tomo I (only volume published), Madrid.

————, 1954, anonymous pamphlet (it is by Fausto Arocena) published with the name Erro as a title by Government of Gipuzkoa, to commemorate the centennial of his death, San Sebastián.

Nicolás Esandi, 1946, *Vascuence y etrusco. Origen de los lenguajes de Italia: Documentos prehistóricos. Estudio comparativo*, Universidad de Buenos Aires.

Juan Fernández Amador de los Ríos, 1909–1914, *Diccionario vasco-caldaico-castellano.* (13 fascicles / up to *at-*.) Pamplona.

Francisco Fernández y González, 1893a, *Los lenguajes hablados por los indígenas del norte y centro de América*, Conferencia del Ateneo, Madrid.

————, 1893b, *Los lenguajes hablados por los indígenas de la América meridional*, Conferencia del Ateneo, Madrid.

————, 1894, *Influencia de las lenguas y letras orientales en las culturas de los pueblos de la Península Ibérica*, Paper read before the Real Academia Española, Madrid.

————, 1902, "Sur la prédominance des éléments sémitiques dans la langue basque," *Verhandlungen des XIII. Internationalen Orientalisten-Kongresses in Hamburg 1902*, Sektion V (3 page offprint).

Aureliano Fernández Guerra, 1872, *Libro de Santoña*, Madrid.

————, 1878, *Cantabria*, Madrid.

Fidel Fita y Colomer, 1879, *El Gerundense y la España primitiva*, Paper read before the Real Academia de la Historia, 2nd ed., Madrid.

Henrique Flórez, 1786, *La Cantabria: Disertación sobre el sitio y extensión que tuvo en tiempo de los romanos* . . . , preliminary discourse to volume XXIV of *España sagrada*, Madrid.

Justo Garate, 1936. *La época de Pablo Astarloa y Juan Antonio Moguel*, Bilbao.

Estevan de Garibay y Camalloa, 1571, *Compendio historial de la Chrónica y universal historia de todos los reynos de España . . . compuesta por . . . , de nación cántabro, vezino de la villa de Mondragón, en la provincia de Guipúzcoa*, Antwerp.

Francisco Xavier de Garma y Salcedo, 1738, *Theatro universal de España. Descripción eclesiástica y secular de todos sus reynos y provincias*, 4 vols., Madrid.

Hans-Martin Gauger, 1967, "Bernardo Aldrete. Ein Beitrag zur Vorgeschichte der romanischen Sprachwissenschaft." *Romanistisches Jahrbuch*, 18, 207–248.

José Godoy Alcántara, 1868, *Historia crítica de los falsos cronicones*, Madrid.

P. Gabriel de Henao, 1689–1691, *Averiguaciones de las antigüedades de Cantabria*, 2 vols., Salamanca.

Lorenzo Hervás (y Panduro), 1778–1787, *Idea dell'Universo*, 21 vols., Cesena. From this work we cite the volumes dedicated to linguistics:

1784, vol. XVI, *Catalogo delle lingue conosciute*.

1785, vol. XVIII, *Trattato dell'origine, formazione, meccanismo, ed armonia degl'idiomi*.

1786, vol. XIX, *Aritmetica di quasi tutte le nazioni conosciute. Divisione del tempo fra le nazioni orientali*.

1787a, vol. XX, *Vocabolario poligloto con prolegomeni sopra più di CL lingue*.

1787b, vol. XXI, *Saggio pratico delle lingue e dialetti, con cui si dimostra l'infusione del primo idioma dell'uman genere, e la confusione delle lingue in esso poi accaduta, e si additano la diramazione e dispersione delle nazioni con molti risultati utili alla storia*.

————, 1800–1805, *Catálogo de las lenguas de las naciones conocidas, y enumeración, división, y clases de éstas, según la diversidad de sus idiomas y dialectos,* 6 vols., Madrid.

1800, I, *Lenguas de América.*

1801, II, *Lenguas y naciones de las islas de los Mares Pacífico e Indiano austral y oriental y del continente de Asia.*

1802, III, *Lenguas y naciones europeas. Naciones europeas advenedizas.*

1804a, IV, *Naciones europeas primitivas: sus lenguas matrices y dialectos de éstas.* 1804b, V, Idem. 1805, VI, Idem.

————, 1808, *División primitiva del tiempo entre los vascongados, usada aún por ellos,* published in Olarra, 1947, 313–354.

Aemilius Hübner, 1893, *Monumenta linguae Ibericae,* Berlin.

Francisco Xavier Manuel de la Huerta y Vega, 1738, 1740, *España primitiva. Historia de sus reyes y monarcas desde su población hasta Christo,* 2 vols., Madrid.

Wilhelm von Humboldt, 1917, *Berichtigungen und Zusätze zum ersten Abschnitt des zweiten Bandes des Mithridates über die cantabrische oder baskische Sprache,* en Adelung & Vater, 4, 275–360.

————, 1821, *Prüfung der Untersuchungen über die Urbewohner Hispaniens vermittelst der Vaskischen Sprache.* We cite this work via the 1959 publication *Primitivos pobladores de España y lengua vasca,* trans. F. Echebarria, prologue by A. Steiger, Madrid. [Editorial Note: This was true of the original, but for this translation the German original was consulted.]

Nicolás Landuchio, 1958, *Dictionarium linguae Cantabricae (1562),* edited by Manuel Agud and Luis Michelena, San Sebastián.

M(anuel) d(e) L(arramendi), 1728, *De la antigüedad y universalidad del Bascuenze en España; de sus perfecciones y ventajas sobre otras muchas lenguas: Demostración previa al Arte que se dará a luz desta lengua,* Salamanca.

Manuel de Larramendi, 1729, *El Impossible Vencido, Arte de la lengua Bascongada,* Salamanca.

————, 1736, *Discurso histórico sobre la antigua famosa Cantabria: Questión decidida: si las provincias de Bizcaya, Guipúzcoa* y *Alaba estuvieron comprendidas en la antigua Cantabria*, Madrid.

———, 1853, *Diccionario trilingüe castellano, bascuence y latín*. New edition by Pío de Zuazua, 2 vols. (The first edition is from 1745.)

———, 1950, *Corografía de la muy noble y muy leal provincia de Guipúzcoa*, Buenos Aires.

Fernando Lázaro Carreter, 1949, *Las ideas lingüísticas en España durante el siglo XVIII*. Supplement XLVIII to the *Revista de Filología Española*, Madrid.

Gregorio López Madera, 1602, *Historia y discursos de la certidumbre de las reliquias, láminas y prophecías descubiertos en el Monte santo y Iglesia de Granada, desde el año de mil y quinientos y ochenta y ocho hasta el de mil y quinientos noventa y ocho*, Granada.

Juan Antonio Llórente, 1806–1808, *Noticias históricas de las tres Provincias Vascongadas*, 5 vols., Madrid.

Alonso de Madrigal or Alphonsus Tostatus, 1506–1507, *Comento o exposición de las crónicas o tiempos interpretado en vulgar. Tostado sobre el Eusebio*, Salamanca.

———, 1728, *Opera Omnia*, 27 vols. in folio, Venice.

P. Juan de Mariana, 1950, *Historia general de España*, books I–XVII, collection organized and revised with a preliminary discourse by D(on) F(rancisco) P(í) y M(argall), I, Bibl. de Autores Españoles, XXX, Madrid.

Lucio Marineo Sículo, 1539, Obra compuesta por..., Coronista de sus majestades *De las cosas memorables de España*, Alcalá de Henares.

André Martinet, 1955, *Economie des Changements phonétiques*, Bern.

Francisco Martínez Marina, 1805, "Ensayo histórico crítico sobre el origen y progresos de las lenguas, señaladamente del romance castellano: Catálogo de algunas voces castellanas puramente arábigas o tomadas de la lengua griega y de los idiomas orientales, pero introducidas en España por los árabes," *Memorias de la Real Academia de la Historia*, IV, 2, 63 and VIII + 86 pages.

Juan Martínez Ruiz, 1970, "Cartas inéditas de B. de Aldrete (1608–1626)," *Boletín de la Real Academia Española*, 50, 77–135, 277–314, 471–515.

Pedro de Medina, 1595, *Primera y segunda parte de las grandezas y cosas notables de España*, corrected and greatly expanded by Diego Pérez de Mesa, Alcalá de Henares.

Juan Francisco de Masdeu, 1783 ff., *Historia crítica de España y de la cultura española*, 20 vols., Madrid. We cite this work by year only: 1784, II, España antigua, first part; 1785, III, España antigua, second part; 1807, VII, España romana, second book, España romana baxo el Imperio.

Gregorio Mayans y Siscar, 1873, *Orígenes de la lengua española, compuestos por diversos autores recogidos por D.* published for the first time in 1737, and reprinted now by the La Amistad Literaria society with a prologue by D. Juan Eugenio Hartzenbusch and notes by D. Eduardo de Mier, Madrid.

M. Menéndez Pelayo, 1941, *Estudios y discursos de crítica histórica y literaria*, vol. I, Santander.

Luis Michelena, 1954, "De onomástica aquitana," *Pirineos*, 10, 409–455.

———, 1961, "La inscripción de Lerga," *Príncipe de Viana*, 22, 65–74.

———, 1964a, *Sobre el pasado de la lengua vasca*, San Sebastián.

———, 1964b, *Textos arcaicos vascos*, Madrid.

———, v. Landuchio.

MLI — *Monumenta linguae Ibericae*, v. Hübner.

Juan Antonio Moguel, 1854, *Cartas y disertaciones sobre la lengua vascongada, Memorial histórico español*, 7, 661–753, Madrid.

Ambrosio de Morales, 1573, *La Corónica general de España, prosiguiendo adelante los cinco libros que el maestro Florián Docampo . . . dexó escritos*, Alcalá.

———, 1577, *Los otros dos libros undécimo y duodécimo de la Coránica general de España . . . Van juntas con esta parte las Antigüedades de España que hasta agora se han podido escrevir.* We cite the *Antigüedades*, which they have separate pagination, with the indication *Ant.*, Alcalá.

————, 1793, *Opúsculos castellanos,* 3 vols., Madrid.

Joseph de Moret, 1665, *Investigaciones históricas de las antigüedades del Reyno de Navarra,* Pamplona.

————, 1684, *Annales del Reyno de Navarra,* I, Pamplona.

Muñoz y Manzano, v. Conde de la Viñaza.

Nieto Jiménez, v. Aldrete.

Arnaldo Oihenart, 1656, *Notitia utriusque Vasconiae, tum Ibericae quam Aquitanicae,* 2nd ed., Paris.

José de Olarra, 1947, "Hallazgo del tratado de Hervás y Panduro *División del tiempo entre los bascongados, usada aún por ellos,*" *Boletín de la Real Sociedad Vascongada de Amigos del País,* 3, 303–354.

Aita Onaindia, 1954, *Milla euskal-olerki eder,* Aldiz-urren aukeratuta, Larrea-Amorebieta.

Juan de Perochegui, 1760, *Origen de la Nación Bascongada y de su lengua, de que han dimanado las Monarquías Española, y Francia, y la República de Venecia, que existen al presente,* 2nd printing, Pamplona.

PL = *Patrología Latina,* ed. Migne.

Andrés de Poca, 1587, *De la antigua lengua, poblaciones y comarcas de las Españas, en que de paso se tocan algunas cosas de la Cantabria,* Bilbao (we cite the edition of A. Rodríguez Herrero, Madrid, 1959).

Miguel Rodríguez-Ferrer, 1873, *Los vascongados. Su país, su lengua y el Príncipe L. L. Bonaparte,* with an introduction by A. Cánovas del Castillo, Madrid.

R. Thurneysen, 1916, "Die Keltischen Sprachen," in *Geschichte der indogermanischen Sprachwissenschaft edited by* von W. Streitberg, II, 1, 281–305, Strasbourg.

Tostado, v. Madrigal.

Antonio Tovar, 1949, *Estudios sobre las primitivas lenguas hispánicas,* Buenos Aires.

————, 1958, "Esp. *amarraco,* vasc. *amar, amai* y el topónimo *Amaya,*" in *Ethymologica W. von Wartburg zum siebzigsten Geburtstag* 831–834, Tubingen.

————, 1959, *El euskera y sus parientes,* Madrid.

————, 1970, "Zur Frage der Urheimat und zum Wort für 'Name' als Kriterium für zwei Sprachwelten," *Indogermanische Forschungen,* 75, 32-43.

————, 1977a, "Comparaciones tipológicas del euskera," *Euskera,* 22, 449–476.

————, 1977b, "El nombre de Pamplona," *Fontes linguae Vasconum* 9, 5–8.

————, 1978, "Typologische Perspektiven des Baskischen," *Sprachkontakte im Nordseegebiet,* Akten des 1. Symposions über Sprach-kontakt in Europa, edited by von P. Sture Ureland, 67–81, Tubingen.

————, 1979, "Vasco y lenguas caucásicas: indicios tipológicos," *Euskera,* 24, 13–33.

————, 1980, "Das Irische und die Typologie," in press *Wechselbeziehung diachroner und synchroner Sprachwissenschaft, Festschrift für O. Szemerényi,* Amsterdam.

A. Tovar, K. Bouda, L. Michelena, W. Vycichl, M. Swadesh, 1961, "El método léxico-estadístico y su aplicación a las relaciones del vascuence," *Boletín de la Real Sociedad Vascongada de los Amigos del País,* 17, 249–281.

Joaquín Traggia, 1802, art. XIII, "Del origen de la lengua vascongada, en la voz Navarra," *Diccionario geográfico-histórico de España por la Real Academia de la Historia,* 2, 151–166 Madrid.

Francisco M. Tubino.

Miguel de Unamuno, 1958, *Obras completas,* edition directed by M. García Blanco, 16 vols., Madrid. We cite simply with the abbreviation OC and the indication of the volume except for the following works that we cite with year and page:

————, 1884, "Crítica del problema sobre el origen y prehistoria de la raza vasca." Doctoral thesis in the Facultad de Filosofía y Letras, read in Madrid on June 20, 1884. Note: The thesis, which was supervised by Antonio Sánchez Moguel, earned a grade of outstanding. *OC,* VI, 87–142.

————, 1886, "Del elemento alienígena en el idioma vasco," first appeared in volume 1 of the *Revista de Vizcaya.* [corrected, it was republished in the *Zeitschrift für romanische Philologie*, 17 (1893), 137–147.] OC, VI, 143–167.

———, 1893, "Sobre el cultivo del vascuence," *Eco de Bilbao*, November and December. OC, VI, 249–267.

———, 1902, "La cuestión del vascuence," *La Lectura*, Madrid. OC, III, 551–581.

Julio de Urquijo e Ibarra, 1918, *Estado actual de los estudios relativos a la lengua vasca, address at the* Congreso de Oñate.

Juan de Valdés, 1969, *Diálogo de la lengua,* edited by Juan M. Lope Blanch, Madrid.

Luis Villasante, O. F. M., 1961, *Historia de la literatura vasca*, Bilbao.

Conde de la Viñaza (Cipriano Muñoz y Manzano), 1893, *Biblioteca histórica de la Filología castellana,* Madrid.

Rodrigo Ximénez de Rada, 1545, *Rerum in Hispania gestarum chronicon* . . . , Granada. I have also seen the edition of the works of El Toledano in the collection of Cardenal Lorenzana, PP. *Toletanorum opera,* III, Madrid, 1793; reprinted in Valencia, Estudios Medievales, 22, 1968.

Index